ILLUSION OF TRUTH

Robert Archibald

Cactus Mystery Press
an imprint of Blue Fortune Enterprises LLC

ILLUSION OF TRUTH
Copyright © 2022 by Robert Archibald.

All rights reserved. Printed in the United States of America. No part of this book may be used or reproduced in any manner whatsoever without written permission except in the case of brief quotations embodied in critical articles or reviews.

This book is a work of fiction. Names, characters, businesses, organizations, places, events and incidents either are the product of the author's imagination or are used fictitiously. Any resemblance to actual persons, living or dead, events, or locales is entirely coincidental.

For information contact :
Blue Fortune Enterprises, LLC
Cactus Mystery Press
P.O. Box 554
Yorktown, VA 23690
http://blue-fortune.com

Book and Cover design by Wesley Miller, WAMCreate

ISBN: 978-1-948979-89-4
First Edition: November 2022

DEDICATION

Margaret Wren Archibald
May she grow up in a world better than ours.

Fiction by Robert Archibald:
Roundabout Revenge
Guilty Until Proven Innocent
Crime Might Pay
Who Dung It?

Reviews for *Roundabout Revenge*
Fascinating plot, thoughtfully developed. Looking forward to what story twists his next book will bring.
Fred Cason, Amazon review

I loved Roundabout Revenge. Author Robert Archibald is a retired college professor whose writing demonstrates that he is a scholar not only in his professional field of study, but also in his observations on society. In this engrossing novel, he sheds light on why law and justice are sometimes at odds with each other. There also are wonderful discussions among the characters about sports, diversity in schools and society, and about how conservatives and liberals have come to hold their beliefs. I look forward to the sequel.
CW Stacks, Amazon review

Reviews for *Guilty Until Proven Innocent*
Another Archibald masterpiece... This quality page-turner encompasses a number of adventures that sometimes end not as anticipated. The expected becomes the unexpected...
If you enjoyed "Revenge," you'll enjoy this too. If you missed "Revenge" pick it up with the knowledge that you'll have two enjoyable books to occupy your time.
Wilford Kale, Virginia Gazette review

Acknowledgments

While it is inspired by things I've seen in the news, *Illusion of Truth* is a work of fiction. Any resemblance between characters in the book and anyone I have known or met is a complete coincidence.

This book benefited greatly from the efforts of friends, particularly my writers' group: Tim Holland, Elizabeth Lee, Caterina Novelliere, Peter Stipe, and Susan Williamson. They read and commented on the vast majority of the manuscript. My friend Kirk Lovenbury read the entire manuscript and gave helpful comments. Also, Rich and Sudie Watkins listened and critiqued the manuscript while my wife Nancy read it aloud. Finally, I included a story told by my colleague Clay Clemons over wine at lunch one day. All of these helpers had nothing to do with any errors one might find in the text.

As always, I would like to thank Narielle Living for an extensive edit that improved the manuscript immensely.

Finally, everything I do benefits from the help of my wife, Nancy.

CHAPTER ONE

Maybe it was at least partly his fault, but Dwight Kelton didn't like the way he'd slinked away from the university, as if he were a monumental failure. He'd been solid five months ago. He was married, he thought successfully, with a secure, high-paying, tenured position. Now he'd been forced to resign and divorce proceedings were well under way. Worse yet, he was headed back to live with his mother in Ohio.

Dwight didn't look forward to sharing the house with his mother, Evangeline, but she thought she needed him. She'd had a stroke two months ago and was slowly recovering. Dwight had visited her in the hospital right after the stroke, but he hadn't been able to stay long because of his teaching schedule. He'd kept in touch with her doctors and his mother when she was able to speak, so he knew some of what to expect. She had a young girl coming in to fix meals and a nurse who visited regularly. Dwight didn't know what he could do to help, but he knew Evangeline wanted him to stay with her.

It had been difficult to tell his mother he was resigning from the university. The call had gone better than he'd expected and ended with Evangeline's invitation, actually command, for him to come back home. Dwight hadn't always gotten along with his parents, so he was a bit surprised. He told himself he'd stay as long as he was needed, then he'd figure out what to do with the rest of his life.

The day he arrived, he used his key, trying to be quiet in case his mother was napping. He was surprised to find her sitting on the couch in the living room. She looked much better than she had in the hospital. A small droop to the right side of her mouth and the walker parked beside her were the only signs of the stroke. She'd always been an attractive woman, but her beauty was fading. Dwight thought she'd stopped trying a little; maybe things had become too difficult to manage. She no longer colored her hair, and she was dressed in a housecoat. She'd never been one to dress casually. He walked over and gave her a brief hug.

"How are you doing, Mom?" Dwight asked as he sat in the chair facing her.

"Better than you, I expect."

"I'm okay. It's a bit of a drive, but not too bad. I feel fine."

"You've made a wreck of your life. You lost your job. You're getting divorced. You're a forty-year-old ruined man."

"Thanks for mentioning it."

"Always the smart aleck, weren't you?"

Dwight took a deep breath to calm himself. It was no use responding, so silence descended.

Evangeline finally filled the silence. "Why don't you give me the details? I could only get the barest outline out of you on the phone."

Dwight had anticipated this kind of interrogation. He leaned back in his chair and stared at the ceiling. "It started with Marjorie's affair. A friend told me she was seeing our department chair. I didn't believe it at first, but I did some snooping. It was true. I stewed about it for around a week. Finally, I confronted her. What started out as a relatively calm discussion devolved into a horrible shouting match. It ended with her storming out of the condo. It was clear our marriage couldn't survive the things we'd said to each other. Being a coward, I wrote out my thoughts, ending with an offer of an uncontested divorce and put it in her campus mailbox. That's how we communicate now, through campus mail."

"They don't force tenured professors to resign just because they're getting divorced. There must be more to it."

He closed his eyes. "You're right. About three weeks after our shouting match, a graduate student knocked on my door one evening. Sarah Jensen. I knew her. She'd heard about my breakup with Marjorie. Sarah called her Professor Smyth, I guess. While I knew it wasn't a good idea, one thing led to another, and she ended up in my bed that night."

"Isn't that against the rules? Making love to one of the students in your program?"

"Yes, there's a prohibition against consensual amorous relations. That's what they call it. It's widely ignored, at least where graduate students are concerned. Sarah was twenty-three, and I could tell I wasn't her first partner. Also, I have to admit, I'm weak. I hadn't had sex for quite a while, and she was very attractive."

"Spare me those details."

Dwight stood up at this point and started pacing. As much as he'd rehearsed his remarks and thought it all made sense, his mother didn't seem to be a receptive audience. After one tour of the living room, he continued. "Things started to fall apart when Sarah failed the qualifying exam. She was devastated. It's a big deal, the qualifier. Students who fail the qualifier are dropped from the program. Sarah appealed, claiming the only reason she failed was because Marjorie was jealous. Marjorie had been one of the graders, and she did give Sarah very low marks, but it wasn't because of Sarah and me. In fact, the qualifier is blind graded. There is no way the grader can know who the student is. Sarah's appeal didn't go anywhere. Unfortunately, her appeal was based on our relationship, which was against the rules."

"So it wasn't, what would you call it, a one-night stand with this girl?"

"It wasn't. Anyway, I got called into the dean's office and given the choice of going through the consensual amorous relations procedures or of resigning and sparing the university all the mess. I took the resignation route with the proviso that the entire episode would be erased from any records, so here I am."

"What are you going to do?"

"I've got a book on Charles Dickens half finished. It's due at the publisher's in three months. As you know, my books have sold very well. I've got quite a bit saved, and there's more coming in. In a year or so, I may look for another teaching job. I don't know. First things first. I want to be sure you're completely recovered."

"Thank you for thinking of me." Evangeline remained on the couch, hands folded in her lap, not looking at Dwight.

He stopped pacing and stretched. "Now that I've dealt with your curiosity, I'm going to get my stuff. I assume I'll be in the guest room."

"Yes. It used to be yours. If you need a place to write, you can use your dad's study. I haven't gotten around to redecorating it."

Dwight made several trips to his car. Although he had given away quite a few books, he still had three heavy boxes of them. He also had one small box of mementos, not much to say for fifteen years of marriage. He'd left the furniture for Marjorie. He just had his clothes, his books, and the one box.

As he returned to his car for the last load, a teenage girl came up the walk. Dwight did a double take. The girl looked just like someone he used to know: Cathy Mellow, the best-looking girl in Dwight's high school class. Every guy in the class, Dwight included, had had a crush on Cathy. This girl looked identical—same blonde hair, same big smile, same slim waist, and the same emerald eyes.

She approached him. "You must be Professor Kelton. Your mother told me you'd be here today."

Dwight shook the girl's outstretched hand. "And you are?"

"Oh, excuse me. I'm Courtney. Courtney Wilson. I cook for your mother. It's time for me to prepare dinner. I'll make enough for you, too." With that, she ran up to the door.

She must be Cathy Mellow's daughter. The resemblance is too strong. After a moment, it made sense. Cathy had married Bill Wilson. Bill and Cathy were the hot-shot couple in his high school class. Cathy was the prettiest cheerleader, and Bill was the star quarterback. Dwight had been in awe of them. He'd been a short, pimply faced nerd before anyone knew the word nerd. He wasn't a football player. He did write for the sports section of the student newspaper and got good grades, so he wasn't a nobody, but he was close.

An hour later, as she prepared to leave after serving dinner in the dining room, Courtney spoke to Dwight as he came down the stairs. "I'm glad I caught you. I told my folks you were coming, and they said they remembered you from high school. They want you to visit some time."

With that, Courtney bounced out of the house. As Dwight watched her leave, he remembered her mother had that same bounce in her step. *I wonder what Cathy is like now.*

CHAPTER TWO

It took Dwight longer than he thought to be productive. Evangeline had no reason to have Wi-Fi. She didn't use the internet, email, or a cell phone. He couldn't live without Wi-Fi. Unfortunately, he wasn't handy, and he didn't know what he really needed. Luckily, he found a computer repair store, and they recommended someone who could install the necessary equipment. Still, it was two days before he successfully logged in to read his email.

He spent quite a bit of time with his mother. It didn't take long to realize she was starved for conversation. Before her stroke, she'd been very active in several groups, played bridge, and frequently went to lunch with friends. Since the stroke, she'd either been in the hospital or the house. She thought she'd eventually recover enough to get back to her life, but Dwight could tell she wasn't sure. She worried she'd never be able to drive again. Dwight told her not to worry. Even if she couldn't drive, there were taxis and maybe even Uber. Explaining Uber took a while.

"But wouldn't I have to get one of those cell phones to use Uber?" Evangeline asked.

"Yes, you would. You'd have to come into the modern age. I've been spending a bunch of time getting the house connected to Wi-Fi, and

I've finally managed it. We can get you a cell phone, and I'll teach you how to use it. I bet Courtney can help too. She's probably a whiz with a cell phone."

"Isn't it really a little computer? I don't know the first thing about computers."

"It's not hard. Look at it this way. There are a whole bunch of people not nearly as smart as you who have mastered the use of cell phones. One of the keys to learning is thinking you can."

"Aren't you the philosopher."

"Well, I have a Doctor of Philosophy, so maybe I am."

After a long pause, Evangeline finally relented. "All right, get me a cell phone."

Dwight was happy and a little surprised by her response. If nothing else, it would give them something to talk about when he explained how things worked.

The next morning, Dwight gave Courtney the Wi-Fi password.

"Thanks so much, Professor. This house is about the only place I visit that doesn't have Wi-Fi. Oh yeah, I'm supposed to invite you for dinner with my folks tonight. They remember you from high school and want to catch up."

"Sure, I'd be happy to come. I haven't kept up with my classmates. I didn't return much after I left for college."

"You thought you were too good for Boynton," Evangeline interjected. "Every summer in college and then graduate school, you stayed at the university. We barely saw you."

"I got jobs as a research assistant in the summers and over Christmas breaks. They were great jobs. The ones I had as an undergrad were critical for getting into graduate school and getting a fellowship to boot. You didn't have to pay a cent for my graduate education."

"I guess you think I should be thanking you for that," Evangeline said, pouting.

"Whatever," Dwight said. "Anyway, I'd love to come to dinner with your folks, Courtney."

"I'll let them know. Six-thirty, I think. I'll text if I'm wrong about the time."

On his way to the store to get his mother a cell phone, Dwight wondered what it would be like having dinner with Bill and Cathy. He hadn't kept up with anyone from high school. For the most part, he'd hated high school. He was the shortest boy in his class, and, since he had a bad case of acne, he'd been a social nonentity. His mother was right. He'd avoided coming home during college.

College had been a completely different experience. Three things made it better. First, miraculously, his face had cleared up. Second, he grew, and by the time he was a senior, he was over six foot. These first two factors made it easy to snag dates. He hadn't dated anyone seriously until Marjorie in grad school, but unlike high school, he had an active social life. The third factor was academics. He took an English literature class as a freshman and fell in love. The professor had really liked one of his papers. At the end of the semester, he'd become the professor's research assistant. While he'd been a good student in high school, it hadn't been a great advantage. In fact, those who got good grades were looked down on. There was no stigma attached to being a good student in college.

Graduate school had been even better. Everyone was there because they were interested in what they were studying. He'd been impressed with his fellow students, especially Marjorie Smyth. She'd been a real hot shot at the prestigious college she'd gone to, and she had the biggest fellowship in the department. On top of that, she was gorgeous, a tall brunette with a great smile. Dwight was thrilled when she wanted to be his study buddy and even more thrilled when the study arrangement turned into something more. That was all behind him now. He was back to high school, at least for dinner tonight.

When Dwight presented Evangeline with her cell phone later that day, she looked at it skeptically. He sat next to her at the kitchen table and showed her how to turn it on, explaining slowly.

"This first screen is asking you for your password. I set it up to be the year of your birth, 1937."

"I wouldn't want people to know that."

"Don't worry, you're the only one who should know your password. Never tell anyone else. Now type it in."

Evangeline looked worried, but she managed to get the password inserted. A screen full of icons appeared.

"What's this?"

"These little pictures are called icons, and each one opens a program for you."

"What do I need programs for?"

"Let me show you. See this little picture with the sun and the cloud?"

"Yes, and there's something written below it, but I can't read it. It's too small."

"It says weather. Press the icon."

She did and then stared at the screen. Dwight continued, "See, here's the weather report. If you drag your finger down the page, it will show you more." He demonstrated how to do it.

"What are the other icons?"

Dwight stuck with the simpler icons. He showed her the calculator and the clock and timer. Evangeline interrupted him before he got any further. "I thought this thing was a phone. Show me how the phone part works. I'll worry about the other things later."

"Okay, point taken. It is a phone, but I was just showing you how much more it could do. I haven't even shown you how to get to the internet."

"I don't know why I'd need to know that. I want to be able to make a telephone call."

Dwight explained how to work the phone. He had her call his cell, which didn't present any problem. Then he called her new phone. Evangeline had a little trouble swiping the phone to receive the call, but eventually she figured it out.

"I'm going to call some of my friends. Where's that piece of paper where you wrote down my new phone number? I want to give it to them."

Dwight handed her the card with the phone number and got up. Given her initial resistance, he thought this first session with the phone was a success. There was so much more the phone could do, but he was glad she wanted to stop. It was better to give her things in small doses.

CHAPTER THREE

That evening, Dwight was surprised to discover the Wilson's house was only two blocks from his mother's. He showed up at six-thirty-five with a bottle of wine. He wondered if the wine was appropriate, but it was what he and Marjorie had always done when they were invited to someone's house for dinner.

Dwight almost didn't recognize Bill Wilson when he answered the door. Bill had put on twenty or thirty pounds, and he seemed several inches shorter than Dwight remembered. He quickly recognized he was probably right about the weight but wrong about the height. His misimpression resulted from the fact that he was so much taller than he'd been in high school. Everyone had towered over him then.

"Dwight, is that really you?"

Dwight recognized the voice. Cathy Mellow. She strode across the living room toward him. She looked stunning in her jeans and tight blue top, a more mature version of Courtney. Her blonde hair was fixed differently, but she had the same dimples, strong cheekbones, ready smile, and green eyes. Much to Dwight's surprise, Cathy enveloped him in a big hug. It was a long-delayed high school dream to have Cathy Mellow's breasts pressed against him, even if briefly.

"Yes, it's me," Dwight said, stepping back from the hug. "I bet I've changed a lot, but you two look just like you did back in high school."

Then, remembering the wine, Dwight held it out. "I hope you like this. It's one of my favorites."

Cathy took the wine bottle and inspected it. "Bill is more a beer person, but I'll enjoy this. I'll open it now. Come on in. We have appetizers over by the couch."

Cathy disappeared into the kitchen and Dwight and Bill sat in the living room, Bill on the couch and Dwight in a chair facing him. A coffee table with drink coasters sat between them. Silence descended. As it began to get uncomfortable, Cathy came in with a beer for Bill and a glass of wine for Dwight before returning to the kitchen.

"Cheers," Dwight said as he clinked glasses with Bill. To avoid another awkward silence, Dwight decided he should start a conversation. "I bet you were expecting me to be shorter. The funny thing is, I grew at least an inch every year I was in college. It was the weirdest thing. Most people are close to full grown by their senior year in high school, but not me."

Cathy came in with her wine and sat on the couch. Dwight noticed she sat about as far away from Bill as she could and still be on the same couch.

"I heard that," Cathy said. "At least an inch a year for four years. That's a lot. I think I only recognized you tonight because I was expecting you. I would have walked right past you on the street. You've really changed."

"For the better, I hope."

Cathy nodded and smiled.

Bill finally spoke up. "Yeah, you were kind of a twerp in high school."

Dwight tried not to be annoyed. "So, fill me in on what's happened to you two."

"Well, I guess you heard about what happened to my football career," Bill said. "I got this big scholarship. The coaches told me they were going to build the offense around me. Anyway, the third game of my freshman year, I finally got to play. Things didn't go well. It was like the line didn't want to block for me. I got sacked four times in less than a quarter. I got mad and yelled at some people. I went from the big recruit to third string in a hurry, and then I got hurt. When I couldn't play football, I didn't know what I was doing in college."

Dwight interrupted, "I remember you weren't very interested in academics."

"It's not that. College, and high school for that matter, were all about spitting back on the test what the teacher said in class. It was all about agreeing with the so-called experts. Most of those experts don't really know what's going on. Look at the experts running our country. They can't get anything right."

Looking a little embarrassed, Cathy jumped in. "We don't need your political opinions, Bill. Truth be told, our college career was interrupted by my pregnancy. I love Courtney to death, but she came at an inconvenient time. We were just at the end of the first semester of our sophomore year when we discovered I was pregnant. We had a quick marriage, and we both dropped out after finishing off that year."

"Did you get a chance to go back to college?"

"No," Cathy continued, looking down at her wine glass. "Bill didn't want to. His father gave him a job selling insurance, and he figured there was no reason for him to have a degree. I was home with Courtney, so I couldn't go back. I guess I could have later, but I never got around to it. I own a dress shop in town, and we've just opened a branch in Clayville."

"That's impressive. Is Courtney your only child?" Dwight asked.

Cathy lifted her glass and drank before answering. "Unfortunately," Cathy answered. "I got pregnant one other time, but I miscarried. It was really tough."

"I'm so sorry."

Bill jumped in. "Courtney's a jock too. She's an all-state field hockey player. She's got a full scholarship, just like me. I hope she doesn't get injured too."

"Wow, a full scholarship. As much as college costs now, I bet that's a load off your minds."

"Yeah, it's nice," Bill said. "Not that we couldn't have swung it. Despite my political opinions my wife doesn't like, I've done all right in the insurance racket. As you can tell, Cathy does good at the store, too. We moved into this neighborhood four years ago."

"Didn't this house used to belong to the Meadows? I didn't know them, just the name. They didn't have any kids our age."

"Yeah, it was the Meadows' place," Bill responded. "He had to go into assisted living. Since I handled their long-term care insurance, I knew about it ahead of everyone else. I was able to jump in with an offer before they even put it on the market."

"I was flabbergasted when Bill came home and told me we were moving. It came out of the blue. I mean, we'd been thinking about looking for another house, but we hadn't even talked to a real estate agent."

Dwight sensed the sudden move was still a source of tension between Bill and Cathy, so he changed the subject. "My story is fairly simple. I went to college and never left. I went straight from undergrad to graduate school and straight from graduate school to a teaching position all at the same place. It was a little odd, shifting relationships. People who'd been my teachers became my colleagues, but it all worked out."

Cathy put her wine glass down with a thunk and turned to face Dwight. "Tell me about your work. Do you do research and present papers and things?

"Yes, that's the part of the job I like the most. I study authors, what makes them tick, and how the time period they lived in influenced what they wrote. Good research topics are like puzzles. You have to fit all the pieces together."

"I bet you're talented," Cathy said. "You were probably the smartest in our high school class."

"I don't know about that, but anyway, I like the research and writing."

Bill filled the ensuing silence by waving his empty beer glass at Cathy. "Would you get me a refill, dear?"

Dwight thought he saw Cathy's eyes roll as she stood up, grabbed Bill's glass, and headed toward the kitchen.

Cathy had a question when she returned with Bill's beer. "Didn't you get married?"

"Yes, I met Marjorie in grad school. We got married as second-year grad students. Luckily, there were two open positions the year we went on the job market. I don't know what would have happened if we'd gotten jobs at different schools. Anyway, we both got tenure, so we stayed."

"Yeah, but you're back here now," Cathy said. "Is this temporary, a sabbatical or something?"

Dwight repeated his sad story much the way he'd told his mother. Bill and Cathy were fascinated. The ways of academia seemed odd to them. It was clear they'd never heard of anything like a consensual amorous relations policy.

When Dwight finished his story, Bill asked, "How can the school outlaw something consensual? I mean, you said this Sarah was twenty-three, and you're way over twenty-one. It's none of the college's business what two adults do on their own time."

"You sound like some of my colleagues," Dwight responded. "It's complicated. There is a power differential between teachers and students. You certainly wouldn't want a professor hitting on a student and then giving the student a bad grade if she, or he for that matter, turned the prof down. What if an amorous relationship ends badly, and the prof takes it out on the student? That wouldn't be right. The whole idea is to avoid conflicts of interest. If the qualifier hadn't been blind graded as I said, Sarah's claim might have had a chance of being upheld."

Bill didn't want to let go of the issue. "But what if the professor is in the English department, and his girlfriend is in the biology department or the law school? I don't see how there can be any conflict. If they are two consenting adults, they should be able to do what they want."

"Again, lots of people would agree with you, and if the across-department amorous relationship continues or ends happily, there is seldom a problem. The difficult cases come when the amorous relationship ends badly. Suppose your biology student breaks up with the English professor. Nothing would stop the English prof talking to his friends in biology about the student. Professors have powers students don't. Disputes can get to something called the hearing committee, which is made up of faculty from lots of departments. It is possible for cross-department situations like you described to involve other people from those two departments. It can be exceedingly messy. The powers that be at the university, the board, decided that banning all relationships was easier than trying to determine which ones to allow."

Bill was about to object when Cathy interrupted. "Bill, I never told you about this, but remember the class I dropped as a freshman?"

"Huh."

"A sociology class. The reason I dropped was the grad assistant in the class. He kept asking me for dates and got really mad when I turned him down. He made it clear I wasn't going to get a good grade. Dwight's right. There are power differentials. I could have tried to complain, but it would've been my word against his. I dropped the class, but it really pissed me off."

"That's a good example," Dwight said. "Lots of the problems involve graduate teaching assistants."

Bill was looking for a way to at least score one point. "Okay, I can see a prohibition about dating undergraduates. Most of them are minors anyway. I just can't see how the same logic pertains to our friend Dwight here."

"Don't worry about me, Bill, I was probably going to resign anyway. I don't think it would have worked out being in the same department as my ex-wife. Also, I can be here to help my mom. In a year or so, I might look for another teaching job. Before that, I have a book to finish."

"Courtney read one of your books, the one on William Shakespeare," Cathy said. "She was really surprised to find out her dad and I went to high school with you."

"That was my first one. It's been a big seller for me. I'm working on a book about Charles Dickens now. It'll be the fifth biography I've published."

"And they're aimed at a middle school or high school audience, at least that's what Courtney said. She read the Shakespeare book a couple of years ago."

"Yeah, my snooty academic colleagues didn't like the way I pitched the books, but my publisher does, and they sell. I think middle and high school students should have good reference books, something more than what they can find on the internet."

"I agree," Cathy said. "I think kids get too much of their information from the internet."

"I disagree," Bill interrupted. "There's lots of good stuff on the internet. I think it's a better source than newspapers and magazines. All you get from newspapers and magazines is the liberal press's viewpoint. The internet is where other people get a chance to tell what's really happening, not just what the east-coast liberals want you to believe."

"I thought we agreed not to get into your crackpot internet sites."

A silence followed Cathy's sharp retort. Dwight figured he'd better change the subject fast. "Are any of our high school classmates still living in town?"

The conversation shifted nicely. It turned out several people Dwight knew from high school were still in town, and others who lived at some distance that either Cathy or Bill kept up with. Dwight remembered most of the people, and Cathy dragged out the high school yearbook to show him pictures of those he didn't remember. The dinner passed uneventfully, with the discussion focused on their high school classmates. Still, Bill and Cathy didn't seem comfortable with each other. Dwight wondered what was going on.

Just before Dwight left, he exchanged emails and phone numbers with Bill and Cathy. They agreed to keep in touch, and Cathy said she was thinking of hosting a little get together with some of his classmates who lived in town.

As Dwight walked home, he marveled at how much his high school self would have liked the goodbye hug he got from Cathy.

CHAPTER FOUR

The next morning, Dwight went for a run. It was the first time he'd exercised since coming to Boynton. As he ran, he recognized it hadn't been a good idea to miss as many days as he had. He wasn't fast, but he enjoyed running. Also, he figured if he kept running, he wouldn't have to worry much about what he ate. He'd worked up a good sweat by the time he finished thirty minutes.

After his shower, he checked his email. Dwight was surprised to find one from Bill Wilson.

> Dwight, Cathy gets all uptight about my favorite internet sites, but she never gives them a chance. I think it's where you can find truth. You should give my favorite site a look, particularly the origins video. VMvoice.com *Bill*

Dwight sent back a quick email thanking Bill and telling him he'd check out the site. Some of the discussion the previous evening suggested he wouldn't be inclined to like the same news sources as Bill, but he thought he should give it a look anyway. Dwight was convinced a large part of the political divide in the country traced to different sources of news offering different views of reality. It caused political arguments that would likely never be resolved. He had a terrible feeling

Bill's site would be one of those offering alternative facts, ones he'd find difficult to believe. Still, if he was going to be thrown together with Bill and his friends, it might be good to know where they were coming from.

He opened VMvoices.com and searched for the origins video. It was easy to find. Dwight clicked on it, and a YouTube video appeared, featuring a tall man in a strange outfit. A Guy Fawkes mask covered his face. His outfit made him look like a medieval warrior. He wore a Viking helmet featuring horns on the side, a robe that came well below his knees, and big boots. *I think he's the one speaking, but I can't see his mouth move because of the mask.* Whoever spoke had a commanding voice, a deep baritone.

The masked man told a fascinating story. He claimed his group originated with the Vikings who came with Leif Eriksson, the first Europeans to land in North America. According to the speaker, these Vikings sailed from Greenland and settled in what is now Newfoundland in Canada. Dwight thought this much of the story was true, or at least he knew about Leif Erickson.

The video went on to say that the site of this settlement had been found by archeologists in the early nineteen sixties. It consisted of several houses, and there was evidence it had been lived in for quite a while. Most people think the Vikings abandoned the settlement and went back to Greenland and Iceland.

Dwight didn't have any reason to doubt this bit of history, but what came next was a different story. The narrator explained that not all the Vikings left, and he can trace his ancestry to those early Viking settlers who stayed. According to him, the settlement was abandoned by the main group of Vikings because they disapproved of settlers who stayed. The major reason for the disapproval was that the Vikings who stayed had taken up with a group of mermaids. Dwight backed up the video at this point and played it again to be sure he'd heard it correctly.

The narrator then explained how, after the main group left, what he called the VM group, VM for Vikings and mermaids, moved further inland and over the years migrated west and south. As he explained, they thrived for three reasons: First, they developed good relations with the native peoples they encountered. Second, the mermaids caught lots of fish in the lakes. The third, and major reason they thrived, involved the Overseers. The Overseers were space aliens who had helped the VM group at the start and visited them several times as they migrated. The Overseers taught the group how to become invisible when it suited them. The power of invisibility came in handy as the group moved through more populated regions during their migration. The group eventually settled in what is now the United States three hundred years ago. The guy claimed this video is the first time anyone from the group has revealed their history to the outside world.

He was sure this was a bunch of hogwash and almost turned off the video. *How could Bill, or any other thinking person, find this anything but funny?* Looking back at the video, Dwight knew that the guy understood where his audience was at this point. He said, "Most of you don't believe me. Let me give you a demonstration. I have three things."

He then took a piece of paper out of his robe and held it up. "I spit into one of those tubes to have my ancestry done. Here's what I got."

The camera zoomed in on the paper the guy was holding. It showed the guy's ancestors were from three groups: Scandinavians, Native American, and Unknown in roughly equal amounts.

"What do you think the unknown part is?" After a pause, he continued, "Second, I have a little video for you."

The video showed a couple of women in bikinis walking into a lake. The women laid down in the water. An overhead camera showed their legs slowly developing green scales as they grew together. Eventually, a longer shot showed the women didn't have legs. They each had one big flipper. The video stopped after they swam around the lake for a couple of minutes.

"Still not convinced?" the masked man asked when the camera returned to him. "Here's more for you." At this point, he took the boot off his right foot, lifted his robe, and poured water on his leg. Very quickly, green scales started to grow on his lower leg and foot.

He couldn't tell how this trick had been performed, or how the mermaids had transformed, for that matter, but he'd seen better magic shows in person. This was a video, and there were lots of ways to alter video. It was clever, but Dwight wasn't sold by any means.

The masked man took a towel and patted down his leg, and the scales faded away. "Enough of this. I wanted you to know I was being honest with you, so I gave a short demonstration. Now I need to explain why I've revealed our secret."

Dwight shifted in his seat, wondering how much more of this he should watch. It was bizarre, but not especially believable. He decided he'd stick it out to the end of the video.

"The Overseers have been guiding the leaders of the United States from the beginning. They think our experiment with democracy is very worthwhile. They are great believers in liberty. They helped Thomas Jefferson write the Declaration of Independence and James Madison write the Constitution. They have been behind most of the decisions that have led the United States to become the greatest nation on earth.

"Unfortunately, we haven't seen the Overseers for over forty years. I have revealed myself because we finally heard from them. As they explained, they are in the midst of a battle with one of their cosmic enemies, and the tide of battle turned against them starting about thirty-five years ago. They have not been able to help guide our country. Their enemies have insinuated themselves into the liberal elite in this country, and this is the reason this country is in such a steep decline."

Dwight knew where this diatribe was going, and he wondered how much more he could stand to watch. *Maybe just another minute or two*, he thought. "Look at what has happened. We're being overrun by people from foreign countries. Jobs, the jobs that the foreigners haven't taken away, are disappearing. Who has more rights today than ever before? Gays and minorities, that's who. Here is a piece of evidence you won't get from the liberal elites and their experts."

At that point, the guy held up a graph. It showed two lines, both of which skewed up at the end. He explained that one line represented the number of vaccines given to the average child in the US by the time they reached eight years old, and the other line gave the estimate of the number of gays in the US.

"The conclusion is clear. All the experts tell you to vaccinate your kids, but as you can see, the result is we get more gays." Dwight shook his head, wondering about this guy's childhood.

"The liberal newspapers and college professors will tell you to listen to experts, but these experts have been wrong more often than they've been right, and they ignore clear evidence like I just showed you when it doesn't suit their purposes. It wasn't too long ago, the experts were predicting a new ice age; now all they can talk about is so-called global warming.

"Right thinking people can see things. They don't need experts to tell them what to do. This is the message the overseer told me to tell you. Don't be taken in by the liberal elites and their experts. They are trying to take away your liberties. Need an example? Listen to what they say about guns.

"The Overseer's message is simple. Remember how your ancestors thrived. They relied on themselves, not the government. They didn't need high-priced college educations to know the difference between right and wrong. They didn't need experts to tell them what was happening around them. They could see it and understand it. The Overseers want us to return to our roots, to the truth as our founding fathers knew it.

"I will amplify this message in additional posts." With that, the guy in the Guy Fawkes mask disappeared from the screen, ending the video.

Dwight sat back and thought about what he'd just seen. *Slick. The video was professionally done, but it lost track of reality soon after it started. The business about the mermaids and the space aliens is complete nonsense.*

Dwight wondered if his biases were showing. After the mermaids and the space aliens, the thrust of the message was conservative. It ran counter to all his instincts. The experts the masked man railed against were Dwight's people. While he wasn't politically active, he was a liberal. He could see how the video appealed to Bill, but it clearly wasn't his cup of tea. He decided not to look at any of the other videos.

After an hour of unsuccessfully trying to get his attention back on Charles Dickens, Dwight gave up and went looking for his mom. Maybe her second cell phone lesson would help him get his mind off Vikings and mermaids. He found her in the living room, sitting in her chair. She'd fixed her hair and was dressed like her old self.

"What's up, Mom? Are you going out?" He took a seat on the couch next to her.

She sat up straight and gave him a small smile. "Yes, as a matter of fact I am. I called Gertrude and Mildred yesterday on my new phone." Her smile faded for a moment before she continued. "It's funny, but I was mad at them. I've known them both for probably thirty years, and they didn't call me when I was stuck in here recovering."

He had to be careful how he phrased this. He didn't want his mother to feel like he was being negative about her condition, but he also didn't want her to think her friends had abandoned her. "It's hard with a stroke, Mom. Remember? You had trouble talking at first. A phone call was difficult for you then. I had trouble understanding you. You've gotten a lot better. Maybe your friends were afraid to call, because they had no way of knowing what they'd get on the other end of the line."

Her smile returned. "You are smart sometimes, despite all your flaws. Yes, that's what they both told me. They told me they'd called earlier, but they couldn't understand me. They were afraid it would be the same thing if they called again. They were thrilled when I sounded better. We're going out to lunch at Johnson's. I've called a cab. It should be here any minute now."

"I guess there's not time for another cell phone lesson."

"No, but both Gert and Mildred have the silly things. They said they could show me how they used them. I've got mine in my purse."

"Great, I bet they can show you lots of things. If you need more help, I'm always here."

A horn sounded outside. "Thank you, dear." Evangeline stood, crossed the room, and peered out the window. "There's my cab." Grabbing her walker, she marched out the door without even saying goodbye.

Dwight marveled at the change in his mother. Watching her walk down the sidewalk, he could tell she hadn't fully recovered. Still, her mood had surely improved.

After his mother left, Dwight wandered up to his father's office and spent a relatively unproductive hour trying to determine what to do with the David Copperfield chapter of his Dickens book. Finally, he recognized he was hungry. Somehow it was one-thirty. He went to the kitchen but didn't find anything appealing. He decided to find out what options Boynton offered. He wondered if Haden's Deli in the center of town was still there.

Dwight found a parking place on the edge of the business district. He walked down Main Street to see what things looked like. Unlike some towns whose main shopping district had been replaced by a mall, or worse yet, a Walmart, Boynton's downtown seemed to be surviving.

As he walked down the street, he saw Cathy's dress shop, Clothes for Me and You. He wondered if she was in the store but didn't check. It would seem weird. He should try to get Cathy Wilson out of his mind.

Haden's Deli was still there, right in the center of town. Dwight had a leisurely lunch, after which he walked the rest of Main Street before turning around, crossing the street, and heading for his car. It was odd. He'd grown up here, but he didn't recognize much of the town. Most of the stores were different, and there were some empty store fronts. He didn't recognize anyone who passed him on the street, and no one recognized him. He saw Cathy's store, on the other side of the street this time.

CHAPTER FIVE

His mother was home when Dwight returned from lunch, sitting in the kitchen with a cup of tea. He declined a cup for himself but joined her at the table. She was full of gossip. For some reason, she seemed to think Dwight would be interested in the goings on of her over-seventy friends. He jollied her along because it was good to see her with more enthusiasm for life. After she began to slow down, he asked her if she had learned anything more about her phone.

"Oh yes. Mildred is very adept with her phone, and it's just like mine. She showed me the flashlight. Who knew a phone could act like a flashlight? And she showed me her email. Can we get me an email address? I think I need it. Mildred keeps track of a bunch of my friends with email. I think I can learn how to use it."

"Sure. Accounts are free. I can set you up with one. You'll have to have a password for the email account, but if I can do things right, you won't have to use it often."

Dwight took Evangeline's phone and started to set up email for her. "There's no use in you understanding what I'm doing now. I'll explain things once the email program is installed. You just want to know how to send and receive email, right?"

"Yes, that's all. I'm impressed at how fast you can type on such a small space."

"I'm not that fast. You should see some of the college students. Their thumbs are a blur."

When the email program was ready, Dwight sent his mother an email. Then he showed her how to look at her messages. "I guess I should have expected something like this," Evangeline said. "You welcomed me to this century. Very funny."

"What did you say a few days ago? Always a smart aleck. Guilty as charged. Now send me a message. Here, I'll show you how."

Evangeline had trouble hitting the right keys, but eventually she was able to send a message to Dwight. Evangeline was tiring, so after he showed her he'd received her message, Dwight suggested maybe they continue her cell phone lessons at some other time.

"You're right. I think I need a nap. Lunch was enjoyable, but I'm not used to being out and about. I think I'll climb up the stairs and take a nap."

"Do you want me to carry your walker up for you?"

"No, no need. I have an upstairs walker and a downstairs one. I can manage the stairs using the banister. It would be too much bother to try to carry a walker up and down the stairs."

Dwight followed his mother upstairs and went to see if he could make any progress on Dickens. For the rest of the afternoon, he reread some of David Copperfield and then managed a solid hour of writing. He was pleased with his progress for a change.

As he got ready for bed, he checked his email one last time. He almost didn't look at one of the five unread messages. He didn't recognize the address. When he did look at it, he found the email was from Cathy Wilson. It was short. She said she had enjoyed seeing him and wondered if he could meet her at her Clayville store for lunch tomorrow. She said there was something she wanted to talk over. She added the address of the store and signed off. Dwight didn't know what to think, but he did know he was free for lunch and intrigued by the invitation. He answered, telling her he'd see her at noon.

The next morning dragged. He helped his mother with her phone for a while, showing her how to delete unwanted emails and how to set up an address book. He suggested she write an email to Mildred asking her for the emails of their friends.

"But I don't know Mildred's email address."

"Whoops, I guess you'll have to call her. I sometimes forget this thing is a phone."

"Okay." His mother smiled at him.

Dwight spent the next two and a half hours accomplishing very little. He answered an email from his publisher, Jim, bringing him up to date, telling him where he was and that he thought he could still make the deadline. He also answered the email of one of his old colleagues, Larry Morgan, who wasn't a fan of Marjorie. It was nice to be brought up to date on campus happenings, but somewhat surprisingly, Dwight wasn't interested. After the emails, he reviewed what he'd written the previous afternoon. Parts of it were rough, and he spent quite a bit of time polishing the prose. He looked up and only one hour had passed. *It's always this way when I'm eager for something*, he thought.

Eventually, it was close to time for him to start for Clayville, so Dwight went to the bedroom to change. He'd been thinking about what to wear, but he hadn't come to any conclusion. Finally, he settled on a lightweight sport coat over an open collar shirt—dressed up but not too much. He still had half an hour to make the fifteen miles, but he started anyway.

He guessed he'd been to Clayville a couple of times in his life, but it had been a while. His GPS directed him to the store with ten minutes to spare, so he decided to drive around town to kill the time. There was a small downtown and a few nice houses. Dwight wondered what kept the town going. Cathy must have thought she'd attract customers, so there had to be something.

At twelve precisely, Dwight walked into the women's clothing store. Cathy was helping a customer, so another woman approached him. "I'm here for lunch with Mrs. Wilson," he said.

Cathy heard him. "I'll just be a second. Mrs. Jacobs has made her selection. Colleen can ring her up."

As Cathy walked toward him, Dwight realized again what a knockout she was. She wore an emerald-green dress, with a scooped top and showing lots of leg—not revealing, but suggestive. She gave him one of her hugs that threatened his equilibrium, but he recovered.

"My car's out back; come on through." As they passed the salesclerk, Cathy said, "Colleen, this is Dwight Kelton. We went to high school together in Boynton. I'll be back in an hour or so."

Dwight shook hands with Colleen and followed Cathy through the door to the rear of the store. They got into a white SUV parked in back, and Cathy said, "I made a reservation at the country club. It's about the only decent place in town."

"Sounds fine. I'm not picky."

The country club dining room had surprisingly few customers. Cathy suggested the hostess take them to a table for two out of earshot of other tables. As he looked at the menu, Dwight wondered what this was all about. Cathy hadn't revealed anything on the ride to the country club.

After the waitress took their drink orders, Chablis for Cathy and iced tea for Dwight, Cathy finally broke her silence. "I understand Bill sent you an email suggesting you look at the VM site."

"Yes, he did."

Cathy stared directly into Dwight's eyes. "What did you think?"

Dwight paused then decided to be honest. "It was nicely produced, and the guy, whoever he is, has a great voice. That said, it was basically a bunch of hogwash."

A big smile spread across Cathy's face. "I knew that would be your reaction."

"Does Bill fall for that stuff?"

Cathy's smile disappeared. "Unfortunately, hook, line, and sinker. He's a big VM believer, and it's getting worse. I think he's sent them money and is starting to try to form a local VM group." She looked down as she placed her napkin on her lap.

Again, Dwight decided honesty was the best approach. "Bill's clearly a political conservative. I could tell that when I was at your house. I guess some of what the guy in the mask was saying would be right up his alley. Still, how can he believe the guy is descended from Vikings and mermaids? Vikings are real, mermaids are not."

A look—frustration? resignation?—passed over Cathy's face briefly before she answered. "Yeah, you only watched the origins video, I bet. It's the mildest one. They get scarier."

Their drinks arrived, and the waitress took their orders, a salad for Cathy and a chicken sandwich for Dwight.

Dwight waited for the waitress to get out of range. "Scarier how?"

"Well, some of it is the Viking and mermaid stuff. That's in all of them. So is the space aliens bit, for that matter. One of the most frightening ones is called Stars and Bars." Cathy stopped and took a large sip of her wine. "The masked guy explains how the alien Overseers come sporadically and missed the bulk of the Civil War. He said they were involved in putting Robert E. Lee in charge of the Confederate army, but then they had to leave. You have to understand, Mr. Lee was a descendant of the Viking mermaid people. The Overseers thought he would prevail, and when they came back in 1873, at least I think it was '73, they were shocked. They thought the South would win easily. The stars and bars video is all about how the south deserved to win. They were on the side of small government and people's liberty, just like the Overseers preach." Cathy finished her wine and signaled the waitress for another glass.

"They weren't on the side of the slaves' liberty," Dwight interjected.

"Of course, but there is not one mention of slavery in the entire video. The war was about liberty versus government control, according to the masked Viking-mermaid man."

"That's crazy."

Their food arrived, along with Cathy's wine, so the discussion ceased while they ate. Dwight was glad he had stuck to iced tea. He'd need to keep his wits about him, because he still wasn't sure what this lunch was about. After their plates were cleared and they ordered coffee, Dwight asked Cathy to explain more of the videos.

"The one that convinced me Bill had drifted from reality is called Witch Doctors, and it's about how modern medicine is a tool of the liberal elite. I think you saw the graph in the video you watched about the relationship between vaccinations and gays. Despite all the good vaccinations have done, like eradicating polio and smallpox, the guy says people shouldn't vaccinate their kids. The Witch Doctor has more stuff like that." She took another healthy slug of her wine, making Dwight wonder if she'd be okay to drive back from lunch. Maybe he should convince her to eat dessert to soak up the alcohol. "It's fake science. The Witch Doctor echoes themes found in the other videos, such as distrust of government statistics. It's health statistics here, but it's other statistics elsewhere." She looked up from staring at her wine glass, her gaze open and concerned. "The weirdest part is the claim that implants allow the government to track people. Each knee or hip replacement, or false tooth for that matter, has a small transmitter linked to a database controlled by the government. With this database, they track a large fraction of the population. The video ends with the command, 'Hold on to your parts. Don't let the doctors replace them.'"

Dwight suppressed a shudder. This type of propaganda could be dangerous. "This is not just run-of-the-mill conservatism," Dwight said. "It's kooky. This kind of stuff makes people think someone, the liberal elite, I guess, is plotting against them somehow."

Cathy nodded, a look of relief in her eyes. "Yes, and the more of it you see, the more frightening it becomes. If people swallow this stuff, it will undermine the country. We need some common underlying beliefs, and we need to trust our fellow citizens. The VM guy is trying to erode what keeps the country together. And my husband believes all this."

Dwight thought for a moment before asking, "Don't you think only a small minority of the country will fall for this nonsense?"

"Unfortunately, no."

He sat back and stared at Cathy. *Why is she telling me all this?*

Almost as if she were reading his mind, Cathy continued, "I think the VM guy has to be stopped, and I think you can help."

Dwight shook his head. What did she think he could do that would stop any of this? "I might be able to show Bill how foolish the VM stuff is. Is that what you want?"

"I don't care what Bill believes. He and I are through. We're only staying in the same house because of Courtney. When she goes off to college, I'm divorcing him."

He was shocked at how calmly Cathy made this declaration. "Wow, I'm sorry. I always thought of you two as the perfect couple."

"Looks can fool you. I'm sure I loved him once, but that's long gone. Ever since he failed at college football, he's become a bitter person. He blames all his shortcomings, and they're numerous, on other people. Nothing's ever his fault."

"But you two look successful. You live in a nice house in one of the best neighborhoods in town."

"Like I said, looks can fool you. We could only afford the house because of what I make from the stores. Bill is running his father's insurance business into the ground. I don't know how he's going to survive after the divorce, and frankly I don't care."

He was still confused about what she wanted. "I don't get what you want me to do."

Cathy reached over and grasped his hand. "I know it's a big favor, but I want you to infiltrate the VM group. Someone needs to expose them. Someone who can write. You told us you liked solving puzzles. There are lots of puzzles. Who are these people? Where are they from? Who funds them? Someone needs to answer these questions."

Dwight didn't know what to think. "How would I even get started?"

"I know Bill will try to recruit you. The VM people have reached out to anyone dumb enough to send them money asking them to put together local groups. As I said, Bill is trying to start one."

He leaned back and considered what she'd just asked. "I don't know. My life just got turned upside down, and this is not the kind of project I know anything about. I'm not sure I could fake believing this stuff. It's so far out."

Cathy looked into Dwight's eyes and smiled. "I think you can do it."

He was falling under Cathy's spell, and part of him didn't care. "I'll think about it. That's all I can promise. I find it hard to believe it's as dangerous as you think."

"I know it's dangerous," Cathy said. She was still holding Dwight's hand. "It's the kind of thing that lots of people will dismiss. Like you said, it seems too kooky. Still, to some it has the illusion of truth. I know Bill, and I know people like him. It's going to catch on, and before you know it, we'll have problems. We need to stop it before it gets started."

Dwight needed time to think, and he couldn't think straight with Cathy holding his hand. He withdrew his hand and excused himself to go to the bathroom. He took his time in there, washing his hands and blotting his face with a wet paper towel. As he walked back to the table, he hadn't made up his mind, but he had developed a strategy. "Here's what I'll do. I'm going to give your proposal serious consideration. I'll look at some of the other videos. Let's meet back here day after tomorrow, and I'll give you a definitive answer."

Cathy reached over and gave his hand a squeeze. "Thanks, I guess that's what I should have expected. I sprang this idea completely out of the blue." At this point, Cathy rose and said, "I'd better get back to work."

When they got to the parking spot behind the store, instead of getting out, Cathy put her hand on Dwight's leg and looked him in the eyes. "Dwight, I thought you underrated yourself in high school. Don't do it again now. I know you can do what I'm asking. You're an incredibly talented person."

Cathy leaned over and kissed him lightly on the lips. "Give my proposal serious thought."

Dwight was stunned, but he was able to gather himself enough to follow Cathy into the back room of the store.

When they got to the sales floor, Colleen looked as if she was a little peeved. "You guys took your time," she said as she took her purse out of a drawer.

"I'm sorry," Cathy said. "I'll try not to be late again."

Colleen walked out the door just as a customer walked in. Dwight turned to Cathy and said, "It looks like you need to attend to her. I'll see you day after tomorrow."

Cathy enveloped him in a hug, a bit longer than usual, and breathed into his ear. "Think about it."

Dwight left the store, wondering just what was going on.

CHAPTER SIX

When Dwight got home, he went into his office and looked at another VM video. Lower Education turned out to be all about the evils of going to college. It started by focusing on three things: student debt, liberal professors, and useless curriculum. The VM guy used data dishonestly. He showed newspaper stories about students who had abnormally high debt. Dwight knew who they were. They were students who'd attended very expensive schools and whose parents hadn't helped. On top of that, the students had gone on to graduate school. As a result, their debts were four or five times the debt of the average student. With the professors, he picked kooks who Dwight thought probably shouldn't be allowed to teach anywhere. While the professors mentioned were bad, they were by no means representative. The examples of courses were similar. The courses mentioned weren't normal. They had way-out titles. Actually, Dwight believed, if the courses forced students to think clearly and write convincingly, the actual subject matter wasn't too important, so there was no way he was buying the argument. When he finished this portion of the video, Dwight could see how it peddled the notion that colleges and universities were tools of the liberal elite, and they couldn't be trusted.

He sat back, taking his eyes off the screen to think about what he'd just seen. He thought it was incredibly biased, too biased to convince anyone. He wondered if someone not intimately connected with higher education would have found the video as unconvincing. It was intellectually dishonest, but that didn't stop it from being effective with people. Lots of people thought college was a waste of time and money. Many dreams of landing a cushy, high-salary job after college had been dashed. Lots of people who went to college didn't finish, so they didn't derive much benefit from it. Then he remembered what Bill had said about his college experience. *He'd probably eat this up.*

In the final part of the video, the masked man claimed that all college did was make graduates think they were better than people without a degree. The fascination with college-based paths to social success implicitly downplayed the importance of people who worked with their hands. "Part of the problem with America today," claimed the masked guy, "is that we have bought into a system that looks down on honest work."

While the guy was a charlatan, Dwight wasn't sure this last point didn't have merit. Again, he thought, *It will certainly appeal to Bill and lots of working-class people.* The country was split, and maybe this person had a point. For the first time, Dwight thought he might be able to play the game Cathy wanted. At least some of what the VM guy was saying wasn't complete hogwash.

Dwight stared at the ceiling, replaying his talk with Cathy. Despite what she said, he thought maybe she wanted his help because of some deep-seated animus toward Bill. Still, even if that were true, she was right. This VM nonsense should be exposed. *Am I the one who should do it? How would I do it?*

One of the things Cathy had said stuck with him. She said he'd underrated himself in high school. The statement had amazed him almost as much as the kiss that followed. He didn't think Cathy Mellow had given him one thought in high school. He wasn't sure they'd ever had more than two or three conversations. Thinking back, he guessed they'd been in lots of classes together. Being an M, she would have sat behind him as a K. He remembered there were no L's and only Doris McDonald between them. He thought the National Honor Society would have been the only club they were in together, and that group never met. Why would she say he'd underrated himself in high school?

Marjorie had said a similar thing to him when they were first dating. She told him he was better than he claimed to be. He remembered being thrilled by her comment. *Why am I skeptical of a similar claim from Cathy? Maybe it was the hand holding, the kiss, and the overlong goodbye hug. It all seemed a little much.*

Still, what if it was sincere? Maybe she likes me for some reason. The physical stuff might be part of it too. She and Bill probably hadn't been intimate for quite some time. Dwight didn't know what to think.

That evening, Dwight caught Courtney in the front room just as she was leaving after preparing dinner. She had one strap of her backpack on and clutched a lacrosse stick in her hand. "I thought you played field hockey," he said.

"I do, but that's in the fall. All of us play both sports."

"Keeps you in shape."

She shrugged the other backpack strap over her shoulder. "Yeah, I guess so. I think I'm only going to play hockey in college. I don't think I can do two sports and make good grades."

Dwight was impressed with her insight. "You're probably right. Please tell your parents I enjoyed getting reacquainted."

"Oh Professor, both my parents enjoyed it too." In typical teenager fashion, she rolled her eyes. "It's about the only thing I've seen them agree on for the past three years."

"Gosh, I didn't know they weren't getting along." Dwight marveled at his ability to hide what he knew. While he was glad to have Cathy's words confirmed, he was unhappy for Cathy.

"They try to hide it when anyone's around, but when they're alone it shows. Back a few years ago, there were terrible arguments. Now it's mostly silence. That's what was so good about your visit. It gave them a chance to relive high school when they were happy with each other."

"I'm so sorry. You seem to have come to terms with it."

"Yeah. I've been living with it for a while, and I guess I can see my mom's side. She's the one who talks to me. My dad's a different story. He never says a thing. Lately, he's been in a different universe with some crazy internet site he looks at all the time. Also, I think he has a girlfriend. He tries to hide it, but I think he does. They're headed for a divorce."

"Again, I'm sorry. Back in high school, we all thought they were the perfect couple. Unfortunately, people can grow apart."

"Your mom said you were in divorce proceedings, so I guess you'd know."

Dwight smiled. "Touché."

Courtney laughed and, hoisting her backpack and her lacrosse stick, left by the front door.

Later that evening, Dwight returned to his office and watched the Witch Doctor video before going to bed. It was just like Cathy had described. Again, the guy cherry picked the data to make his points. It was completely intellectually dishonest, but again Dwight could see how it could be convincing. The theme continued in the other VM videos. So-called experts, physicians in this instance, but more generally college-educated elites, made lots of mistakes, and they looked down their noses at the working class. It wasn't right.

The closing section of the video really disturbed Dwight. The speaker claimed some nefarious representatives were polluting the drinking water. He asserted that the additive had the surprising effect of making children more rambunctious and adults more docile. They were spreading this additive, which was currently undetectable, in public water supplies all over the country. The VM guy said the Overseers were working on an antidote, but it wasn't ready yet. Dwight thought this was complete nonsense, but he could see how it fit.

The next morning, he figured he'd better settle down and do the work he'd been avoiding. To determine just how effective the VM videos were, he'd have to plow through the comments associated with the videos. Dwight hated comments. He had published several papers in online journals that allowed readers to post comments. He couldn't help himself from reading through what was posted on those papers. It had usually been a waste of time. Some people were on-target and helpful. Others had an ax to grind, so they were off topic. Still others found some way to be nasty, on-topic or off-topic. Dwight didn't think people should be allowed to post comments unless they were willing to put their name on them, but even in the academic world people could be anonymous.

The comments on the origins video were mostly negative, though some were positive. Thankfully, there weren't many crazy riffs on some topic unrelated to anything in the video. As he suspected, the Stars and Bars video elicited many more comments, and they were almost all positive. A few people mentioned slaves, but they were shouted down by the people who claimed the war wasn't about slavery at all. The Witch Doctor video garnered even more comments, and they were overwhelmingly supportive of the video's claims. Many of them were long descriptions of times when the medical community had misdiagnosed some illness. Many of them were gut wrenching. As Dwight continued, looking at the comments in the order the videos were released, they grew more and more positive. He figured like-minded people were the only ones who would bother to keep looking at the videos.

He took a break from the comments to view the last two videos. The first one was focused on race relations and affirmative action. Keeping up the thrust of the previous videos, the masked man recounted stories about good, solid, working-class white citizens losing jobs or promotions because of affirmative action. Colleges and universities came in for another bashing in this video. Dwight didn't think this video broke much new ground. As he suspected, the comments were overwhelmingly positive. The viewers loved this video.

The last video Dwight looked at, the most recently released, focused on guns. Ominously, it was titled "The Solution." The masked man traced the American love of guns through American history, starting with the Minutemen. He then described the attempts to limit the use of guns as being driven by the liberal elites. He argued, and found scholarly studies to back up his claim, that guns stop crime. Again, Dwight thought he cherry-picked his examples, and he never once mentioned accidental shootings. The ending of the video was chilling. "Keep your guns safe," he said. "They will be needed for the final solution."

Turning to the comments, Dwight became frightened. All the comments were supportive. They told of love for the second amendment, gun club memberships, and somewhat off target, martial arts academies. Militia groups pledged their support.

Dwight knew there were underground groups in the country who were violently anti-government, but he thought they were mostly isolated survivalist crazies in the West. Reading the comments made him feel like he was drastically underestimating the number of heavily armed people who hated the government. This VM masked man was gaining their allegiance. He could see why Cathy was frightened. What bothered him was the fear that the VM propaganda might be too far gone to stop. *What can I do?*

Dwight decided to get out of his office and go for the run he should have done earlier. He left his mother chatting happily on her phone and walked out the front door. When he was growing up, lots of kids lived nearby. He looked for signs of young children, swing sets, Big Wheels, and bicycles, but he didn't see many. He guessed the neighborhood had become too pricey for young families with kids.

As he ran, he made a decision. He'd take the first steps implicit in Cathy's plan. He'd email Bill and tell him he'd enjoyed the origins video and looked at a couple of the others. That put the ball in Bill's court. If Cathy was right, Bill would get back to him about some local group. He wasn't sure how far he wanted to go with this, but there was little risk in approaching Bill. *I can't ignore what's happening. I'll figure this out as I go.*

CHAPTER SEVEN

The next day, Dwight drove to the country club. Cathy was already there, standing beside her SUV and looking fabulous. She had on a short skirt, a red top that exposed a little of her midriff, and red sandals. When he got a little closer, Dwight thought maybe it wasn't a short skirt but rather a blousy pair of shorts. He remembered Marjorie calling such a thing a skort. *Whatever, she looks great.*

Dwight pulled up beside her and got out of his car. Cathy flew into his arms, hugging him tightly. This wasn't one of her hello hugs, it was way more. Hugging back, Dwight's arms touched exposed skin on her back. It sent a thrill through his body.

She whispered into his ear, "I'm so glad you're going to help." After a big squeeze, she broke off the hug, took Dwight's hand, and led him toward the door.

As he followed her into the country club, Dwight felt like a puppy being led by his master, but somehow it didn't bother him.

After they were seated, again in an isolated table for two, Dwight said, "I see you monitor Bill's emails."

Cathy beamed at him. "Yes, he and I used to share an email address, and he hasn't been smart enough to change the password. I have a new address—one with my own password. I check his once in a while to keep up with what he's doing."

"And you saw my email."

Cathy reached her hand across the table and took Dwight's. "It was really good, just the right mix of enthusiasm for the VM videos and a little skepticism. Bill's going to think you're on the edge, and he can push you over."

"That's what I was aiming for."

"It worked. You got invited to a meeting tonight."

Cathy removed her hand as the waitress came with their menus. Dwight ordered a beer this time, and Cathy stuck with Chablis. They both ordered the same food they'd had the last time they were there.

After they ordered, Dwight spoke up. "I had a talk with Courtney the night before last, and she thinks you and Bill are headed for a divorce. I was surprised at how nonchalant she was about it. There wasn't a hint of emotion."

Cathy blew out a breath and sat back. "Courtney's a sharp kid, and she's been living with Bill and me all her life. She's seen us drift apart, and she couldn't help overhearing a fair number of arguments. We confide in one another. She knows Bill and I are just keeping up appearances. I don't think there's any drama, as far as she's concerned."

Dwight nodded, feeling as if he'd entered a minefield. "Okay, I guess it makes sense. I was surprised, that's all."

"I can see how. It's been settled in my mind, and I suppose Courtney's too, for quite some time."

He didn't want to, but he knew he had to tell her what her daughter had said. "She thinks Bill has a girlfriend."

"Yes, I know about her from his email, and in a funny way I'm happy for Bill. Her name is Stacy Bonnett. I guess you'll probably meet her."

Dwight still had a nagging question. He figured it was time to get it out. "I don't understand why you're so interested in stopping the VM people. It's not about getting back at Bill, I can see that. What is it?"

The waitress arrived with their drinks, so Cathy waited until she left to answer him. "It's a fair question. Let me give you a little background. My father was a captain in the army. I adored him. When I was eight, he was killed in Iraq. It was terrible for us, but he died for a cause he cared deeply about, protecting this country. I guess it sounds hokey, but I'm a patriot. I don't want to see this country destroyed. I think the ultimate aim of the VM movement is a rebellion, and I think they may be able to get enough supporters. I don't want that to happen."

This time, Dwight reached across the table and took Cathy's hand. "I don't either. And I think you're right about the rebellion. They just about came out and said it in the 'The Solution' video."

Cathy squeezed Bill's hand and released it. The waitress was back, this time with their food.

When she left, Dwight said, "You've got an eager volunteer for the cause."

Cathy smiled. "I'm so glad."

As they ate, Dwight told Cathy he'd read the comments on the videos, and he found them very disturbing. "Quite a few people have bought what the VM guy is saying. I'm sure lots of them already leaned that way before the VM guy, so they may not have been too hard to reel in. No matter, he's got them now."

"Did you see the comments that were signed BW?"

"No, I didn't pay attention to the signatures. Except I did see lots of them weren't signed."

"Bill wrote the BW ones. It might be good for you to read them before the meeting."

"Will do."

As they were walking out after lunch, Cathy took Dwight's hand and led him toward her car. When she got to the driver's door, she looked around. They were alone in the parking lot. She turned, took Dwight in her arms, and kissed him. Dwight was surprised. This wasn't a little peck like before, it was a full-on kiss. He kissed back enthusiastically.

When the kiss broke off, Cathy smiled up at Dwight. "I'm looking forward to seeing you again."

"Me too," stammered Dwight. "I'll email you with a summary of what I learned in my meeting with Bill."

"Great, and we can arrange to get together after that and plan our next steps."

Dwight took the initiative this time and stepped toward Cathy and kissed her. This kiss lasted a little longer than the first one. When they broke apart, Cathy smiled, winked at Dwight, and got into her car.

As he watched her drive off, he wondered what he'd gotten into. He was sure he liked it, but he wasn't quite sure what it was.

Dwight spent the afternoon helping his mother with her phone, writing a couple of pages in the Dickens book, and reading the BW comments. Bill's posts started out quite short. They were mostly laudatory, saying the VM guy understood the truth about America. Later they continued the theme but with a greater sense of urgency. Bill was asking what he could do to right the wrongs the videos pointed out. Dwight thought Bill was one of the more enthusiastic commenters.

In the evening, Dwight drove to the Red Dolphin, a bar on the outskirts of Boynton. He'd never been to the bar, but he remembered it had a rough reputation. Some of his high school acquaintances who had fake IDs told wild stories about the goings on there. When he arrived, it was only half full. He easily spotted Bill sitting with four other people at a table with chairs for eight. They had a pitcher of beer, and there were two empty glasses.

Bill waved him over, and he sat in front of one of the empty glasses. Bill announced, "This is my friend Dwight. I was telling you about him. He just got fired from his job for the oddest reason. Dwight, I'll let the rest of these guys introduce themselves."

Dwight looked closely at the people as they introduced themselves.

"I'm Pete," a short, scruffy guy who looked to be in his fifties said, and they shook hands. "Here, I'll do the honors," Pete said as he filled a glass for Dwight.

"I can see your name from your shirt," Dwight said, pointing to the oil-stained uniform Pete was wearing.

"Yeah, I work over at the JM Garage."

"I'm Roscoe Shrimp," a heavy-set guy Dwight's age announced. The guy had a crushing handshake. "Tank? Is that you?" Roscoe "Tank" Pearlman had been one of the linemen on the high school football team quarterbacked by Bill. It would have been stretching it to say he and Dwight had been friends. Since Dwight had been so short in high school, he remembered Tank used to enjoy tormenting him.

"Yeah, long time no see."

Bill spoke up. "Dwight, Roscoe, and I went to high school together."

"I'm Styles," the next guy said, holding out his hand. Styles was completely bald and had an impressive beer belly. Dwight couldn't tell how old he was.

The final person to offer a name was the girl plastered to Bill's side. "Call me Stacy," she said. Dwight thought the skinny brunette was overly made up, but she wasn't bad looking.

"Nice to meet you all," Dwight said.

"Tell us how you got fired," Tank said. Dwight was sure Tank would like to hear anything that made Dwight look bad.

He'd prepared for this question. "Here's the deal. I was a professor at a university. The long and short of it is that it became known I was sleeping with one of the coeds. The school has a policy that prohibits what they call consensual amorous relations between staff and students, so they fired me."

Bill filled the silence. "That's a bare-bones account. What Dwight left out was the coed was a graduate student, and she was twenty-three. I don't see how it's anyone's business what two mature adults do with their time. How can they have rules against consensual behavior? Consensual means they both consented to whatever they were doing."

"I think we all know what they were doing," Styles said with a leer aimed at Dwight. "Heck, I never been to college, but I thought professors and students got it on all the time."

"Yeah," Tank said. "There was a guy at the junior college where I first went who was famous for shagging the coeds. One of my girlfriends called it a lay for an A."

Everyone laughed. Dwight forced himself to join their laughter, knowing it would look bad if he didn't.

At that point, an older man joined the table. He had gray hair and walked a little slowly. Dwight figured he was in his seventies. He sat down, waved at all the others, and held his hand out to Dwight. "I'm Len," he said.

"Dwight, nice to meet you." Dwight poured a beer for the newcomer.

At this point, Bill started the meeting. "That's everyone I think is coming. I got an email from VM headquarters. There are three things they want us to do at this point. First, they're going to start an online message board where people can exchange ideas. They'll send me the address, and I'll pass it on. It will give us a chance to see what other people are thinking. The second one is kinda neat. It's a hand signal they want us to use to identify other believers. It works this way—make a two with your right hand."

"Like a V for victory," Tank interjected.

"Yeah, but in this case it's not for victory. Next, bend your wrist and put three fingers down."

Bill demonstrated and everyone mimicked what he was doing. Dwight played along, feeling mildly like he was in a juvenile club of some type.

"It's a VM," Stacy said, laughing.

"Yes, it is," Bill continued. "They say you can flash the sign, and it will identify you to another member. When he sees the sign, he will show it back to you. If you flash the sign to someone who doesn't know what's going on, no big deal. He won't know what you're doing."

"What else did they want?" Len asked.

"Just keep doing what you've been doing. Try to get people you know to look at the videos. That's how I got Dwight here. He watched the origins video and got interested."

Dwight piped in, "That's right, then I watched most of the rest of them. It sure gives you a different view of stuff." He figured he'd been vague enough. He wasn't sure he could cross the line and say he believed in all of it and look believable.

"It does," Stacy said. "Especially about doctors. My mom always followed the doctors. When she got cancer, she went right on chemo like they told her to. It was awful, worse than the cancer, and she died anyway. Those doctors didn't know their ass from a hole in the ground, and what burned me up was they didn't care. I saw two of them laughing to each other in the hallway when I was rushing to see my mom. I got there too late. She was already gone."

"The VM guy is right about a lot of stuff," Len said. "The part I like is sprinkled through the videos. We don't control our lives. Other people do. You think you have a lot of money saved up. Unless you're smart enough to have it in gold or silver, it's just blips on a computer screen somewhere. Someone else is in control, not you."

Dwight debated drinking his beer in a single gulp, but he needed to keep his wits about him. He took a sip, watching everyone carefully. The group was starting to get riled up.

"And those other people," Pete said. "Those liberal elites look down their noses at poor working stiffs like me. I get my hands dirty at work, and I'm proud of it, no matter what they say. I think I can get a couple of my buddies at work to look at the videos. I just have to find the right time to ask them."

Bill leaned forward. "Do that, Pete. All they can do is say no. I've asked four people and snagged Dwight. I think that's about how it will work. If we can get one out of four, we'll be okay."

"I'm here because Len got me to look at the videos," Styles said. "I know some people I'm going to ask."

"Are the VM people going to start having rallies?" Stacy asked. "I mean in-person stuff. I like big rallies. It really gets you going to be with a group of people all into the same thing. It could kinda be like a rock concert, but one about the truth."

Bill smiled at her and pulled her closer. "I don't know. But it sounds like a good idea, hon."

The group broke into separate conversations. Dwight told Len his story about being fired for engaging in consensual amorous relations. Len was astounded. Just like the others, he said it flew in the face of the word consent. Since the two people involved were adults, it seemed crazy to Len. That introduction allowed Len to parrot much of the Lower Education video. Dwight recognized the arguments and was able to add things that kept Len going.

The meeting broke up at about nine. On the way out, Dwight thanked Bill for inviting him.

"Sure, no problem. Next time maybe we can come together. It wouldn't work this time. I'm going over to Stacy's." He gave Dwight a nudge in the ribs. "You know how it is with that ball breaker Cathy."

Dwight nodded, not sure what to say, and went out to his car.

CHAPTER EIGHT

Dwight's next day was unproductive. He did get in his morning run, but for most of the day he spent too much time thinking about his coming meeting with Cathy. The only thing of consequence he accomplished was buying a pack of condoms. He didn't know if he'd need one, but he wanted to be prepared just in case.

The previous evening, he'd sent Cathy a short description of the meeting with the VMers after he'd returned from the Red Dolphin. An hour later, Cathy replied, suggesting they meet for dinner the next night. She told him to meet her behind the Clayville store at six-thirty. She knew a nice restaurant a short drive away.

Dwight was really keyed up when he parked beside Cathy's car at six-thirty on the nose. She was still in the driver's seat, and her window opened as he got out of his car. "Get in, Dwight, I know where we're going." He had been looking forward to a hug hello, but he did as she suggested. When he got into the car, Cathy gave him a big smile. "Fasten your seat belt. I want you safe."

Cathy's beauty always shocked Dwight. Tonight was no exception. She had on a bright red dress with lace at the top showing some cleavage. The dress had a long skirt, but from where he sat, Dwight could tell it had a substantial slit. Cathy glanced at him staring at her legs. "Eyes up, buddy," she said with a smile.

"I could get in trouble there too?" Dwight responded.

"Fair enough," Cathy said with a laugh. "The restaurant is about a twenty-minute drive, so control yourself. Now that you've talked to some of them, can you explain the appeal of the VM stuff? For the life of me, I can't figure it out."

"I've been thinking about that a great deal, and there are probably lots of answers. First, I wonder about the Vikings and mermaids and space aliens. It's nonsense, so why does the guy start off with that?"

"I have no idea."

Dwight looked out the window, pondering Cathy's question. They were passing through a small town he'd couldn't remember seeing before. It didn't look very prosperous. After a couple of minutes, he responded. "My thought is that it gives him instant status as someone special. Someone who should be listened to. Most people will think it's crazy, but he isn't concerned. It gives him a filter. People who buy the Vikings' and mermaids' story will probably fall for the rest of his stuff."

Cathy looked grim. "Makes sense, I guess. If you're gullible enough to fall for the Viking and mermaid bit on the first video, you'd fall for almost anything."

"That's what I'm thinking, and there are deeper reasons for his appeal after someone's interested. I'll give you one. It doesn't cover all his followers, but it fits some. Anyway, increasingly our economy rewards brains more than it rewards muscles. The highly paid jobs are in finance, IT, and management. Sure, there are some good worker jobs, like plumbers and electricians, but they're highly skilled. The low-skilled-high-pay jobs in factories are almost all gone. The paths to the middle class for the C and D students in high school just aren't there anymore. Some people put it this way. Our economy now rewards people who manipulate symbols—you know, letters and numbers—

not people who manipulate things. I think VM appeals to people left behind by the modern economy. People who aren't going to be good symbol manipulators. They need someone to blame, and VM gives them plenty."

"Okay. I can see that. Yes, and you think that fits the people you met?"

Dwight stretched in his seat and thought back to the meeting. *I don't know much about the people who'd been there. Then again, maybe they did have one thing in common?*

"I don't know them well enough to say, but I left out part of it. These left-behind people think they are looked down upon by the others. They think the liberal elite, in VM's words, think they're dumb or something. They resent being looked down on."

Cathy paused the conversation, mulling over what Dwight had just said. Then she continued, "That's certainly not everyone. Not everyone looks down on those people."

"They don't, but there's just enough truth there to generate potent feelings. Let me tell you a story. It's about my colleague Jim. One day last year, I told him I'd just heard from an alum, a student we both taught who announced he'd just taken a job in a fire department. Jim's response was: 'Gosh, I thought he was smart.' I thought it was an awful response, but it's a response consistent with the idea that the liberal elites, like my college professor colleague, look down their noses at people in some kinds of jobs."

"I see. I just thought the VM people were crazy. You're saying they might have a legitimate beef with society. It puts a whole new light on it."

"Don't give them too much credit. I think these guys are on the fringe. They believe the solution to their hurt feelings is a revolution. All I'm saying is that for something like the VM business to appeal to people, there has to be some truth behind it."

"Interesting. Ah, here we are."

They had just crossed a bridge over a small river, and Cathy pulled into a parking spot at a restaurant with a balcony overlooking the river. When she stopped, Dwight jumped out and ran around the car so he could open Cathy's door. He gulped when he got a full look at Cathy in the red dress. She was stunning. Dwight reached out to give her a hug.

Cathy hugged back briefly and then gently pushed him away. "There'll be enough time for that later, big boy," she said with a big smile. Cathy took Dwight's hand, and they walked toward the restaurant.

Over dinner, Cathy quizzed Dwight about his meeting, asking him to describe the people who were there. When they exhausted his meager knowledge about the meeting, Cathy shocked him by asking him about his wife, Marjorie.

Dwight thought for a minute. "Well, there were two sides to Marjorie. When we first met, she was fun and so smart. I fell in love with that Marjorie. Later, when we were professors, I saw another side of her. She is insanely competitive. I guess I noticed it a little before, but she was always the smartest one, so it didn't come out. It started with my Shakespeare book. It was a big success. I sold more books than the rest of the department combined. My colleagues, Marjorie included, looked down their noses at it. They said it wasn't really a scholarly effort. I used too many secondary sources."

"What?"

"My references were almost all other books written about Shakespeare, not original sources."

"Oh, I get it."

"And they didn't like the way I pitched the book at middle and high school students. Anyway, the money and praise kept rolling in, and it burned Marjorie up. I could tell in lots of ways, little put downs, snide remarks, and snubs. She didn't like being second fiddle. Frankly, I was almost glad when she took up with the department chair."

When they returned to the car, Cathy checked to see if they were the only ones in the parking lot. When she saw they were alone, she turned her back on her door, pulled Dwight to her, and gave him a deep kiss. As they broke apart, she said with a gleam in her eye, "Now for the other part of the evening."

Dwight almost stumbled as he went around to his door. On the ride back, they didn't talk much. Dwight didn't know what to say, and Cathy seemed content to drive in silence. Back at the lot behind her store, Cathy got out before Dwight could get around to open her door. She grabbed his hand and led him to the back door of her store, took out a key, opened the door, and almost dragged Dwight inside. After she closed the door, she took Dwight in her arms, kissing him eagerly, pushing his back against the closed door. When the kiss ended, they went right into another embrace. Finally, Cathy whispered in his ear, "I want you."

He nodded and continued kissing her, this time letting his hand slide up her side to her breast. After this kiss, Cathy led Dwight down a hallway into an office. The office had a couch, and Cathy pushed Dwight so he was seated and stepped back. Dwight couldn't figure out what was going on until Cathy, looking him in the eyes and smiling, reached around behind her neck and unfastened the hooks holding her top together. He was mesmerized watching her undress. When she finished, she knelt beside him, kissed him, and started unbuttoning his shirt.

CHAPTER NINE

The next morning, Dwight awoke hearing Courtney and his mother chatting as Courtney served breakfast, but he didn't get up. He couldn't help reviewing the previous evening. It had been wonderful. Their first bout of lovemaking had been almost frantic—quick for both of them. The control Cathy had exhibited during her striptease vanished when Dwight's clothes came off. The only awkward bit was when he took out the condom. Cathy had batted it away, saying, "Not needed."

Afterwards, when he was cradling her in his arms, Dwight thought he heard her sobbing. He remembered asking what was wrong.

Cathy answered, "Nothing, absolutely nothing. It's just been so long, and it was so good."

She'd switched from crying to laughing when he'd responded, "Your lack of recent practice wasn't evident."

They'd shared a long kiss after that, followed by several others. When they made love again, it had been slower and gentler, but just as satisfying.

As much as he didn't want to stop replaying his time with Cathy, he decided he'd better get on with the day. He got out of bed and checked his email on his phone. The most interesting new email was from Bill, giving the particulars for the VM message board. Dwight decided he'd read through it later.

After his shower, he dressed and went downstairs to see what Courtney had left for his breakfast. He was surprised to see his mother still seated at the table, reading the paper and drinking coffee. "Good morning, Mother."

Evangeline ignored him, so Dwight went into the kitchen to see what he could find. A few minutes later, he came out with a plate of scrambled eggs he'd reheated in the microwave, and two pieces of toast. He took a seat across from his mother, who'd been looking at him as he came to the table.

"What's her name?" she asked.

Dwight was stunned. "What are you talking about?"

"I asked what her name was. It's simple. Night before last, my friend Mildred saw you turn into that awful place, the Red Dolphin. Then last night it was almost one o'clock before you came home from wherever. Finally, you're walking around this morning with a shit-eating grin on your face. I repeat—what's her name?"

"Mother, I never heard you say anything like that. Where did you ever hear the expression shit-eating grin?"

"Your father used to come home and tell me the strange things he'd heard on the shop floor. You wouldn't believe what some of those workmen would say."

"I've always thought that particular expression was weird. Who would smile while they were consuming excrement?"

"I've never thought about it, but it fits you this morning. And you still haven't answered my question."

"Well, I'm not telling you a thing."

"It's not nice to keep secrets from your mother."

"How did Mildred know it was my car? A white Toyota Camry is about as nondescript as it gets."

"Out-of-state plates."

"Sure, I should have thought about that. Maybe I'll go over to motor vehicles and change my plates. I'm not interested in being so easy to spot."

"So, there is some woman, but you're not willing to tell me her name?"

"I didn't say anything about a woman, but if there were one, I wouldn't tell you her name." With that, Dwight gathered his breakfast dishes and went to the kitchen to clean up.

Later that morning, he went to motor vehicles, changed his registration, and got new plates. He hoped his car would be parked behind Cathy's store many nights. There was no reason to make it stand out.

When he got back, he looked at the VM message board. It didn't have many entries yet, so it didn't take long. Most of the entries appeared to be people introducing themselves and expressing support for the VM videos. Five reported on the size of their local VM groups. Dwight was surprised that two of them claimed to have over twenty members. As far as he could tell, Bill hadn't posted anything.

He was scheduled to meet Cathy at seven in Clayville, so he had the afternoon to spend on Charles Dickens, whom he'd been ignoring lately. He'd taught a class on Dickens more than once, so he had his lecture notes as a guide. Unlike many authors, Dickens was very popular in his own time. Often his novels were published a chapter at a time with his readers eagerly awaiting each new installment. Because of this, there was a vast amount of contemporary commentary about Dickens and his books. Dwight's task was condensing all the available material into a book that would be easy for middle- and high-school readers.

He became engrossed in the work, and the afternoon passed quickly. When he heard Courtney come in to cook dinner, he started thinking about her mother, and progress on Dickens ceased. *Interacting with*

Courtney is going to seem odd. I don't know quite how to be with her. I can't mention I'm going to be seeing her mother later in the evening, let alone talk about what we'll be doing.

After dinner, he primped more than he needed to before driving to Clayville. Cathy's car was parked behind the store, and the back door was unlocked. He found Cathy in the office. Her outfit grabbed his attention. She had on a very short skirt and a top that left little to the imagination. She got up and came into his arms, giving him a big kiss, then she pushed him away, saying, "Here, sit on the couch. We need to talk."

"Okay." Dwight wondered what was coming. He didn't think he was up for a long talk. The outfit she was wearing didn't suggest conversation.

"I want to start our relationship on the right foot," Cathy said. "I don't want any lies involved. Unfortunately, I started things off with a lie. When you came to our house for dinner, I said something like, I wouldn't have recognized you if we'd passed on the street. That wasn't honest. A couple of years ago, Courtney showed me the Shakespeare book, and it had a picture of you on the back cover. I have to admit, I hardly recognized you then. I even took out the annual to see if there was a resemblance. There was, but you'd changed quite a bit. After looking at the picture, I Googled you and found several other pictures, so I knew what you looked like well before you rang our doorbell that night. I have to admit I fantasized about you a little."

Dwight was astounded and didn't know how to respond. Finally, he said, "It's no big deal. I have a similar admission. When Courtney passed along your invitation for dinner, I didn't give one minute's thought about seeing Bill again, but I sure thought a lot about seeing you. I guess you might not have been aware, but I had a big-time crush on you all through school."

"You were so shy then. I guess I was so into Bill, I didn't think much about other guys. I mean, I knew you were the smartest guy in the class, but you were so shy, and little. Things have changed now. Bill isn't in the picture anymore, and you've overcome your shyness."

Cathy paused, looked Dwight in the eyes, and gave him her brightest smile. "Now, I'm hot for the smartest guy in the class."

"Enough talking," Dwight said, sliding closer to Cathy.

"Absolutely."

After making love, they got dressed. Dwight noticed Cathy did not put on the same outfit she had on when he came in. "Different clothes now," he commented.

"That little number was for your eyes only, Dwight. I'm certainly not going home in it."

"Makes sense. I'm a little at loose ends on our project to infiltrate the VM group. There's a meeting next week, but there hasn't been much action on the website. Is there anything you think I should be doing?"

"I only have one idea, and it's a long shot."

"What is it?"

"Well, if we're going to stop this nonsense, we have to know who's behind it. That may eventually be revealed, but I wonder. I think we should try to figure who's behind the mask."

"There are some hints. I think the guy's an actor or a magician. At least someone with experience with stage productions or television, or something. The videos are too slick. This guy's no amateur."

"You're probably right, but I was thinking along other lines. Remember the Origins video where the mermaids swam off in the lake? I'm thinking we should try to identify the lake. As I remember it, there was a minute or two just showing the mermaids swimming around. That could give us enough video of the lake to work with."

"Aren't there millions of lakes? Heck, Minnesota claims to have ten thousand."

"Yeah, but you can eliminate lots of them. It wasn't Lake Michigan for sure. I think we ought to be able to determine the rough size of the lake. That will limit the search."

"Still, there are scads of smaller lakes."

"You're right, but I have an ace in the hole. Courtney has a computer geek girlfriend, Yolanda Gomez. I heard them talking about how easy it is to identify places pictures were taken. The internet is a treasure trove of pictures. Just think about Google earth. I bet we could enlist Courtney and Yolanda. According to Courtney, Yolanda is an absolute whiz at searches."

Dwight's stomach tightened at the thought of talking with Cathy's daughter. What would she think about him being with her mother? "I don't think we want Courtney to know about us. Do we?"

"No, you're right. At least not yet. I'll have to leave you out of this part of it."

"I think so, but it's a great idea. If we can identify the lake, we can visit it to see if the VM guys left any clues. Yeah, it's good, and if this Yolanda is as good as you say she is, it just might work."

"So, your assignment is to look at the video of the mermaids again. Look closely at the surroundings. There might be types of trees that will help us focus on certain regions, or there might be something else that gives it away."

"I'm sort of a dunce at identifying trees. Anyway, I'll try. I have to admit, when I looked at that video, I spent more time looking at the mermaids than the surroundings."

Cathy rubbed up against him. "So, you were looking at the girls, huh. Somehow, I'm not surprised. I thought you might be the kind of guy who liked women."

"You know it," Dwight answered, taking her in his arms and giving her a long kiss.

After breakfast the next morning, Dwight looked at the Origins video again. He fast forwarded to the mermaid demonstration. He got angry with himself when it became clear he was focusing on the mermaids more than their surroundings. One of them, the bustier one, had a distinctive swimming stroke.

He backed the video up and put it on slow motion, focusing on the surroundings. The lake didn't look very large. At least it wasn't very wide. The mermaids had started off on a beach, but the far side of the lake was wooded. The trees looked to be deciduous, maybe maples or oaks. Dwight didn't know. At least they weren't pine trees.

When the camera panned out as the mermaids were swimming around completely transformed, Dwight could see the right-hand edge of the lake. There was a house or cottage or something on the shore, and they had a short boat dock or fishing pier. It looked to be the only house on the lake. Of course, he couldn't see the other shore, so there might have been more houses.

Dwight looked at the video in slow motion several times, but he didn't see anything else that he thought would help. Mostly the camera focused on the mermaids. Lots of the shots were designed to show the scales growing on their legs, and they were no help at all.

Finally, he emailed Cathy, telling her what he'd discovered. He apologized again for not being able to identify the trees.

An hour or so later, Cathy replied that she hadn't had much luck either. She did say she'd set up a meeting with Yolanda and Courtney for after school. They were going to come see her at the Boynton store. She promised to report back the results of the conversation, and she apologized for not being able to see him that evening. She had a meeting she couldn't get out of.

Dwight already knew about the meeting, but he didn't like it. He figured he'd better take a longer than usual run.

CHAPTER TEN

When Dwight got back from his evening run, he showered and checked his email. As usual there was a great deal of junk, but there was also an email from Cathy. She reported that Courtney and Yolanda had found the lake. It was in the western part of Michigan, south of Grand Rapids. She attached several pictures of a small lake called Lake Granger. Dwight thought it matched the pictures from the VM video, but he couldn't be sure.

The pictures showed a small beach behind a big house. The house had a large yard sloping down to the beach. Dwight thought the beach might be where the mermaids started their swim. It would have been easy to set up a camera to get the views in the video. The one house with the boat dock was in the far side of the photos too, and there were three other houses on the part of the lake not visible in the VM videos.

Dwight went to Google Maps, where he learned Lake Granger was only a six-hour drive from Boynton. It would be easy to get there in a day, but a one-day round trip wasn't going to be possible. He wondered how he and Cathy were going to handle it. People in a small town like Boynton would start to talk if they went on a trip together or if they were both gone at the same time.

He returned an email to Cathy, telling her to congratulate the girls and asking what time the two of them could get together tomorrow to figure out what to do with their new information. Cathy must have been sitting in front of her computer. Her response was almost immediate. It said, "Dinner and… Meet me behind the C-ville store at 6:30."

Dwight replied, "…indeed. See you then."

The next day, Dwight accompanied his mother to her doctor's appointment. The doctor was pleased with Evangeline's progress. She did a great job on the brief quiz the nurse had given her, and she easily answered all the doctor's questions. Dwight could tell she was getting a little antsy as the appointment dragged on. She didn't like being poked and prodded by the doctor as he tested her reflexes.

As they were walking out of the doctor's office, she finally unloaded. "I don't know why they have to take so long. The doctor could tell I was greatly improved. Heck, he said that the first thing when he got to the examining room. And I don't know why you had to come along. You just sat there like a lump on a log."

Dwight knew it wouldn't do any good to respond, but he couldn't help himself. "We already discussed it. I came along because it's always good to have two sets of ears at a doctor's appointment. I guess it turns out I wasn't needed this time, but you never know."

Instead of responding, Evangeline pushed her walker a little faster. She stayed in a bad mood on the drive home. As he took her walker to the open passenger-side door when they were in front of the house, he broke the silence. "I'm not sure why you're so glum. You had a great appointment. The doctor doesn't want to see you for two months."

Not mollified, his mother responded. "I guess I should be looking at the bright side, but I can't. It's just, well… I was hoping I'd be more thoroughly recovered. For instance, I want to get rid of this damn walker."

"The doctor told you to work on that when the nurse comes."

"Yeah, yeah, I know. Don't bug me about it."

Dwight knew when to stop talking, so he went to his office. He had every intention of working on the Dickens book, but he didn't. He looked at the photos of Lake Granger. After he'd reviewed them, he found the lake on Google Maps. He zoomed in to try to figure out the road system around the lake. There were roads on all four sides of the lake, and he wrote down the names of the roads. Next, he switched to street views and looked at the houses from the street.

The house in front of the beach, 2051 State Road 15, was the newest and largest house on the lake. It was painted white and had dark green shutters. There was a large barn or storeroom or something behind the house. Its neighbor with the dock showing in the video turned out to be a double-wide trailer. Its yard was a mess, and there was a shabby looking pickup parked next to it the day the Google camera drove by. The other dwellings on the lake were small cottages. Dwight thought they might just be used in the summer.

Next Dwight tried being an internet sleuth. He looked at the website of the Michigan county that included Lake Granger. The website had information on all the land in the county. He found the plat for the lot at 2051 State Road 15. It was a large lot, almost three acres. The current house was built four years ago on the site of an older house. Searching around, he found could only find a list of plats for the street. He was hoping to find something giving the owner's name, but he came up empty.

For the rest of the day, he made some progress on Dickens. He couldn't really get going though. His mind kept diverting to Lake Granger. At one point, he set aside the book and trolled the county website again. He didn't find anything useful. He would need more information in order to figure out the name of the property owner.

At six thirty, he pulled up beside Cathy's SUV. The back door to the store was locked, so he knocked. Cathy answered a minute later and pulled him through the door and started kissing him.

"I missed you so much," she said when they came up for air.

"Likewise," he stammered, breathing hard.

Cathy pushed him away, straightened her clothes, a pair of slacks and a green knit top that matched her eyes. "We'd better head off to dinner. It's a bit of a drive, and I have a reservation for seven."

"I'll drive this time," said Dwight. "And that means we'll have to return here to get your car."

"Great plan," Cathy said with a big smile and a wink.

On the drive, they discussed the possibilities for a trip to Michigan.

"If I give my staff notice, I can get away for a couple of days. I have store managers for both stores, and they're good. I don't think I've taken more than a week off for six or seven years, so I can do a couple of days with no problem."

"My situation is easier. My mother doesn't really need me, and my work on the Dickens book is eminently interruptible. But we'd better be careful about traveling together. In fact, I don't think we should. We want to keep our relationship secret from Bill. If I'm going to be a member of his VM group, he'd better not suspect we're together."

"You're right, we should travel separately. Too bad. I was looking forward to being with you."

After a pause, Dwight had a proposal. "Why don't I tell people I've got to go back to the university for something. Instead of heading to Pennsylvania, I'll drive to Grand Rapids. You can fly to Grand Rapids the next day. Then we can take a day scouting around the lake. Afterwards we'll drive back, and I can drop you off at your car at the airport."

"So, I just buy a one-way ticket."

"That's my suggestion."

"I think I can make that work. It's three days before your next meeting with Bill. You should go to the meeting, so let's say you leave the next day, and I'll come the day after. That leaves me enough time to get my staffing right."

Dinner at a little hole in the wall place a couple of towns south of Clayville was surprisingly good. Their discussion focused on friends from high school Cathy had just heard from. Dwight marveled at how easily they could talk.

When they drove back, Dwight told Cathy about what he'd found out about Lake Granger and the house at 5021.

"I would have never thought about the county website," Cathy said. "Sometimes they have quite a bit of information. It's surprising how little privacy homeowners have, at least about their house."

Silence followed. Dwight couldn't think of anything to say. He was thinking too much about what was ahead of them.

When they walked to their cars after they'd spent a delightful time in the office at the store, Cathy kissed Dwight one more time, stepped back, and said, "That's quite a grin you have on your face there."

"I can't help it. You do that to me. In fact, my mom accused me of having a shit-eating grin on my face the morning after you and I first made love. She wanted to know the name of the woman."

Cathy shook her head. "There's two disturbing things about what you just said. First, I would never believe Evangeline would say shit-eating grin. Second, you didn't tell her, did you?"

"No, I didn't tell her, and yes, she did say it. I almost flipped out."

"Astounding."

The next three days passed uneventfully. Cathy and Dwight did get together at the Clayville store late one night, but otherwise Dwight couldn't think of any highlights as he drove to the Red Dolphin. When he entered, he noted the place had a sort of worn look. Nothing looked new, and the whole place smelled like stale beer. Only three tables were occupied, and there were five men at the bar, no women.

Bill, Stacy, Len, and Styles were at the same table. This night there were ten glasses around the table and two pitchers of beer.

"We're expecting a bigger group," Dwight said as he flashed the VM sign to the assembled foursome.

Stacy giggled as she gave Dwight the sign, and the others did so without the giggle. Soon Pete and two guys in similar shirts walked in. Pete made the introductions. Dwight's was the only name he missed. His two friends were Jack and Jo Jo.

Jo Jo said, "My real name is Joseph, but I've gone by Jo Jo ever since I can remember."

A few minutes later, Tank and a guy he introduced as Rex filled the last two seats. When everyone was settled, Bill started the meeting. "Did any of you get a chance to look at the message board they set up?"

Len answered first, "Yeah, I did. There wasn't much new stuff."

"Weren't you surprised at the size of some of the groups?" Dwight asked. "I sure was. I guess they must be in bigger places than Boynton."

"Dwight's right," Bill said. "Some of the groups are large. There's no telling where they're from, and they may have already been in some other group that switched over to VM."

"I think we should introduce ourselves to the new folks, and then learn something about them," Styles said.

"That's a good idea," Bill responded. "Why don't you go first, Styles."

They went around the table, and Dwight learned more about the people he'd met. When his turn came, he gave a brief intro, ending with, "And you wouldn't believe how I lost my last job. I was fired for violating the consensual amorous relations policy. I was fired for engaging in consensual behavior with someone who was twenty-three years old."

"Tell them what kind of consensual behavior," Stacy said with a giggle.

"He had sex with a twenty-three-year-old graduate student," Bill said.

The introductions continued. Rex, who came with Tank, said he was

Roscoe's neighbor. Dwight figured he was about five years younger than Tank. He was a plumber's assistant. He thought he was going to have a career in the army, but it didn't work out. Jack and Jo Jo, who were both short, maybe five six or five seven, worked with Pete, and they gave only the briefest of introductions. Neither of them spoke very loudly, so Dwight didn't catch much of what they were saying.

After the intros, Bill told the group there was a big announcement coming on the VM website. He didn't know if it was a new video or something else. He just got an official email telling him to have his group check the website every day.

"Do you think they're going to announce a list of people to vote for?" Pete asked.

"They might," Len responded. "It makes sense. There are some politicians who would agree with what the VM guy's saying. I think it would be smart for them to put out a list."

"I don't know," Bill responded. "I'm not sure the VM guy thinks our problems are small enough to be fixed by voting. The right people aren't going to get the press they need to be successful in politics. The liberal elites control the media."

Bill's statement was red meat for his audience. Several members of the group jumped in with examples of biases they'd observed, both on television and in newspapers. Dwight sat back and listened. Len was the most well-spoken of the group, and he seemed to have a better command of his facts. Unfortunately, he spoke too long. Dwight could tell he was losing respect among the group.

As he drove home, Dwight thought Bill had done a poor job of winding up the meeting. He had trouble controlling the discussion, and he let it go on too long. He didn't recognize when people were repeating themselves. Dwight was thoroughly tired of the meeting well before it broke up.

CHAPTER ELEVEN

As Dwight drove to Grand Rapids the next morning, he reviewed his time in Boynton. He'd gone there with little hope of enjoying himself. He couldn't have been more mistaken. It was marvelous how rapidly he and Cathy had gotten together. They both were ready, he guessed. He'd spent the last two and a half months at school estranged from his wife and regretting his brief fling with Sarah. Cathy had been celibate for much longer. Living in a small town like Boynton wasn't easy, particularly since she and Bill were trying to keep up appearances.

Sex drive was clearly part of what had sped things up, but it was more. Looking back, he realized his feelings about Cathy were more than a boyhood crush driven by his libido. He remembered thinking she was smart as well as gorgeous. In high school, she was out of his league in every dimension. The big surprise was that she even remembered him from high school, let alone fantasied about him after she'd seen his picture on the book cover.

The shared VM project brought them close rapidly, too. He wondered what would have happened if he'd decided against helping her. Dwight didn't want to go there. He was thoroughly involved, and he agreed with Cathy. Something should be done to stop the VM guy. If his nonsense grew, it wouldn't end well. He still wasn't certain how they could stop VM, but they could cross that bridge later.

Dwight decided to drive by Lake Granger before he went into Grand Rapids. The house at 5021 was impressive, a two-story Dutch Colonial with green shutters and a detached garage. Slowly driving by, he snapped a picture with his phone. He could see part of the barn or whatever it was behind the house. As far as he could tell, no one was home. He drove on to check out the cottages. As he'd suspected from Google Street Views, they were older and smaller than 5021. One of them seemed to be occupied. Dwight thought the other two might be full on a weekend.

He turned around and drove toward 5021 again. As he approached, a big van turned in the driveway, so he slowed down. Three guys and one girl got out before the van drove into the garage. He couldn't tell for sure, but they all looked to be in their twenties or early thirties. Dwight wondered if the girl was one of the mermaids. She certainly had the figure for it. A minute later, the driver joined the group. He looked to be a bit older than the others. Dwight sped up and drove by as the people were letting themselves in the front door.

After a left turn, he paused in front of the trailer for a few minutes. Silence met him, and he was almost positive it wasn't occupied. In fact, he didn't think anyone had been in it for quite some time. Grass had grown up in the tire tracks where a vehicle would park. Given the height of the grass, no one had been there for more than a month. Dwight decided to park and take a close look at 5021's back yard.

He quietly got out of the car and crept up to the trailer's windows to peer inside. The inside was a mess. Rotting food sat on the little kitchen counter, with flies swarming, and the place smelled like the inside of a dumpster. When he got to the far side of the trailer, he saw some of the reason for the odor. Apparently, whoever lived in the trailer just dumped his or her trash out a window. There were full plastic trash bags and quite a bit of loose trash. Dwight gave the trash dump a wide berth and spotted a tall bush of some kind he could hide behind. It should provide a good view of the house next door.

Nothing was happening in 5021 for the first five minutes he sat behind his bush. He got some pictures of the back of the house and its yard. Finally, the back door opened, and the three younger guys came out. They went to the barn structure, pulled up a garage door, and disappeared inside. Dwight got enough of a look before they closed the door to see the barn housed a woodworking shop. Fairly soon after the guys went inside, he heard a table saw.

Ten minutes later, just when Dwight thought he'd seen everything worth seeing, the back door opened again. The girl stepped out, wearing a bikini and carrying a towel. She headed for the beach. Dwight figured he'd have to slide around the bush, or she might be able to see him. After he shifted position, he realized he'd lost his sightline to the barn, but it wasn't a big deal. As the girl walked past, within forty feet or so of his bush, Dwight stopped breathing. He didn't want to be discovered.

Now Dwight was stuck behind his bush. The girl on the beach would see him for sure if he tried to walk back to his car. Also, it was possible she could see his car if she looked that way. There was nothing he could do about it. *I sure hope she doesn't take a long swim.*

He figured there were worse situations. He had a chance to look at a pretty girl in a bikini. Somehow it didn't thrill him the way it might have in the past. Cathy dominated his thoughts. Other women, no matter how scantily clad, didn't spark his interest.

He watched as the girl dipped her foot in the water and then got in. When she started swimming, Dwight thought she had an odd-looking swimming stroke—one he'd seen before. It was in the mermaid video. It made sense. This girl had definitely played one of the mermaids. Dwight whipped out his cell phone and took a short video of her swimming. Her swim was short, and Dwight stared at her as she walked in the shallow water heading back toward the beach. He continued the video as she toweled off before heading back to the house.

When the mermaid girl was inside, he crouch-walked his way to the trailer. He tried to keep trees between himself and the house. There was a chance someone would see him out one of the windows. He made it to his car, got in, and drove away, happy with what he'd discovered.

Daniel Vilsac almost slept through the spying mission. At least that's what it had seemed like. Up to this point, he'd been on the most boring assignment he'd ever had as the head of security for the Mincy stores. Old man Mincy had wanted Daniel to keep an eye on his son and his friends at the lake house in Michigan, but Gregory didn't want Clem to know he was being watched. Daniel had established a base across the lake from the house. There were plenty of trees, so he didn't think anyone in the house knew he was there.

Until today, nothing had happened. He'd become familiar with the rhythms around the house. There was one highlight as far as he was concerned: the babe's swims in the lake. Luckily for him she swam twice a day, and he got a good look at her.

This time, she was a little early, but he roused to the familiar noises. He was surprised to see a car parked close to the trailer. Getting out his binoculars, which he usually had trained on the girl, he searched the property. He didn't see anything out of place. When the girl got out of the water, he followed her into the house. Then someone appeared from behind a big bush and headed for the trailer. Daniel got a good look at him. As the guy drove away, Daniel took down his license number—513-34K, a new Ohio plate.

Daniel didn't know what to think as he wrote down the information in his notebook. He'd be sure to mention it in his report to Greg this evening.

◇◇◇

The hotel had WiFi, so Dwight sent Cathy a brief email describing what he'd found and sent her a picture of the house. It was awkward not being able to phone, but with Bill still in the house, they couldn't risk it. She answered an hour later, congratulating him on being so resourceful. He was tired. Driving didn't feel like much work, but it tired him out just the same. He guessed any type of activity involving six hours of concentration would tire anyone. He got a quick dinner in the hotel and went to bed early. The king-sized bed felt enormous. He thought, *It will be so much nicer with Cathy in it tomorrow night.*

The next morning, he went to the county offices. He told the clerk he was interested in trying to buy property on Lake Granger. He said he'd been by the lake and seen some nice cottages and a double-wide trailer. The trailer looked abandoned, and he was thinking about seeing if he could buy the lot it sat on, so he needed to identify the owner. The clerk said she knew the place he was talking about.

"The trailer's right beside the Mincy place. They've got such a nice house, it's a shame to have that trashy trailer there. Let me see who owns the lot." She went to the back room. About five minutes later, she walked out with a book of deeds. After turning a couple of pages, she handed the book to Dwight and pointed to a page. "That's the lot."

"Are the other Lake Granger lots in this same book? I might want to ask about one of the cottages if the trailer guy doesn't want to sell."

"Sure, they're all there. Take the book to the table over there and take down any information you want."

Dwight found the deed for the lot occupied by 5021 and took down the owner's information:

Gregory Mincy
59 North 12th Street, Indianapolis, IN

He also got the names and addresses for the trailer lot and one of the cottages. He didn't want to turn back the book too early.

When he returned the book, he thanked the clerk and said, "It looks like all the owners are out-of-towners. Are all the houses out there summer places?"

The clerk pushed her glasses up on her nose. "As far as I know, the Mincy place is the only one that's winterized. I think the owner's son lives there some even through the winter. I'm not sure though."

Dwight thanked her again and walked out, feeling triumphant.

He returned to his hotel room, fired up the internet, and started to see what he could find about Gregory Mincy of Indianapolis. He found that Gregory was the owner of a small chain of department stores. Mr. Mincy was in his late seventies and still oversaw the day-to-day operations of the stores and kept his position as chair of the board. He was prominent in politics and involved with several charities. There were a few pictures of Mr. Mincy with his wife at his side at charity events. He had even published a few op-eds in the local paper. While it was clear he had mainstream pro-business conservative views, he didn't sound as extreme as the VM guy.

I wonder if I could find information about the son who the clerk thought lived in the Lake Granger house. It took a while, but he found Gregory Mincy had two children, a son Clement and a daughter Paula. Clement was the younger, about thirty-five now. He was an actor, and there were several mentions of him being in plays at local theaters. His acting didn't appear to take him away from Indianapolis. Also, he might well be the same guy who advertised himself as "The Great Clement," a magician. Dwight couldn't be sure. He remembered thinking that the VM guy had a great stage presence. This made sense if Clement Mincy was the guy.

He couldn't find anything about the daughter Paula, and except for her pictures at some charity events, there wasn't anything about Gregory Mincy's wife.

Dwight went to lunch and then headed out to Lake Granger. He drove by the front of 5021 again. This time the garage door was open, and he saw a sedan, a Lexus with Indiana plates as well as the van, which had Michigan plates. He drove around the lake to avoid passing the house again and found a parking place that hid his car more thoroughly from anyone in the house. It was a longer walk to the trailer, but he didn't mind. The weather was nice.

When he got close to the trailer, he saw another car parked beside it. It was a great looking silver Audi TT with Indiana plates. He approached cautiously. One glance inside told him no one was in the trailer. He made his way around it on the side away from the trash dump and saw a woman in a green shirt and jeans hunkered down behind the bush he'd used yesterday. Just when he was about to retreat, Dwight stepped on a stick. It snapped. The woman looked up and stared him in the eyes. Dwight turned around and made his way to his car. When he was halfway there, he could hear running steps behind him. He turned around and saw the woman only about fifty yards behind him and closing fast. Dwight stopped. The woman seemed determined to catch him, and he didn't see any reason to run away.

The woman slowed to a walk and came up to Dwight. "What were you doing back there?"

"I think I should ask you the same question," Dwight replied. The woman stared at him. Dwight guessed she was in her late twenties, and except for being a little out of breath and wearing very thick glasses, she was a good-looking slim brunette in her late twenties or early thirties. She had long hair fixed in a ponytail.

After an awkward silence, Dwight asked, "Shall we flip a coin?"

The woman laughed. "No, I'll go first. I was spying on the house next to the trailer. My ex-boyfriend lives there, I think. He owes me money for rent. He walked out of our apartment last year, and I got stuck with the bills we used to share. I need to find him."

Dwight decided she'd given him a straight response. "I was going to do the same thing for a different reason. You were behind the same bush I used to spy on the house yesterday."

"So, what was your reason?"

"I'm trying to find someone who's behind some crazy right-wing stuff on the internet."

"Oh, you mean the VM stuff?"

"Bingo."

"Well, you found it. In fact, I broke up with Clem over those posts. It started out as a joke, or at least I thought it was a joke."

"Wait a minute," Dwight interrupted. He narrowed his eyes, squinting at her. "Were you one of the mermaids in the first video?"

"Guilty as charged," she responded, shifting slightly. "When I got wind of Clem's plans, the seriousness of them, I got really angry with him, and he walked out. I thought the mermaid bit was funny, but Clem wasn't playing it that way. If he didn't owe me so much, I wouldn't want to have anything to do with him. I was trying to find out if he was here, so I could give the bill collectors a good address."

Dwight pointed at the house. "Yesterday I saw five people there," Dwight said. "Three young guys, maybe in their late twenties, one guy a little older, and the other mermaid, at least I'm pretty sure it was. Does one of them sound like your Clem? By the way, Clem is Clement Mincy. Right?"

"Yes, you got the name right. He was the slightly older one. The other guys are the ones who build sets for him and generally help out. The woman is Katerina. You're right, she was the other mermaid."

He nodded. "Yesterday I saw her swimming and she has a funny stroke just like one of the mermaids. The guys building sets makes sense too. I heard a saw going when the three young guys went into that barn or whatever it is."

"Okay, mister…"

"Dwight Kelton. And you are?"

"Marcie Green."

They shook hands, and Marcie asked, "Just why are you interested in Clem and the VM stuff?"

Dwight hesitated. What would Cathy think of him telling this woman what was going on? Would she be upset with him? He wasn't sure, but it seemed like taking a chance and talking was his best option. "I think he should be stopped. What he's doing is dangerous. He's getting a bunch of people riled up with his propaganda. I think he wants to cause a revolution."

"Really?"

"Yes. Have you been following the VM posts? They're getting more and more radical, and he's got thousands of followers forming into local groups or clubs. Lots of people buy his line of thinking."

Marcie's face crinkled in confusion. "But the Viking and mermaid stuff is so wild."

"It fits right into the mindset of people who think the liberal elite control the news media. It's easy for them to believe the media would suppress information about the Vikings and mermaids. It's all part of a conspiracy to keep conservative people in line. Believe me, I've infiltrated one of the groups. The people in our group aren't phased by the weird stuff, even the space alien bit."

"So how did you find Lake Granger?"

"My girlfriend has a daughter in high school, and the daughter has a computer whiz friend. Somehow, they were able to match the lake in the mermaid video with images of Lake Granger. I think they used Google Maps."

Marcie looked over at the lake. *I guess the shoreline is distinctive*, she thought. *Still, there are thousands of lakes in Michigan. This one can't be that different. These guys must be really good.*

"Clem thought he was so smart. He said there would be no way we'd ever be identified. He stayed behind a mask all the time. Katerina and I weren't masked, but almost all the shots of us were from the waist down. It was tedious. We had lots of short takes while Clem slowly putt the scales on us. Then someone smoothed it all out, making it look like we were growing the tail. I thought it looked great when it was done. I guess you could see more of us when we were swimming around with those silly tails on."

"Listen Marcie, there are a ton of questions I want to ask you about Clem, but this may not be the right venue. I have to go pick up my girlfriend at the Grand Rapids airport in an hour or so. Is there somewhere we could meet in the evening? We're staying in Grand Rapids tonight."

"Yeah, I'm staying there too. What about dinner at Mario's? It's a nice Italian place on Second Street, I think."

"We'll find it. Is six-thirty reasonable?"

"Sure. I'll call for a reservation right now," Marcie said, taking out her cell phone. They shook hands, separated, and walked toward their cars.

Dwight waved at Marcie when he drove past her. He could see she was headed back to spy on the Mincy guy again.

Daniel Vilsac witnessed the girl's arrival in the nice-looking Audi. He thought it was interesting when she hid behind the same bush as the guy yesterday. After she'd been there for a while, a guy showed up walking along the road. Daniel looked back and spotted his car, verifying what he thought. *It's the same guy as yesterday.*

CHAPTER TWELVE

Marcie watched Dwight drive away and headed back to be sure Clem was in the house. She felt good about her encounter with the guy. He'd been smart enough to find Lake Granger, so he might be able to slow Clem's VM business. She agreed with Dwight. VM might be dangerous. Clem should be stopped.

When she peeked around the trailer, she saw Katerina in the lake. Dwight was right, she did have a distinctive swimming stroke. As Marcie headed to her hiding place behind the bush, Katerina turned, and their eyes locked. Marcie froze. She didn't know what to do. She could tell Katerina had picked up speed as she turned for shore. When Katerina got to the beach, she called out, "Marcie, is that you?"

Marcie turned and headed for her car as fast as she could go. When she reached it, she jumped in, started the engine, and drove away. She had to slam on the brakes a moment later, because Clem's Lexus came to a skidding halt at the intersection, blocking her path.

Stunned by the suddenness of events, she sat in the car trying to decide what to do. Meanwhile, Clem leapt out of his car and ran to her driver's door. Katerina and one of the carpenter guys, Jake she thought, ran through the woods toward the two cars.

Clem jerked open her car door. "What the hell are you doing here?"

Marcie stared at him, seeing rage in his eyes. She got her back up. "I was looking for you. You ran out, sticking me with your half of the rent and a bunch of other expenses. I wanted to be sure I knew where to send the bill collectors."

"What?"

"You haven't responded in any other way. I've left messages on your cell, but you've ignored them. You haven't answered any letters or emails. I couldn't find you in Indianapolis, and your parents wouldn't tell me where you were. I came here to find you. Now I've done it. Let me go."

"I don't think so," Clem said as he hauled her out of the car.

Jake and Katerina had arrived, and Clem tossed his keys to Katerina. "Here, put my car in the garage. Jake, drive Marcie's car and park it in front of the house."

With that, Clem put an arm around Marcie and marched her toward the house. She thought about struggling, but she didn't know what she'd do if she managed to get away from Clem. They had her car.

Inside, Clem pushed Marcie onto a couch and told her to sit still. A few moments later, Katerina and Jake came in. Clem, who had been pacing in front of Marcie, asked Katerina, "Where did you see her?"

"She was over by that trailer. I think she was headed to hide behind a tree or something. Remember yesterday, I told you I thought it was funny that a car was parked near the trailer. Today I saw her car when I started my swim, but I didn't see her. I looked pretty close. Anyway, when I was in the water, I saw another car go by on the road. Then a few minutes later, I spotted her walking from the trailer. I guess she was headed to her spying spot, but she took off when she could tell I'd spotted her. That's when I yelled and ran to tell you."

"Who was in the other car, Marcie? Was someone else with you?"

Marcie thought fast. *How much do I tell him?* "There was a guy who was also spying on you, but I don't know who he was. I was behind a bush by the trailer, and he came around the trailer and almost tripped over me. He took off. It must have been his car Katerina saw yesterday."

"You don't know who this guy is. Is that right?"

"No, I don't."

"Why don't I believe you? If you were behind the bush and the guy bolted when he saw you, why did Katerina see you walking away from the trailer toward your hiding place?" Clem stopped his pacing and stared at her.

"Let me go, Clem. You can't hold me here against my will."

"We'll see about that. Katerina, why don't you and I go talk this over. Jake, watch her."

Marcie was terrified. *What are they going to do with me?* She figured she'd always gotten along with Jake, so she gave him a big smile. "Why don't you just give me my keys, and we can forget about this whole thing?"

Jake smiled back at her and shook his head. "No way. You're staying right here until I hear different from Clem."

In the backyard, where Clement and Katerina had gone to talk, Clem still paced. "We can't just let her go. She knows where we are, and there's no telling who was in the other car. This is making me nervous."

"We can't keep her here either," Katerina responded. "We're going to be headed out on the road in a week. We've got to get rid of her."

Clement stopped his pacing. "What do you mean, get rid of her?"

"I mean kill her. Buck up, boy. We can't have anyone knowing who we are or where we are. The whole thing is only going to work if we maintain the mystery. She knows too much. She's got to go. There's no alternative."

Clem resumed his pacing. "You mean just kill her right now?"

"I don't see another way to go."

"I'm going to have to call my dad. It's too big a decision to make, but you're right. I can't see any way around it."

"I know a way to take care of her. Then we can stash her body in her car and dump the car somewhere a long way from here."

"You're a cold-blooded one, aren't you?"

Katerina interrupted Clem's pacing and wrapped him in a big hug and kissed him. When they separated, she said, "That's why you like me, right?"

That evening, after keeping her on the living room couch with Jake on guard, Katerina and Clement took Marcie to her car. Clement drove Marcie's car with Marcie as a passenger, and Katerina followed in Clem's Lexus. They didn't tell the others where they were going or what they planned to do.

When they got to their intended destination, Katerina pulled up behind Marcie's car. Clement went around and pulled Marcie out of the car roughly. He spun her so her back was toward Katerina and wrapped his arms around her, holding her fast. Before Marcie knew what was happening, the wire from Katerina's garrote slipped around her neck. Katerina pulled hard. It didn't take long for Marcie to die.

Katrina extracted her garrote from Marcie's neck and turned to Clem with a big grin on her face. "That was a real thrill. I can't believe it."

"Let's do a good job of cleaning up after ourselves and get out of here," Clement responded.

When Clem and Katerina returned home two hours later, they didn't give any explanation of what they'd done or where they'd been.

<◆◆◆>

Earlier that afternoon, Dwight had been thrilled when he saw Cathy coming in the group of people who'd been on her plane. She flew into his arms, kissing him. He took her carry-on, and they walked out of the terminal arm-in-arm.

When they got into the car, Dwight said, "I've had an incredibly productive day. I found out the name of the VM guy, and I met his ex-girlfriend. We're having dinner with her tonight."

"Wow, I hope your hotel's close. I have some plans for you, and then I want to hear all about your great day. You say you know the masked VM guy's identity. Fantastic."

After they tried out the king-sized bed, and Cathy was thoroughly briefed about what Dwight had discovered, they headed to dinner. Marios was a short drive from the hotel, and they arrived five minutes early. They did some window shopping before presenting themselves to the hostess at six-thirty. She found the reservation under Green and escorted them to the table. Dwight positioned himself so he could wave to Marcie when she came in. They ordered drinks, red wine for Dwight and white wine for Cathy. Ten minutes later, the waitress came by, asking if they wanted to order.

"No, we're waiting for our friend," Dwight said.

"I wonder where she is," Cathy commented.

"I don't know. She suggested this restaurant, and we agreed on six-thirty."

"The hostess had the Green reservation down for six-thirty. She must have been held up for some reason."

Twenty minutes later, they finally ordered. The meals were good, which compensated for the feeling they'd been blown off by Marcie. Dwight was kicking himself for not getting her phone number or giving her his number. *She'd seemed so eager to help, and then she doesn't show.* Dwight couldn't figure out what was going on. *I hope nothing has happened to her.*

They even dawdled over dessert, hoping Marcie would show, but no such luck. Finally, they drove back to the hotel.

CHAPTER THIRTEEN

The next morning, Dwight and Cathy watched the news on the big-screen TV in their hotel room. They propped themselves up with the extra pillows, enjoying a slow morning. They only had a six-hour drive in front of them, so there was no hurry. When the national news cut to the local station, the first story was about the discovery of a woman who'd been murdered. She'd been choked to death and then dumped in a car that had been shoved off the road. The name of the victim was being withheld pending the notification of the next of kin. Dwight jumped when the TV showed the victim's car being pulled from the side of the road. It was a silver Audi TT with Indiana plates.

"It's Marcie's car," Dwight blurted.

"Oh my God!"

Dwight got out of bed and started pacing. "When I left her yesterday afternoon, she was headed back to spy on the Mincy house. They must have seen her."

"You think they killed her and stashed her in her car?"

"I don't know, but it seems like a strong possibility. Clement Mincy knew she could identify him as the VM masked man. He's never identified himself, as far as we know. Like I said, the other mermaid is still hanging with him, and there haven't been any other people in the videos."

"But killing her seems extreme."

"It sure is, but it's no more extreme than what he's advocating in his videos. Remember the last one—The Solution."

"I guess you're right. This is scary. We'd better be careful around these people."

Dwight continued to pace. "We should call the police. Usually, they have a way for people to give them anonymous tips. We could say we saw the silver Audi TT parked close to 5021 State Road 15 yesterday afternoon."

"Will it really be anonymous? They can probably trace the call."

"I don't know, but they claim you can be anonymous. I think the first thing is to see if Grand Rapids has such a crime line, or whatever they call it."

Cathy took out her phone and found the number for reporting crimes. "The website says you don't have to give your name. I think you just leave a message. There might not be anyone to talk to."

"Let's pack up, and then I'll leave the message from one of the house phones in the hotel."

On the way out of the hotel, Dwight left his message. As they headed to the car, Dwight said, "Let's go to breakfast at the place we saw last night. Then I'll drive you by Lake Granger to show you the setup. It's not too far out of the way."

After breakfast, Dwight approached the lake from the side with the trailer. When he got to the corner, he could see a police car parked in front of 5021.

"They got your message," Cathy said. "I wonder what's going on."

"We can't wait around to see, but we can monitor the Grand Rapids news sources. I hope this puts a big crimp in the VM guy's style."

Daniel Vilsac wondered what was going on with the police car at the house. He'd talked to Greg the night before, so he knew what Clem had done. It seemed like a risky move, but Greg said he'd approved it. Now the police were here. *How in the heck had they caught on to Clem so fast?*

The entire month before, he'd been bored stiff staking out the house, but this last three days there had been lots of action. The guy with the new Ohio plates one day, the same guy and the girl in the silver Audi the next day, and the police today. Just when he thought he had seen everything, he saw the Ohio car drive by and pause at the intersection. This time the car had two passengers, the guy and some woman. The car didn't stop. Daniel didn't know what was going on.

On the drive back, Dwight filled Cathy in on more details about the Mincy family. He'd forgotten to tell her anything about Gregory Mincy, Clement's father.

"He could be behind it," Cathy conjectured. "I don't see how what we've learned about Clement suggests he could fund much of an operation. Really good video cameras and sophisticated editing equipment aren't cheap. Also, his crew has to eat. I bet they've been together for all those videos. Keeping this project going must have run up quite a tab. I don't think a guy who works in local theater productions could have made much money. You didn't find anything about Clement holding any kind of job, did you?"

"No, but I didn't have time to do a thorough search. I can't fault your line of reasoning though. The VM thing must have some backers, and Gregory Mincy is a logical guess. When we get home, I'll see if I can find anything more about Clement's employment history, and I should look more closely at those op-eds Gregory wrote."

"You said they were right wing but not extreme. Maybe as a store owner he thought exposing his extreme right-wing views wouldn't be good for business."

After they'd driven for a while, Cathy opened up about how she and

Bill had drifted apart. She had two major complaints about Bill. First, he never seemed to be able to see anyone else's viewpoint. He just stuck with his views, even if there were clearly two sides of an argument. "It's like when you were telling us about your problems at your old job. You could see both sides: the problems with power differentials and the notion that consenting adults should be free to do what they want. Bill could only see one side. He just went on and on about consenting adults. He's like that all the time. He just sees his side of any argument. I think it's why he been taken in by VM."

"What's your second complaint?"

"He never takes responsibility for his mistakes. The way he explained his football career that first night is a good example. He got into a game in college, and he got sacked a bunch of times. I think he told you the line wouldn't block for him. That's his story now, but I remember the coach yelling at him for hanging on to the ball too long. Bill's story blames other people, not himself. After living with him, I saw it wasn't just football. It's been the same with his job. Everything that goes wrong is someone else's fault. The last straw was the miscarriage I told you about. It wasn't my fault. It wasn't anyone's fault, but Bill blew up at me."

Dwight thought Cathy was tearing up. He reached a hand over and stroked her leg. She held his hand there. "That had to feel like a big betrayal."

"It did."

"I guess I saw a little of what you're talking about, even in high school. You might remember, I was the sportswriter for the student paper. I paid attention to all the games, at least when I wasn't watching the cheerleaders." Dwight smiled at Cathy.

"Anyway, we had a great line, and Dwight always had a lot of time to select a receiver. I'm not sure he was sacked more than two or three times all season. I interviewed him after one game in which he'd been sacked once and hurried a few other times. He complained about the line. I didn't think much about it at the time. I couldn't use it in my article. You can't put negative stuff about another student in the student paper, but it rings true with what you're saying."

"You're different. When you told us about your troubles, you took responsibility. You said it was a big mistake to sleep with that graduate student. I'm not sure I've ever heard Bill say anything he ever did was a big mistake, and there have been some whoppers."

Dwight smiled and squeezed Cathy's hand. "Oh, I make big mistakes all the time. Who thought that ability would get me the girl of my dreams?"

"Don't be silly. And don't make lots of mistakes. Just admit to them when it happens."

"You can count on it."

Dwight dropped Cathy at the airport so she could pick up her car. They decided she'd drive right home, but Dwight would stay away one more day. That way his trip would clearly be longer than hers.

Earlier that morning, Clement and Katerina had been surprised when a patrol car pulled up to the house on Lake Granger. They were in the house, and the guys were out back putting the finishing touches on the sets. Clement answered the door when the cop knocked.

"Hello Officer, what can I do for you?"

"I'm Richard Sauers with the county police. Can I come in for a few minutes?"

"Sure, come on in."

After they were seated in the living room, the officer took down their names. Then he said, "Someone has reported that a Silver Audi TT with Indiana plates was seen at this house yesterday afternoon. Do you know anything about that?"

"Yes, the car you're talking about belongs to Marcie Green. She is an ex-girlfriend of mine. We had some business to discuss. She thinks I owe her rent money. I told her she was mistaken. It was a very unsatisfactory talk, and I think she was fairly mad at me when she left."

"What time was that? When she left, I mean?"

"It was about five o'clock, I think. I'm not sure."

Clement turned to Katerina, who sat beside him on the couch. "Katerina, what time did Marcie leave? Do you remember?"

"I think it was after five, maybe five-thirty. I couldn't swear to it."

Clement leaned back, crossing his feet in front of him. "Do you mind if I ask you why you're interested, officer?"

"Ms. Green was killed some time after she left your house."

"What?" Katerina shrieked.

Clement immediately leaned forward, put his arm around Katerina, and said, "You don't think we had anything to do with it. She was alive and well when she left here. She wasn't very pleased with me, but she was alive and well. What happened to her?"

"Someone choked her and pushed her car off the road."

"Around here?"

"No. By the bridge, over in Knox County. You say Ms. Green was your ex-girlfriend. Can you think of anyone who would have wanted to kill her?"

"We broke up more than a year and a half ago, and yesterday was the first time I've seen her since. It wasn't a pleasant breakup. I don't know who she's been hanging with lately. I'm not sure I can be of much help."

"Didn't she have a strained relationship with her brother?" Katerina asked.

"Yeah, but I don't think he'd kill her."

The officer looked at his notes. "Did you two go anywhere last night?"

Clement shook his head. "No, sir, we stayed here."

"Okay," the officer said. "If you hear anything about what happened to Ms. Green, let us know. Thank you for your help."

After the officer left, Katerina turned on Clement. "I was shocked when you told the cop all that. Why didn't you just clam up? Tell him you didn't know anything about a silver Audi TT?"

"I couldn't. It was all going to come out. They're going to investigate Marcie's background. Lots of people know we used to live together. She had that car then, and the bit about her thinking I owed her money was good to include. She could have told someone that's why she headed this way."

"I see it. It just surprised me. I hope I played along okay. I tried to take your lead."

"You did fine, hon. As long as we got all of our fingerprints off Marcie's car, we're going to be fine."

"We're set then. We wore gloves and wiped it down. Still, it really threw me when it was the police at the door. How did they suspect us so soon?"

"Don't worry. Someone saw Marcie's car here, like the guy said. An Audi TT is distinctive. We're in the clear. The police don't really know anything. Now let's see if the boys have the stage set up yet."

Clement and Katerina went out to the where Jake, Wilhelm, and Enrique were setting up a stage on a gravel pad they'd created beside the workshop. The stage was big, designed to be used in outdoor venues. It came in four parts, and the crew was attaching the final section. As Clement and Katerina watched, they plugged in the main power supply and stepped back to admire their work.

Katerina took over at that point. She went stage right and slipped into a control room built under the stage. The stage was over seven feet tall, so there was ample room for her to sit. "Enrique, why don't you get in position. We'll try your entrance."

Enrique, a slim, black-haired Hispanic, disappeared under the stage.

"Ready," he shouted.

Katerina pressed a switch, and Enrique popped up through a trap door and stood on the stage with a big smile on his face.

Clement and the other two workmen clapped, shouted, "It works," and danced around. Katerina came out of the control room and embraced Clement.

After they'd calmed down, Clement said, "We've got to test the rest of this, and then we'll have lots of rehearsing to do. Jake, let's try your entrance next."

The group worked the rest of the day trying out the mechanisms and tweaking the set when they found little problems. By the end of the day, they were satisfied. Things were working very smoothly.

CHAPTER FOURTEEN

Bill's group at the Red Dolphin had grown to fifteen, so they had to pull two tables together for the meeting. Bill had big news. The VM people were going to be doing in-person rallies. The group leaders received an email announcing the first three events: Birmingham, Alabama; Knoxville, Tennessee; and Cincinnati, Ohio. Bill had copied the email and passed it out, so everyone would have the dates.

Stacy couldn't contain herself. "It just what I wanted. I think I said it before. The videos are nice, but there's nothing like a rock concert or a good rally with lots of people."

Bill agreed. "The VM people want chances for like-minded people to meet each other. They want to start a movement to put this country back on the right path. To start a movement, you need to get people together. These in-person events are the start."

Len spoke next. "I have a friend in Birmingham. I think he'll put me up, and I bet I can get him to go to the VM thing with me. I want to go to the first one."

"Great," said Bill. "I was thinking we should all go to Cincinnati. It's by far and away the closest. It's four weeks from now. If you want to go to one of the others, or both for that matter, I think it's great."

"I can't get away from my job to go to the others, but I'm up for

Cincinnati," said one of the new people, Lydia. "We should carpool. I've got a van that will hold about six of us, maybe seven."

Dwight was a little glum, so he didn't join in the discussion. It was animated enough without him. He just nodded along. Last Sunday had been the Boynton High School graduation. He and Evangeline had gone to support Courtney. They'd sat beside Bill and Cathy. It was excruciating being so close to Cathy and not being able to touch her. Also, it bothered him to see Cathy interacting with people as Bill's wife. He knew she was playacting, but it bothered him just the same. Now he was upset because he'd been bothered. He just couldn't keep a level head about Cathy. She hadn't given him any reason to doubt her, but somehow, he couldn't help it. It didn't make him feel good about himself.

The meeting broke up a little later than usual. It was cumbersome with so many people, but the mood was buoyant. Everyone was hyped up about the VM event in Cincinnati. Some people thought they could bring friends, and Bill encouraged them. He wanted to have a big showing.

The next night in the office behind the Clayville store, Dwight filled Cathy in on the big news from the meeting. "I guess I'll be going to Cincinnati, but I don't suppose I can take you."

"I don't know. I'm good at disguises. If it's a big crowd, I can probably stay far away from Bill and Stacy. I'd love to see what's going on."

"That's a great idea. It would be wonderful to have you come with me. I can book a hotel nowhere near where Bill and the rest of the Boynton crowd are staying."

"It's a date," Cathy said with a big smile.

Changing the subject, Dwight said, "I've struck out on the other two things we were interested in. There has been nothing in the Grand Rapids papers about the Marcie Green murder the last four days. Also, I've had no luck uncovering anything more about the Mincys, either Gregory or his son Clement. I may eventually have to go to Indianapolis to find out more."

"Maybe we can make another joint trip."

"That sounds good. Also, I haven't made any progress figuring out what to do with the little bit of information we have. We have the guy's name, but I don't know what to do with it yet."

Cathy hugged Dwight. "I'm sorry you've run into a brick wall, Darling. Let me see if I can brighten your mood."

When Katerina drove the semi onto the fairgrounds in Birmingham, she thought the set up was going to work. There was a nice flat place for the stage marked off just like she'd asked for. She parked beside it and got out. She wasn't surprised the rest of the crew weren't there yet. They'd stopped to exchange their van with Michigan plates for a rental with Alabama plates. Twenty minutes later, the crew and the new van appeared.

Assembling the stage was hard work. It was made harder because Clem had told the crew they had to wear their Guy Fawkes masks as they worked. He didn't want any of them to be recognized or to have anyone to take photographs of them. Clem wanted to preserve the mystery.

Katerina had made all the arrangements with the fairgrounds people. She didn't wear a mask, but she'd dyed her hair bright blue and added padding that made her look considerably overweight. Some fake tattoos completed a weird look. Katerina thought even her close friends would have trouble recognizing her.

The most difficult part of Katerina's job was interfacing with the fairground's workers while keeping them away from the stage. She needed them to collect the twenty-dollar entrance fee from every attendee and give out the tickets. The tickets included instructions for the people to register at a VM site. One of the reasons for the event was to collect email addresses. Another group of fairground workers would be there to provide security, and yet another group would deal with parking. She had worked out all these details over the phone, so she didn't have to interact with too many people as the day progressed.

◇◇◇

Bill scheduled a special meeting the day Len returned from Birmingham. Len was more than eager to report to the group. Before he let Len start, Bill told the group he'd scoured the Birmingham papers to see if there was any report of the event. "There was nothing. It's more evidence of the liberal elite's hold on what we're allowed to know. I guess the *Birmingham Times* isn't supposed to be left-wing, but it's part of the mainstream that's been taken over by the liberals. There's lots about the event on the VM message board, but we don't have to rely on that. Our friend Len was there. Take it away, Len."

Len decided to stand up to tell his story. His audience of thirteen gathered at two round tables. "The VM people set up a stage at the fairgrounds. There were about a thousand seats, but the audience must have been twice that large, so lots of people were standing. The standers were all herded to the back. I was there early, so I got a seat in the fifth row.

"The event was supposed to start at seven thirty, but people were still drifting in, so it started a little late. The first thing was a loud boom and a big puff of thick smoke in front of the stage. When the smoke blew away, the VM guy was standing center stage. We were all shocked—it was like he'd appeared out of nowhere. Finally, there was clapping and cheering. The guy flashed the VM sign and there was another burst of applause. Finally, he put up his hands for silence."

Several discussions started at once. Wanting to get the meeting under control, Bill spoke up in a loud voice, "Let's give Len a chance to finish. I do have one question before that. Was the guy you saw the same guy from the videos?"

"Yeah, he sure looked the same. He had on the same outfit—the Viking helmet, the warrior garb, and the mask. And he sounded the same. I recognized the voice. It's hard to miss. Anyway, he talked for about thirty minutes. Some of it was the stuff we've heard from the videos, but a lot of it was new. I liked it because he got into more specifics. He mentioned particular politicians who represented what was wrong with America, like the governor of California and the mayor of New York City. He gave examples of how wrong they've been so many times. He also spoke at length about the abomination of the transgendered. I don't remember that from the videos, but it might have been there. The guy had a way of getting the crowd stirred up. Everyone was excited, and he had to stop because of the cheering three or four times."

"Was that it—a speech?" someone interrupted.

Len smiled. "No, I haven't got to the best part. At the end of the talk, he said, 'If we want to defeat the liberal elite, we have to keep the faith. Keep the faith, repeat that, keep the faith.' When the crowd wasn't loud enough, he encouraged us again, raising his hands as we shouted. Then there was another boom and a puff of smoke. When the smoke cleared, the VM guy wasn't in the middle of the stage. He was off to one side, the right, I think. He raised his hands again, like he'd done before, and we all shouted keep the faith."

"Was he running from side to side?"

"No, it was like he was disappearing from one place and reappearing in another place. It was spooky. After the same guy on the right side led the cheer, there was another boom and more smoke, and the guy was on the other side of the stage leading the cheer. Everyone was cheering and clapping as well as shouting along with him.

"Then things went crazy. Booms were going off, smoke was erupting, and the guy kept popping up at different spots on the stage. Each time he appeared, he led the cheer. Just when you thought he couldn't keep it up, two VM guys appeared and the cheer got louder. The next time, it was just one. He kept appearing and disappearing. I don't know how many times we all shouted, 'keep the faith'. The finale was four VM guys leading the audience in the cheer, then there was a bigger boom and more smoke. And that was it. The stage was empty. The crowd was all on their feet at this point. When we recognized it was over, we all cheered and clapped and kept shouting 'keep the faith.'"

People around the tables seemed restless. They shifted in their seats. Dwight could see varying reactions to Len's report. Some were clearly enthralled. Others looked skeptical.

After a moment, while Len was trying to collect himself, he continued, "It was thrilling. If the Cincinnati show is anything like this one, it will be an evening to remember for the rest of your life. I've never seen a crowd so together. I met lots of folks. Some were already committed. They'd seen all the videos and read the message board. Others were just curious, dragged there by their friends, but they all came away incredibly enthusiastic."

Dwight was impressed by what he heard. Apparently Clement Mincy put on quite a show. He knew Mincy was a good showman from the videos. Now he could see he knew how to get an audience involved. What Len described required some elaborate staging. The workmen Marcie Green talked about must have built the sets. Part of him was looking forward to the Cincinnati show, just to see how they did it.

The meeting broke up later than normal. Len and Bill stayed until everyone had a chance to ask questions. Dwight excused himself early and left to report to Cathy, who was waiting in the back of the Boynton store. They figured one meeting there wouldn't arouse suspicion. It was late at night, and Dwight parked several stores away. He sent a text saying he was parked, and very carefully made his way up the alley. He was sure no one was around to see him. Given the warning text, Cathy answered his knock quickly.

After he reported on what Len had told the group, Cathy said, "Sounds fascinating. Now I'm sure I want to go to Cincinnati. I hope they have a larger crowd there. I don't want to stand out."

"I bet the crowd is going to be larger. The VM message board lit up with positive comments from people who were at the Birmingham rally, or show, or whatever you call it. If the comments on the Knoxville event are half as good, there will be a big crowd in Cincy. I think we ought to finalize our plans for our trip to Indianapolis."

CHAPTER FIFTEEN

*D*wight felt it was okay to leave his mother for his trip to Indianapolis. She'd done well when he'd gone to Michigan. Since she'd reconnected with her friends, she didn't need, or even want, much of his time. She had managed the high school graduation without a walker, though she did use his arm. He told her he had to spend some time at an archive at the University of Indiana, but she didn't seem to care. "Have a good time," was all she said.

As before, Dwight drove, and Cathy followed a day later by plane. Dwight and Cathy had done as much investigating of the Mincy family as they could using the internet. They'd concocted stories that would allow them to ask questions. They decided to split up, Dwight focusing on the elder Mincy and Cathy on the younger one. Dwight planned to pose as a graduate student working on a master's thesis about the history of local department stores. Cathy's plan was similar, but her focus was on the history of local theaters.

They had discussed the questions they planned to ask. It was easier for Dwight. He could interview Gregory Mincy himself. Cathy couldn't interview Clement. They decided to give him a wide berth. Any information about Clement would have to come indirectly when she asked questions about productions in which he'd played lead roles.

Dwight arrived in Indianapolis in the afternoon, checked into the hotel, and went to visit the first person on his interview list. The gentleman, a Mr. William Hobson, who'd founded a department store fifty years ago, was now in a nursing home. Although he was in his eighties, he'd sounded very spry over the telephone. Hobson, who was grossly overweight and bald as a cue ball, turned out to be an engaging speaker. The interview, a stroll down memory lane for the old gentleman, was interesting. Based on the telephone conversation, Dwight suspected he might be in for a long interview, and he was right. When he finally got around to asking about competitors, he got an earful about Gregory Mincy. According to Mr. Hobson, Mincy was a son of a bitch, and it wasn't just that he was a tough competitor. Hobson characterized Mincy as ruthless and unprincipled. He didn't have much nice to say about his other competitors, but Mincy came in for most of the scorn.

Dwight had a large collection of useless notes when he finished with Mr. Hobson, but he had gained some insight into Gregory Mincy, so the visit wasn't a complete waste of time. Because he wasn't sure how long it would take to get to Indianapolis, he'd only scheduled one interview for the afternoon, so he headed back to the hotel. He took a long late afternoon run, found a nice spot for dinner, and turned in early.

The next morning, Dwight had an interview with Mr. and Mrs. Wallingford, an elderly couple who still lived in their grand old house. He was surprised when a maid answered the door. The maid ushered him into a fancy room, a parlor, Dwight guessed, and she introduced him to the Wallingfords. They both were thin and frail with very weak handshakes. They weren't as talkative as Mr. Hobson, which pleased Dwight. When they got around to his questions about competitors, the Wallingfords both indicated disdain for Gregory Mincy. "A most unpleasant fellow," Mrs. Wallingford said.

Her husband wasn't as restrained. He called Mincy, "an awful right-wing bastard," and recounted a story about how Mincy had used his connections with a very conservative city council member to block a road cut Wallingford had wanted for one of his parking lots.

After the Wallingford interview, Dwight went to the hotel to see if Cathy had arrived. Since they were going to be doing different interviews, they'd decided she should rent a car. She wasn't there when he got to the hotel, but ten minutes later, she texted him from the rental car counter. Thirty-five minutes later, she arrived at the hotel.

Over lunch, Dwight told Cathy about the two interviews he'd conducted, focusing on the information on Gregory Mincy. "Based on my sample of two, Greg Mincy isn't well liked. Neither of his competitors had anything good to say about him. I'm scheduled to talk to him late this afternoon. I think it will be very interesting."

"Sounds like a real sweetheart. I'm nervous. You can ask a direct question about Gregory, but I can't. I hope this isn't a waste of time."

"You'll do fine. Three of the four people you're interviewing are guys. Guys are shallow. They'll tell a pretty girl lots of stuff just to keep her attention."

Cathy looked a little embarrassed. "I guess you're right. I do seem to get a lot of time with the male clothing manufacturers, but then some of them are gay. I don't do so well with them. I could run into the same problem with theater people."

"Pay your money, take your chances."

Cathy's first interview was with a theater manager at a place where Clement Mincy had performed lead roles in two shows. She found the office behind the stage in an old theater building downtown. The manager, a Mr. Bill Curtis, was a short, middle-aged blonde who wore an ascot. He greeted her warmly. Cathy was a little taken aback with the hug Curtis gave a complete stranger, but she guessed theater people were different. She went through the standard questions she and Dwight had rehearsed, writing down notes. Finally, she asked about particular productions. The second play she asked about was one in which Clement Mincy had a lead role.

Mr. Curtis paused before responding. "That one was tough," he finally said.

"Why was that?"

"Well, the lead actor was difficult. As rehearsals went on, it got worse and worse. He drove away some of the understudies. He was abrasive at times and didn't seem to know how to keep things on a professional level."

Flipping pages in her notebook, Cathy looked up and said, "Would that have been Clement Mincy?"

"Clem, yeah it was Clem. Yeah, he did a great audition. He's got a voice made for the stage—a big baritone. Unfortunately, there's a lot you can't tell at an audition."

Cathy looked at her notes again. "I don't understand. My notes say he was in another one of your productions a year later. If he was so difficult, why use him again?"

"That tells you a dirty little secret about life in a struggling small-city theater. Clem's dad is rich. He owns a couple of department stores in town, and he's a sponsor of the theater. Gregory, that's the father, made it known he'd increase his annual donation if we gave Clem another try. I didn't want to, but the theater's board overruled me."

"I get it. Was he any better behaved the second time?"

"Only marginally. He'd been fairly successful as a magician, the 'Great Clement' he called himself, and that gave him more self-confidence. I think he was insecure in the earlier play. Anyway, I wouldn't say it was easy to work with him. The biggest problem was his politics. He's extremely right wing, and he didn't know when to shut up about it."

Cathy went through the interview asking about other plays, so Curtis wouldn't think Clement Mincy was the only one she was interested in.

After a while, she looked at her watch, thanked Mr. Curtis, and told him she had to run to her next interview.

Cathy was right about running late. She showed up five minutes late at the community theater in the suburbs. The theater's director, a Mrs. Earnest, didn't seem to mind her tardiness. Mrs. Earnest was a regal-looking woman who had obviously played the lead in many plays. They had a pleasant chat as they discussed Cathy's questions. None of their discussion revealed anything about Clement Mincy. He'd had a small role in a play four years ago, and his name didn't come up when they talked about the relevant play. Cathy walked away from the interview exhausted. She wasn't used to being in extended discussions like this. At the store, she could get the customer in the dressing room and take a little break. This had been nonstop.

Dwight only had one interview scheduled for that afternoon, but it was the big one, Gregory Mincy. About the same time Cathy was winding up with Bill Curtis, he went to the Mincy store. It was a half hour before the interview. He wanted to get a feel for the store. It took up the first four floors of an old downtown building. The carved figures in the corners indicated a storied past, but the current look of the store suggested something very different. In the past, the store probably had a very upscale clientele, but now it was a discount place. The other Mincy store, in a mall on the edge of town, was quite different. Dwight had seen pictures of the mall store. He figured this location must carry the merchandise the store in the mall couldn't sell and other discounted stuff.

After riding the escalators to the fourth floor, Dwight arrived at Gregory Mincy's office five minutes before his scheduled interview. He greeted the secretary whose desk sat in front of the frosted glass door with gold letters announcing it was the office of Gregory Mincy, President. The secretary had Dwight sit in a chair facing her until his appointed time.

Gregory Mincy was a tall, gray-haired elderly gentleman. Dwight knew from the bio on the store's website that he was seventy-seven. Dwight had several questions he'd asked the other store owners, and Gregory Mincy gave very full answers. He was proud of his stores, and he was happy to tell the story. When Dwight got around to asking about his competitors, Mr. Hobson and the Wallingfords, Mincy didn't have much to say. He seemed to want to give the impression he was above them in some important way.

Toward the end of the half hour, which was all he was allotted, Dwight asked about a succession plan, hoping he'd learn something about Clement. Mr. Mincy seemed nervous about the question, saying, "My son, who'd be the natural one to take over, is more interested in being an actor than a store owner, so the store is going to my daughter and son-in-law. The son-in-law will really run it. He's already a vice president."

Dwight took a chance and probed further. "You don't seem too happy about that? I mean, your son not following in your footsteps."

"No, well... I guess I was at first, but he's got other interests. Actually, I'm thrilled about his newest interest. I'm very involved, but I can't talk about any of that."

Dwight was pleased as he walked out of Gregory's office three minutes later. Gregory was involved with Clement and very interested in the project. He must be the financial support, as they thought.

As he left, Dwight noticed the guy sitting in the chair, reserved for Gregory's next appointment, because the guy was staring at him intently. It seemed weird to Dwight. Going out the office door, Dwight heard Mincy's secretary say, "You can go in now, Daniel."

Daniel Vilsac went in and shook hands with Gregory, who'd come out from behind his desk to greet him. When they were seated in a couple of chairs at the far corner of the office, Daniel asked, "Who was that guy who just left?"

"Some graduate student from Purdue. Said he was writing a Masters' thesis about the history of small department stores. Why do you ask?"

"I couldn't be sure, but he looked a lot like the guy I saw at the Michigan place a couple of times. You know, the Ohio car I told you about. I only got a fuzzy look at him through my binoculars in Michigan, but the guy who just left sure looked similar."

"Yeah, I remember. Did you ever get an answer from your Ohio cop friend, the one who was going to run the plate?"

"I did. It was a new plate, and new ones only get in the registry after a month or two. They have some antiquated computer system. It does things in batches. He'll be able to get me the information when it appears. Give me the name of the Purdue guy, so I can compare it with what comes from the license plate."

Gregory got up and grabbed his calendar off his desk. "Nathan Porter, that's the name of the guy who just left."

Daniel wrote the name down in his notebook.

When Gregory returned to the corner, Daniel spoke. "I went to the Birmingham event, and I've got to say, Clem puts on a good show. He had the people in the palm of his hand by the end. It was really slick."

"It's good to hear that from an unbiased source. Clem was really excited when he called. He called it a slam dunk, but he's always gung-ho about everything he does. I can't trust his opinion."

"I've got to agree with him this time. Everything went off like clockwork, and they had a big, enthusiastic crowd. I followed them to Knoxville. I tell you that Katerina runs a tight ship. As far as I could tell, she rules the roost, and things get done."

Gregory gave Daniel a funny look as he leaned back in his chair, staring at the ceiling. After an uncomfortably long silence, he continued. "Yeah, I wasn't sure about her at first, but I guess she's a good influence on Clem. What you're telling me is all good news."

"I'm glad it is. You owe me big time for watching that house for the last month. Boring. Nothing happened most days. If Katerina hadn't taken a swim in her bikini twice a day, I'd have gone mad. At least they're on the road now. It's a lot better. I'll pick them up for the Cincinnati show and follow them back up to Michigan."

"Yeah, I appreciate you being up here to give me an in-person report. Why don't you give me your blow-by-blow report about the Birmingham rally? You told me you had pictures."

"Yes, I do and some videos too. You're sure Grace can't hear us?"

"She can't, that's why I always take you over to this corner for your reports."

When they'd reported to each other in their hotel room, Dwight and Cathy decided they'd learned about as much as they could in Indianapolis. Gregory was the source of the funds behind Clement. They both were right-wingers, and Clement had some experience as a magician. If they'd had any doubts about Clement being the VM guy, their doubts had been erased.

"Actually, we've just confirmed our suspicions," Cathy said.

"I guess you're right, but it feels like progress. I say we bag the other interviews. I don't think we can learn any more, and I doubt anyone will be upset if we call and cancel. I'd rather just be with you."

CHAPTER SIXTEEN

At the next meeting at the Red Dolphin, Bill had to arrange three tables to accommodate all the people who showed up. He began at seven on the nose. "Let's go around and tell everyone our names. Start on this side," he said, pointing to his left.

Dwight recognized some of the people from previous meetings, but there were lots of new people too. The VM message board had gone crazy with people praising the Knoxville event, which had happened two days before. People who had been to both events said the Knoxville one was better, and, if they were to be believed, the crowd was more enthusiastic. Bill had trouble controlling all the people who wanted to talk about what they'd read on the message board. Finally, the tables broke into separate conversations. Bill just sat back and smiled.

After about twenty minutes, Bill called the group to order again. "I've got a pad of paper for each table. We need to get organized for Cincinnati. I need to know your name, email address, whether you're driving—Yes/No, and whether you need a hotel reservation—again, Yes/No. I'll go home tonight and arrange carpools. Len has volunteered to make hotel reservations. He and I will get together after the meeting to see how many rooms we need."

Someone shouted, "What if I want to room with my wife? Should we both put down we need a hotel reservation?"

"Jo Jo and I will room together," Pete said. "It'll cut down on the cost."

Len answered, "Just write a note about any shared rooms. I'll figure it out."

There was a buzz in the room as people filled out the information and asked each other about possibly rooming together. Dwight just put down his name and email and indicated he was driving but he didn't need a hotel reservation. People left after they'd filled out the form. Everyone seemed eager to go on the Cincinnati trip.

When Dwight returned from the meeting, he found a short email from Cathy waiting for him. It just said she had something for him to read and included the url for a story in the Knoxville *News Sentinel*.

The story, by a reporter named Charlotte Mangum, was about the VM rally. Ms. Mangum was impressed with the show but not with the message, which she described as directly out of the extreme right-wing playbook. She described the VM guy's outfit and the same finale Dwight had heard about from Len. She'd obviously viewed the videos because she said the impresario claimed in internet posts to be a descendant of a union between a Viking and a mermaid. She seemed surprised at how fervently the crowd responded to this unknown person. She had polled several audience members, and not a one of them knew who the guy was.

The story was short, but it was the first mainstream media mention of the VM movement. He returned Cathy's email, asking if she thought they should contact the reporter and tell her what they knew. Cathy answered back, suggesting they talk about it tomorrow night when they met.

The next evening, Dwight arrived at the Clayville store at seven o'clock. He knocked on the back door and it was opened by an older woman wearing a long black dress. Expecting something like this, Dwight looked at the woman closely. Finally, Cathy broke down laughing. "You didn't recognize me, did you? Admit it. You didn't."

"You're right, I didn't. I mean, given the way you bragged about your ability with disguises and our late start time, I expected something. Still, you fooled me for a moment, and I was looking hard. How long does it take to put on the makeup and hair dye?"

"Now that I've done it once, I can probably get it done in half an hour."

"Actually, more to the point, how long does it take you to change back? The real you is much better looking."

"It's easier to take off than to put on. The hair is a wig, and the makeup comes right off. Give me five or ten minutes and then we can go to dinner."

Over dinner, they discussed how to deal with the Knoxville reporter. Cathy was eager to talk with her, and she pulled a piece of paper out of her purse. "Here's the contact information for Charlotte Mangum."

Dwight smiled and pulled a small tablet from his back pocket. "Yeah, I've got the same stuff here. I guess it won't be much of a discussion. We're both agreed, we should contact her. I say we tell her everything we know. As long as she promises to keep our names out of it, the more she knows, the better her stories will be."

"I agree, and if she doesn't know anything more than she had in the first story, she won't get a chance to write another one. We need to give her enough to convince her editor there's potential for something big."

"A story revealing the name of this VM guy should gain quite a bit of attention. Her editor should like it."

"I hope knowing that the VM guy is a failed actor from Indianapolis will cut into his popularity. I don't know if Bill can keep his group going when the information comes out."

Dwight sat back, looking at what he'd written on his tablet. "This is one of the times I'd say we're on the same page."

They laughed.

At nine-thirty the next morning, Dwight called the reporter's number. Unfortunately, he reached her answering machine. He left a message saying he knew the identity of the VM person, and he wanted to talk to her. He left his name and number and then hung up.

He tried to ignore the call he was waiting for and get back to work on Dickens. Despite having everything laid out for a productive morning, he couldn't do it. He got up and paced around the room, but it was no help. He spent several completely unproductive minutes staring at his cell phone, willing it to ring. Finally, he thought, *It's a cell phone. I can take it with me.* Putting his phone in his pocket, he abandoned his Dickens work altogether.

He'd done some exploring of his old neighborhood on his runs, but it was different as he walked. He remembered some of the names of the families who'd lived in the houses but not many. The neighborhood had aged well. He guessed it had been the fanciest part of town when he grew up. The lots were big and so were most of the houses. Things changed a few blocks from his mother's house. The lots and houses were smaller, and some of the lawns needed work. It was funny, Dwight didn't remember noticing the change in the neighborhood when he was growing up. *Surely it had been there.*

As he walked, his mind turned to Cathy. He was deeply in love with her, and he was sure the love was reciprocated, but neither of them had come out and declared the obvious. Maybe it had something to do with their pending divorces. Maybe it was about the power of words. Dwight wondered when he'd have the guts to say the three words.

As he pondered what to do, his phone rang. He struggled to retrieve it from his back pocket then swiped to answer. "Dwight Kelton."

"This is Charlotte Mangum from Knoxville. I got your message."

"Thanks for returning my call. Do you have a few minutes now?"

"Yes."

"I guess that was a dumb question. You wouldn't have called if you didn't have any time," Dwight said nervously. "Anyway, a friend of mine's husband is hooked on the VM stuff, and she asked me to help her expose the VM guy for the fraud he is. I've looked at all the videos and have even joined a local group. Her husband leads the group."

"Your message said you know who the guy is."

Dwight stopped walking for a moment and looked around. The street was deserted, so he kept going.

"Look, Charlotte, I want your assurance that you can keep our names out of any story you write. I wouldn't want anyone to know we've talked. Is that okay?"

"I can live with that. Tell me how you found the guy."

"My friend's daughter has a friend who is a computer whiz. The kids were able to match the lake in the origins video, the one with the mermaids, to a lake in Michigan. I think they somehow used Google Earth information. To make a long story short, I went to the lake, and using county real estate records, I found out who owned the house in front of where the mermaid videos were taken."

"Clever. Are you sure it's the VM guy's house? He could have just rented the house or used a friend's."

"While I was there, I ran into a young woman who verified everything for me. She had played one of the mermaids, but she wasn't a part of the group anymore. She was trying to track down the VM guy because he owed her some money. I'm sure the guy behind the mask is Clement Mincy from Indianapolis."

Dwight had made it home by this point. He decided to sit on the front steps to finish the call. "That's fabulous. I fought my editor to get a chance to cover the VM rally in Knoxville, and he liked the story. The thing is, as far as he is concerned, it was a one-shot deal. If you'll give me an exclusive on what you've told me, I think I can get him to let me do a follow-up story. This is exciting."

"You're the first person we've contacted. Sure, you can have an exclusive. Just don't use our names."

"Wonderful."

"There's something I should warn you about. The VM guy is very dangerous. I think he killed the young woman I talked to you about. I'm not sure, but it certainly looks like it. I left her beside the house, and we arranged a dinner. She never showed up for dinner. The next morning, I saw a report of a murder. The local news showed the police pulling the victim's car from a ravine. I'm sure it was the girl's car."

"Why would he kill her?"

"She used to be his girlfriend, and she knows all about what he's doing. I think he must have seen her as a threat. Let me be clear. I didn't see him kill her, but the timing is very close. I knew she was spying on his house in the afternoon, and she's killed that night. It's possible someone else killed her, but I don't think it's likely."

"Thanks for the warning. I guess I should expect these guys to play rough."

Dwight filled the slight pause. "My friend and I are going to the Cincinnati rally. It would be great if we could meet up there. Do you think your editor would foot the bill for a trip for you?"

"I don't know, but I might come anyway. It looks to me like this VM stuff is growing by leaps and bounds. I've been monitoring their message board, and the number of followers is exploding. I think they could become dangerous very soon. There are lots of militia groups out there who are armed to the teeth. If the VM guy starts his own militia or links up with one of the ones already out there, I don't know what would happen."

Dwight stood up and headed for the front door. "I've had the same thought. The videos have high production values, and they play into lots of people's prejudices. It's not surprising they attract followers, and, as you know, the in-person rallies are slick too. This guy, Clement Mincy, used to be a magician. From what I've heard, some of what he does is like a magic act."

"Yeah, you're right. Wait a minute... Someone is signaling me, so I've got to run. I'll have a chance to talk to my editor later today. I'll call you this evening."

"Make it seven o'clock. I'll be with my friend then."

At the computer in his office, Dwight quickly sent a short message to Cathy with details of his talk with Charlotte.

That evening, Dwight and Cathy waited in the back room of the Clayville store. Dwight looked at Cathy and was amazed all over again at his good fortune. She'd changed into the very abbreviated outfit she'd worn one other time. She was absolutely gorgeous. He scooted closer to her on the couch. She gave him a kiss, but then pushed him away. "Wait a little. We've got a phone call coming soon."

"With you dressed like that, it's hard to care about phone calls."

Cathy got up and did a walk around the room, including a little spin. "So, you like my outfit?"

"You know I do."

Just then Dwight's cell phone rang. He did not recognize the number of his caller ID.

"Hello."

"This is Charlotte Mangum. Is this Dwight Kelton?"

"Speaking, and my friend, Cathy Wilson, is here too. I'm going to put you on speaker."

"Fine. Hello, Cathy."

"Hello," Cathy answered.

"I have big news," Charlotte said. "My editor agreed to let me follow up on the information you've given me. It wasn't an easy sell, but I'd taken some video of the VM rally. I think it's what finally convinced him. Anyway, I have a small budget, and I'm thinking of going to the Cincinnati rally."

"Wonderful," Dwight answered. "As I told you, Cathy and I are going too. We can meet up. It will give us a chance to get acquainted. I guess I really haven't introduced myself."

"Let me stop you," Charlotte interrupted. "I Googled you, so I know who you are. What I don't know is how you got interested in the VM stuff."

"That would be my doing," Cathy said. "I convinced him to get involved. My no-good husband is a real VM supporter. He's started one of the local groups here in Boynton, Ohio. Anyway, when Dwight came into town, I asked him to infiltrate the group. It has to be stopped. I think they can be really dangerous."

"But you did more than that."

"Yes," Dwight responded. "After I went to a few meetings and looked at all the videos, I became convinced the VM guy was trying to start a cult or something. If he succeeds, his group could be a source of evil. As I told you, we found the little lake in Michigan, and I tracked down the owners of the house next to the lake. Also, and I didn't have a chance to tell you this, Cathy and I went to Indianapolis and learned more background on Clement Mincy and his father, Gregory. It appears that Gregory is financing the VM operation."

"Wow, I'd love to talk to you too. You've done lots of investigating."

The conversation continued for a half an hour. Charlotte had lots of questions. By the end of the conversation, Dwight and Cathy had told her just about everything they knew. They ended the call by arranging to meet at the Summit Hotel in Cincinnati. Cathy and Dwight had reservations there. They had chosen it because it was on the other side of the city from where Bill and the Boynton group were staying.

When the phone call ended, Cathy went into Dwight's arms and gave him a deep kiss. Thereafter things proceeded just as the two of them wanted.

On the day she left for Cincinnati, Cathy didn't even have to concoct a story about where she was going. Bill hadn't stayed at the house the night before. She guessed he was probably at Stacy's. She did tell Courtney she had to make a short trip for work, but Courtney was used to Cathy's buying trips. It wasn't the first time Courtney had been left alone.

Dwight had faced a curious set of questions from his mother. He'd finally made her think his recent trips had something to do with the woman she'd been asking about. This had the advantages of being partially true and making his mom think she was smart. She gave him a smirk as he headed out the door with his small suitcase.

Dwight picked up Cathy behind the Clayville store. He was surprised at the size of her suitcase, but then he remembered her disguise. The dress or whatever was large, and she probably needed extra makeup. Anyway, his trunk was large enough.

He knew the arrangements Bill and his group had made, and he and Cathy had a two-hour head start on them. There was no chance of running into them on the road. The trip went uneventfully. They were both excited about meeting Charlotte.

After checking into the hotel, they unpacked and wandered down to the hotel's café for their rendezvous with Charlotte. She said she'd be wearing a red blouse, and Cathy said she would too. At the café, a very tall, skinny woman with a red blouse stood up and waved at them. She had black hair and wore glasses. By the time they reached her, she was seated again, so Dwight and Cathy slid in the booth.

They shook hands, and Cathy and Charlotte started to talk at the same time. After they laughed, Cathy said, "You go first."

"Okay, I play this game with myself. I try to guess what people will look like in situations like this. You know, when you've talked to someone on the phone, but you haven't seen them. I saw photos on the internet of Dwight, but I didn't find any of you, Cathy, so I had a chance to play my game. Let me say, I flubbed. I had you shorter and heavier, with dark hair and glasses. That's not you at all."

"Yeah, and you told us you were tall," Dwight said. "Still, I didn't expect you to be taller than I am."

"I'm six three, and it's a real bother when you live somewhere where the women's basketball team is such a big deal. When I was younger, I can't tell you how many people around Knoxville came up to me and asked questions about Pat Summit."

"I always thought she had a great name for a basketball coach," Cathy commented.

"I guess you're right. I never thought about it. Anyway, much to the coach in my high school's dismay, I was never any good at basketball. I didn't even try out for the team."

The rest of their meal continued in a similar vein. The conversation was light as they exchanged life stories. Charlotte was accustomed to encouraging people to talk, so she learned quite a bit about Dwight and Cathy, but they also learned some things about her. Charlotte was born and raised in a small town between Knoxville and Nashville. She went to the University of Tennessee and interned at the Knoxville paper. She almost blushed when she told them she'd been the only intern they'd hired right after her internship. She'd worked at the paper for ten years, mostly covering local news. She'd done some investigative reports, but she felt like this could be the biggest story she'd ever worked on. Charlotte wasn't married, but she did have a steady boyfriend who was a pastor at a Lutheran church. She thought he was going to propose, but he hadn't yet.

As they were getting up, Cathy arranged to go to the VM rally in Charlotte's rental car. She warned Charlotte about her disguise, so she'd recognize her in the lobby at the appointed time. Dwight was going in his own car, so there would be no problem if he ran into the Boynton group. He wanted to sit with them if he could. He planned to leave earlier than the women, so he'd have a better chance of linking up with the group.

CHAPTER SEVENTEEN

The fairgrounds parking lot already had about fifty cars when Dwight arrived. He parked and sat for a moment. He was nervous. *Somehow coming to the rally is a big step. I hope it's not a mistake.*

He finally got out of his car and made his way to the entry. After he paid his twenty dollars and got his ticket, he looked around but didn't see any familiar faces. In his sports coat, he was overdressed. It didn't bother him. He had a reason for the coat. The seats were filling from the front, and Dwight hustled to a row three rows back from where people were seating themselves. He put his sports coat on the aisle seat and counted over fourteen seats and put a towel on the seat.

Daniel Vilsac saw Dwight's car pull into the lot. He was pretty sure the license was the one he was looking for, but he checked his notebook anyway. Yes, 513-34K, a new Ohio plate. He couldn't use his binoculars to check out the guy. Even with his naked eye, he could see the guy had on a beige sport coat. He'd be easy to spot in the crowd.

Dwight stood in the middle of the seats he was trying to save, planning to tell people they were taken. It wasn't long before he had to execute his plan. It worked with the first group. They weren't bothered to be one row further back. Dwight's luck held. He'd only received two dirty looks before he saw Bill and waved at him.

"Wow Dwight, you're our hero," Bill said.

Stacy released herself from Bill's arm and hugged Dwight. The rest of the group, most of whom Dwight recognized, shook hands with him as they filed into the seats he'd saved. Dwight took the aisle seat and put his sport coat back on. The towel he'd used on the other end was passed back to him. Dwight wished he had a view of the entrance, but he didn't. There was no way he would be able to see Cathy and Charlotte's entry. He did get up a few times to see how big the crowd was, but he didn't spot the women.

Daniel saw the guy in the sport coat save a bunch of seats. It worked, probably because the guy's group showed up soon after he claimed the seats. From his vantage point, he couldn't be sure, but he thought the guy from the car might be the same person he saw coming out of Greg's office, the one who'd claimed to be a graduate student. *I'll have to find out who he is.* If it was the same guy spying on the Michigan house and interviewing Greg, he could spell real trouble for everyone.

As they filed in, Cathy and Charlotte saw Dwight, and Cathy pointed out Bill and Stacy. She and Charlotte were lucky to get seats in the last row. The event wasn't scheduled to start for twenty minutes, and there was a steady stream of people coming in.

"There's going to be a big standing room only crowd," said Charlotte. "There are forty in each row, and I counted fifty rows of seats. That's two-thousand seats, and almost all of them are taken. I bet they have that many in standing room. The set up here is just like Knoxville."

"Dwight thinks it's about a magic show protocol. There are some angles where the tricks won't work."

"Yeah, sure, it makes sense. From the sides, you might be able to see how the VM guys appear and disappear."

Dwight looked around as the crowd assembled. The VM masked man was going to have a large audience. When he looked at the stage, he saw a guy off to the side who seemed to be staring at him. *Of course, I can't be sure it's me he's looking at,* Dwight thought, so he turned around. Seeing nothing unusual behind him, he looked back and the watcher averted his eyes. The guy looked familiar, but Dwight couldn't place him.

As Dwight was puzzling over the guy who'd been looking at him, there was a boom and a burst of smoke, followed by the VM guy. Dwight had a good view, but he expected people in the back, like Cathy and Charlotte, didn't. He wondered what the standing room people could see. The guy was only greeted with scattered applause until he flashed the VM sign. People who were already standing gave the sign back, and the entire audience erupted in a loud cheer.

Finally, the guy in the mask settled the crowd down and started his speech. After the first ten minutes, Charlotte nudged Cathy and said, "This is the same stuff from the Knoxville rally."

A little later, the guy changed things up. He asked members of the audience to stand if they'd served in the military in Viet Nam, Iraq, or Afghanistan. Quite a few men, and even a few women, stood. "Give them a big round of applause," the masked man said.

After the enthusiastic applause, he continued, "As much as I admire your service, I think you shouldn't have had to serve. These wars, maybe particularly the war in Viet Nam, are a good example of how the liberal elite manipulates everything. I doubt if many Americans could have found Viet Nam on a map, but the liberal elite and their dupes Kennedy and Johnson sent massive amounts of men and boys over there to fight. For what? For nothing. Did it make our country better off? No, it didn't! We lost that war because we should never have been there in the first place. The liberal elite made money off the war, while regular people lost their sons. Again, I admire those of you who served. Because of the draft, another idea pushed by the liberal elite, most of you didn't have any other alternative.

"Some of you will say, but what about Osama Ben Laden? Didn't we have to go into Afghanistan to get him? I say no. How did we get him? We got him with a Seal team mission into Pakistan, not Afghanistan, and our men were bogged down in an endless war in Afghanistan. How did that war help us here in the United States? It didn't. Protracted foreign wars are a terrible example of how the liberal elite manipulates common citizens who volunteered to protect this country. Again, let me say it. They volunteered to protect this country. But where do they end up? They end up dying in some God-forsaken country like Iraq or Afghanistan or Viet Nam."

Charlotte nudged Cathy again. "I've never heard this stuff before."

"I'm not sure everyone in the crowd liked it," Cathy commented. "I bet he returns to his regular shtick to get them back."

Cathy was right—the masked man returned to themes from his videos, and by the end, he had the crowd behind him. The finale was a repeat of what he'd done in the other rallies. The crowd responded as they had before, shouting "keep the faith" when the masked men raised their arms. Cathy and Charlotte stood with the rest of the audience, but they didn't join in the cheer.

"Wow," Cathy said when the four masked men finally disappeared in a cloud of smoke. "That was some show."

"That last bit was just like Knoxville," Charlotte said. "And you're right, it was quite a show."

She looked around to see if anyone was listening to them before continuing. "These people ate it up. I think you and I were the only ones not shouting along. What the hell does keep the faith mean? You know, in this context."

"I don't know, and I bet if we asked any of the shouters, they wouldn't know either."

"Whatever, it sure works on these people."

"Let's get out of here. I want to be sure not to run into Bill."

Meanwhile, Dwight and the Boynton group stood around talking to other people in the crowd, which was disbursing slowly. They had been seated with other people who were in local groups. Dwight joined in the discussions. He found it was easy to play his role as an ardent VM supporter.

Daniel had the guy in the sports coat spotted and was ready to follow him. He'd watched the guy during the rally and didn't think he behaved differently than any of the other idiots. *Clem sure knows how to rile up a crowd. This VM business is clearly catching on. The crowd here must be twice the size of the one in Knoxville.*

Just as the guy in the sports coat and his crowd were leaving, Daniel's phone vibrated. He took it out and saw a message from Katerina. She needed help at the door behind the stage. Daniel abandoned his plan to follow the guy and hustled to the back of the stage to see what was going on.

He found six or eight people crowded around the door, and some bozo was knocking on it. Daniel pushed his way through the crowd, grabbed the guy's shoulders, turned him around, and asked in a commanding voice, "What the hell do you think you are doing?"

The guy looked startled. "I just wanted to talk to the VM guy."

"Nobody talks to him. And by the way, why did you think we set up those ropes you crawled over to get here? People aren't supposed to be back here, so get out before you get in trouble."

The guy looked cowed, turned around, and walked away. He was joined by all but one of the people standing around the door. The lone remaining person, a big man dressed in camo, approached Daniel.

"You the security around here? Daniel Vilsac?"

"Yes." Daniel was on edge. There was no way this random guy should have known his name.

"You look way undermanned. You need help."

"I think I handled the situation back here. What makes you think I need help, and how'd you know my name?"

"Your rallies are going to get larger, and they're going to attract guys a lot tougher than the one you just shoved around. I'm from a militia group, and we'd like to volunteer to be security at your rallies. I thought your boss would've told you about me. James Bigelow sent me."

Daniel didn't have the faintest idea what the guy was talking about. He didn't know any James Bigelow, but the guy might be right about needing more security. "I'll talk it over with the others. You might be right. Do you have a way I can contact you by email or text?"

"Yeah, by the way, my name is Billy Rae Husted." Billy Rae stuck out his hand.

Daniel shook the outstretched hand.

The guy shuffled through his wallet and gave Daniel a business card.

"Thanks. If we decide to use you, I'll contact you in plenty of time to get to our next event. We don't have anything scheduled yet, but I'm sure there will be other rallies."

They shook hands again, and the militia guy walked back toward the ropes he'd crawled over before. As he hurried around to the front of the stage, Daniel was mad at Gregory. If Husted was right, Greg should have told him about the militia. When he got to the front, he saw the crowd had almost all left. He hopped up on the stage to see if he could spot the car he was interested in. He didn't have any luck. Cars were jammed together trying to get to the exit, and they'd raised a lot of dust in the process. Daniel couldn't tell one car from another.

Dwight got back to the hotel and found Cathy and Charlotte

sitting on a couch, waiting for him in the lobby. Cathy had gone to the room and removed her makeup and changed clothes. He gave her a brief hug, shook hands with Charlotte, and they all sat down.

"What did you think of the rally, Charlotte?"

"Cathy and I were just talking about that. Actually, most of it was like the Knoxville rally. The only difference was the bit about wars in far-off countries. I don't think it went over as well as the rest of the stuff."

"I found it interesting, and you're right, the audience wasn't ready for it. Still, I think it fits with the theme. This guy appeals to people who think they're being shoved around by the people in power, what he calls the liberal elite. Wars in far-off places aren't something his people started. They were started by politicians and military brass, and they were supported by the people making money from the war effort. None of the people he wants to appeal to are in those groups. His people supplied the frontline soldiers who paid the price for the decisions made by others. It makes sense to me."

Cathy responded, "Yes, I can see that, but some in his audience didn't understand it the way you did. I think they resented the VM guy for saying the soldiers were essentially duped into fighting in those wars. He might have been better off just sticking with Viet Nam. The draft played a big part in that war. It's different with an all-volunteer army."

"Fair enough, and you're right about the current army. Even if the wars are ill considered, the soldiers signed up for whatever the brass decides to do."

Dwight held up his hands, indicating they should stop talking. "I think those people might have been at the rally," he whispered, nodding toward a group approaching the front desk.

After the group left, Charlotte continued, "I think we'll see a video explaining his position further. The guy is savvy enough to recognize his stuff about foreign wars wasn't as well received as the other stuff."

After a pause, Charlotte finished her thought. "It will be interesting to see what happens next. Now I've got to figure out what to do with my next story."

"I think you should expose Clement Mincy," Cathy said. "His brand of nonsense works much better with mystery surrounding it. Once he is exposed as a mediocre actor from Indianapolis, I think he'll lose some of his punch."

"I wish I was surer of that," Dwight commented. "I think lots of what he says hits his followers as truth. They want to hear his message that the liberal elite is the cause of their problems. He's just articulating what they think."

Charlotte broke in at this point. "I'm inclined to take Cathy's side on this, Dwight. I think all the smoke and mirrors, the jumping around making it look like he's in four places at once, makes him feel larger than life. Exposing him will make him seem ordinary, like a talking head. I want to write this story."

"I can see where you're coming from," Dwight said. "I sure hope it works."

CHAPTER EIGHTEEN

After she backed the semi-trailer on to the pad by the barn, Katerina parked the cab next to the abandoned double wide. At the house, Clement opened the door for her and gave her a big kiss. "We've been here for three hours. What took you so long?"

"That rig is slow going up hills, and I don't speed like you guys. I don't want to be pulled over by some cop who wants to know what I'm hauling. Also, I had to pull over for the weigh station when I got to Michigan, and there was a long line. I'm bushed. I hope you've got the bed ready."

The next morning, Clement called the group together for a meeting When they'd all collected around the kitchen table, he started, "I got an email from Daniel, and he ran into a guy who said his militia was willing to provide security at our events. Katerina, he said you might know something about them. What do you think?"

Katerina answered, "I don't know anything about them, but I think it's a good idea. When those guys wanted to get in, they wouldn't take a no from me. I had to call Dan, and he ran them off. There weren't that many of them, so one person could handle it, but it might not be as easy next time. I say we take them up on the offer."

"You'd have to be the one who dealt with them," Clement said.

"That's fine. I'll be happy to be the one who organizes them, and maybe Dan can help. I've done the rest of my job three times now, so I think I can add one more thing."

"All right, you can email Daniel. Now let's move on to the next item of business. I could tell my bit about foreign wars didn't go over as well as the rest of it. I think I need to do a video to explain myself. I'll work on the script, and we can get it done in a couple of days."

Jake said, "Good idea Clem. No matter how many times you said you respected the veterans of those wars, I don't think it sunk in. You don't want to lose any people."

Clem got up from the table and started to pace. The group knew he didn't like criticism, so everyone was nervous. Knowing she was the only one who could talk to him when he was upset, Katerina said. "It's no big deal, honey. I think you left out the part about fighting for big oil companies, not fighting for your country. It's a good line, but you left it out. I think you should be sure to include it in the video."

Clem hung his head. "You're right on both counts. It's a good line, and I forgot it. It was the first time I'd done the foreign wars bit, and I just forgot the line."

"It happens to the best of actors, sweety. Just be sure to get it in the video. I think we all agree that you should do the video."

"Good, anything else we have to do?"

"Let's take a day off," Enrique said. "We've been busting our butts for three weeks now. I think we need a little time off. I'd like to go into town and see if I can pick up a chick."

"Okay, but you know the rules. Don't bring anyone back here, and don't tell anyone what you do or who we are."

"No problem."

Gregory Mincy opened the door to his office for Daniel. It was late and his secretary had gone home, so Gregory stayed behind his desk and Daniel took the chair facing the desk. "How did it go?"

"I'm not sure. The crowd in Cincy was the biggest yet, but the new part of Clem's spiel didn't go over as well as the old stuff. Being against foreign wars came across as being against our troops. I don't think that's the way he meant it, but some of the audience didn't get it."

"Yeah, he talked to me about that. He's going to do one of his videos to try to straighten out the problem. I have to admit, it's partly my fault. I lost a brother in Viet Nam. It still makes me mad. William was lost, but for what? We had no business being there. And maybe they're communists now, but who cares."

"I don't think the negative reaction was widespread, but I hope Clem can correct what he said in the video."

"Me too. Anything else?"

"Yeah, Katerina had to call me to break up a bunch of guys who were banging on the back door of the stage. It wasn't any big deal. They went peacefully when I leaned on them, but it could happen again. After they left, I met a guy who said he represented a militia. He said you'd know about him and mentioned somebody named James Bigelow."

Gregory stood up and went to stand in front of his big window, looking out onto downtown Indianapolis. When he turned around, he said, "I'm so sorry, Dan. I should have told you about the militia guy. It completely slipped my mind. Anyway, what do you think?"

"I think if you trust this Bigelow person, we should take them up on their offer. The larger the crowds get, the more likely we are to have problems. Some of the people Clem's stuff attracts aren't the most well-behaved."

"I can vouch for Bigelow. Anyone he recommends should be top notch. Go ahead and contact them. I don't know where or when the next rally will be. It doesn't matter. Bigelow will be handling their expenses."

"Okay. I'll tell Clem and Katerina about the security. There's one more thing. You remember I got the license plate of the guy who was snooping around in Michigan?"

"Ohio plates. Is that the one?"

"Yeah, I spotted his car in the Cincinnati lot. He got there early. I swear he looks a lot like the guy who interviewed you. You know, the one who said he was from Purdue. Anyway, he got there early and saved a bunch of seats. His group was big, thirteen or fourteen. I was going to tail him out of the lot when I got the call from Katerina about the business at the back door, so I couldn't follow him. I sure hope I can figure out who he is soon. I have a bad feeling about him."

Gregory narrowed his eyes, his gaze sharp and feral. "I agree. If it is the guy from Purdue, I don't think I told him anything important. Still, he seems way too interested in us. Find out who he is as soon as you can."

"Will do."

Back in Boynton, Dwight found a surprise in the mail. He didn't get much mail because he used email for important correspondence. The letter was from Marjorie's attorney in the divorce proceedings. Dwight was shocked when he read Marjorie was asking for twenty-five percent of the royalties from the books Dwight had published while they were married. According to the attorney's letter, she claimed she was an integral part of the writing process, so she deserved a share.

After reading the letter, Dwight stomped around his office, steaming mad. When he'd calmed down, which took a while, he called his lawyer. "Jim, this is Dwight Kelton. I just received a letter from Marjorie's lawyer. She wants a share of my royalties. I don't think it's right. I gave her the condo and all the furniture. It was the only thing of value we jointly owned. She has her car, and I have mine. All our retirement funds are in our separate names. There's no way she should be able to claim a share of my royalties."

"Calm down Dwight. I got a copy of the letter, and I was expecting this call. I agree. You've been more than generous with Marjorie. You have every right to object. The issue will come down to whether she actually contributed to the authorship of the books. Did she help you write them in any way?"

Dwight tightened his grip on the phone as he paced the room. "No, she didn't. In fact, she actively opposed the idea of those books. She told me I was wasting my time writing children's books. Marjorie only values scholarship that involves original research. She considers my books derivative. I was explaining the scholarship of others, not producing anything original."

"Is that right?"

"Yes, but that's not the point. I wrote the books so middle and high school students would have access to good biographies. I wasn't trying to do original research. Marjorie and a bunch of my colleagues resented the fact that my books sold way better than theirs. I actually make money. The idea that she thinks she deserves some of the royalties is hypocritical."

"Was she included in the front of the book? You know, where the author thanks all his friends for supporting him or reading drafts. What do you call it?"

"The acknowledgements. Yes, I guess so, but only for being a supportive spouse, not for having anything to do with the production of the book. I'll have to look to be sure, but I don't think I said anything much. Anyway, lots of my colleagues know what Marjorie thought of my books. She openly ridiculed them on several occasions. I don't want her to have a penny from the books." Dwight took a deep breath and finally sat at his desk.

"Okay, I'll contact her lawyer and make all the threats I can. You have to understand though, if she keeps her demand, and you want to fight it, the divorce will be held up. It's going to cost you a bunch in my fees."

"I don't care. It's just so wrong. Tell her lawyer, I'll fight her tooth and nail. I lost my job, and she kept hers. She doesn't need the money. I do. And she didn't have anything to do with the production of the books."

"I'll get back to you after I've talked to her attorney."

"Thanks, Jim."

The call hadn't mollified Dwight, but it was all he could do. He texted Cathy, asking if she could get away for lunch. He needed to talk to her. The phone rang five minutes later, and he explained what he'd learned.

"That's horrible. I can do a short lunch. I can understand why you're upset. Let's meet at the country club."

"Thanks. I love you."

"Oh Dwight, I love you too."

Dwight gulped. "I guess we've never said that before. It just sort of slipped out, but it's true."

"It's true for me too."

"See you at lunch."

Dwight wondered if the three words would make a difference, and at lunch it appeared they had. Cathy gave him her complete attention as she listened to his complaints about the letter from Marjorie's attorney. She stared at him with a big smile on her face.

"Darling, I know I shouldn't be smiling. What you're talking about is serious, but I can't help it. I didn't realize how much I wanted to hear you say you loved me. I guess it was a big thing. I feel the same way, but somehow, I was afraid to say it."

"I don't know what took me so long. I've been feeling it for quite a while, so when it just slipped out on the phone today, it seemed natural."

"Whether it seemed natural or not, it was thrilling to me. I've been feeling it for a long time, and I was pretty sure you felt the same way. Still, it was great to hear."

"It's a good thing I see the waitress coming, or I'd be jumping across the table at you."

Cathy looked up and released Dwight's hands and winked at him. "The feeling is mutual."

Over lunch they discussed their divorces. Cathy assured Dwight he shouldn't worry about the letter he'd just received. "I'm sure you can straighten it out. You've given her the condo. She's already received more than her fair share. Even if it's more of a hassle than you'd anticipated, I bet a judge would take your side. There is no way she deserves any of the proceeds from your books."

"I hope you're right, but it brings up something you have to think about. Are the stores in your name only or is Bill a part owner?"

"Luckily, I was starting to sour on Bill when I decided to buy the store from Mrs. McNulty. She was the previous owner. I've always had a big savings account. The money came from life insurance on my father. I'd kept it separate from the joint accounts Bill and I had. Anyway, I used that money for a big down payment and took out a loan in my own name. Luckily, Bill doesn't have any claim on my business income."

"Marjorie shouldn't have any claim on my book income, but she's trying. I hope Bill doesn't want to pull anything like that with you."

"I don't think he will. If he does, I'll fight him to the bitter end, just like you're going to."

When they got to the parking lot, they were glad to see it was almost deserted, so they shared a deep kiss. After the kiss, they said in unison, "I love you."

Three days later, Dwight and Cathy received an email from Charlotte. It contained a draft of her story, revealing the identity of the VM masked man. Charlotte had put their discoveries to good use and done more investigation on her own. The result was a good story. First, it described the videos and the in-person rallies. Then it turned to identifying Clement Mincy. The discussion had several steps. Charlotte showed two pictures of the lake, one taken from the mermaid video and the other from Google Maps. She then described how the lake was identified as being behind a house owned by Gregory Mincy and lived in by Clement Mincy. Next, Charlotte relied on an anonymous source who stated that Clement Mincy was the man behind the mask. The final part of the story was about Clement Mincy. Charlotte described his career as an actor and a magician. She must have made a side trip to Indianapolis because she had been able to get some quotations from people who knew him. For the most part, these quotations were not flattering. One person stated that Clement was a "…right wing kook who wasn't a very good actor."

Dwight thought the story was great. He emailed Charlotte with his congratulations and copied Cathy on the email. Ten minutes later, he got a copy of Cathy's email to Charlotte. She had been equally complementary.

Charlotte Mangum's story had been picked up by several other papers, and Daniel Vilsac was surprised when he saw it. He quickly attached the story to emails he sent to Gregory and Clement.

"Holy shit," Clement said after he'd read the story on his cell phone.

Katerina, who sat beside him on the living room couch looking over his shoulder, took his phone and said, "Just a minute. Let me finish."

"How the hell did this reporter from Knoxville figure out who I was?"

"I think it had to be your old girlfriend, Marcie. She was the only one ever involved who isn't still with us. We caught her snooping around here. She must have talked to the reporter before she came here. She surely didn't talk to anyone after we took care of her."

"What are we going to do about it?"

"We have to figure out how to issue a denial. I think it has to be more than a statement from your father. Surely it will help for him to tell the Indianapolis papers he doesn't know anything about VM, but we have to have more."

"I can attach a denial to the new video I'm doing to placate the veterans. It wouldn't be difficult."

"I think we should do that, but there has to be more. We need something that will grab the papers' attention. This article is going to have wide circulation. We need something splashy to counteract it."

CHAPTER NINETEEN

Two and a half weeks later, Dwight and Cathy drove together to the VM rally in Toledo. Again, they left earlier than Bill and the somewhat smaller group from Boynton. It had been a rocky two and a half weeks for the Boynton VM group. Charlotte's story had hit them hard. The revelation that the man behind the mask was a thoroughly mediocre actor from Indianapolis stuck people the wrong way. Bill wasn't deterred. He printed off the email the leaders had received. It included a complete denial of the story. It said flat out that Clement Mincy wasn't the VM guy. Several members of the group were skeptical, and Bill got mad at them.

The new VM video, which focused on foreign wars, was very well received by the members who still were hanging on, and many of them called the members who had fallen away urging them to look at it. Mostly they told them to look at the end of the video. Right before he disappeared, the VM guy mentioned the Mincy story. He denied being Clement Mincy and promised to prove it at the next rally scheduled for Toledo, Ohio. This wasn't convincing for the skeptics, but it was enough for Bill to recruit eight people to go to Toledo.

A week before the Toledo rally, Dwight had gone to a meeting with Marjorie and the two lawyers. The only issue in dispute was the royalties. The meeting had been acrimonious, but Dwight had won. Marjorie's lawyer laid out the bogus claim that as a supportive spouse, she deserved to share in the royalties. Dwight's lawyer threated to call witnesses who would testify that Marjorie frequently ridiculed Dwight's books. After a short conference with her lawyer, Marjorie dropped her claim. Dwight knew Marjorie would hate to be shown up in public that way, so he was not surprised the tactic worked. Still, it had been a nerve-wracking meeting. He was delighted to make it back to Cathy and Boynton.

Cathy was also involved in divorce proceedings. She and Bill were now officially separated. He had moved in with Stacy. Under their separation agreement, Cathy and Courtney would stay in the house until Courtney went to college. After that, the rights to the house would be settled in the divorce. Cathy wasn't sure she wanted the house anyway, but she didn't indicate as much to Bill. Their official separation turned some heads in town, but not too many. Rumors about Bill and Stacy had been around for a long time.

Dwight and Cathy met with Charlotte in the hotel lobby in Toledo. "How are you holding up?" Cathy asked.

"It's been a rough couple of weeks. My editor is standing by me, but I've had a couple of tense meetings with him. Gregory Mincy is threatening to sue the paper unless we print a retraction. The editor thinks it's a bluff, but he doesn't really know."

"I'm willing to reveal myself as your source if it comes to that," Dwight said.

"That's awfully nice of you. I don't know if it will be necessary. Still, if it looks like the legal proceedings are really going to happen, I might have to call on you."

Cathy broke in, "Actually just letting Mincy's lawyers know you have a person who can back up the story might be enough to make them think twice about going forward."

"Come to think of it, I've got some evidence I forgot to tell you about," Dwight said.

"What?" the two women echoed.

"I have a video of the woman, I think Marcie told me her name was Katerina, swimming. She and one of the mermaids share a very distinctive swimming stroke. Marcie told me she and this Katerina had played the mermaids. Anyway, my little video looks just like part of the VM video."

"That could be helpful, but it also points out one of the difficulties we might have. Our best evidence is based on what Marcie told you. It's hearsay. Granted, we have other evidence to corroborate our story, but it's all circumstantial. We really don't have any direct evidence."

"I can see how we might have trouble in court," Cathy said.

"I just hope it doesn't come to that," Charlotte concluded.

After that, the three friends turned to a discussion of what they thought was going to happen at the rally. They had all seen the VM video in which the masked man promised to convince everyone he wasn't Clement Mincy.

"I don't think he's going to remove his mask revealing his identity," Dwight said.

"Me either," Charlotte responded.

"I bet it will somehow involve plastic masks, like the *Mission Impossible* movies," Cathy said.

"That's possible," Charlotte said. "We know Mincy was a magician. We've already seen him make the masked man appear and disappear, so I wouldn't put anything past him. Whatever he does, I bet it's slick. I don't think it will be easy to poke holes in it. Frankly I'm worried."

An hour later, they shared an early dinner at the hotel. After dinner, Dwight left to save seats the way he had in Cincinnati, Cathy went to the room to put on her disguise, and Charlotte cooled her heels in the lobby.

◇◇◇

Before people started to arrive, Daniel and Katerina met in front of the stage with the Midnight Patrol militia group. There were eight men dressed in camouflage. Daniel told them they had one job, with two parts. "First, keep people off the stage. I don't want them rushing the stage during the performance, and I don't want them inspecting the stage before or after. Second, keep people from trying to get into our set after everything is over."

Looking at the guy he'd met before, Billy Rae, he continued, "You know, like the bozos I had to run off in Cincinnati. I'll come and relieve you when you are no longer needed. Just so I'm clear: I want all eight of you in front before the performance. When things start, kneel and face the crowd. Then after things finish, you can stand up and maybe three of you can move to secure the back."

The group leader nodded.

Katerina spoke up at this point. "There's three things Dan left out. First, there's a seat with a ribbon on it in the front row. Don't let anyone remove that ribbon. About ten minutes before things get going, a man in a suit will come out with me to take the seat. Second, see that camera there? Don't let anyone disturb it. Maybe one of you should stand by it until right before we start. Third, I have badges for all of you."

Katerina reached into the bag she was carrying and handed out badges, which were small replicas of Guy Fawkes masks. "Wear these. They will tell people you're official."

Dwight arrived at the fairgrounds parking lot and thought, *Either I'm really early, or this is going to be a much smaller crowd. This lot doesn't have fifty cars yet.*

He took his time walking to the entrance, paid his twenty dollars, and found he could block off the seats he needed in the sixth row. The Boynton group would have a great view. He was surprised to see the big guys in camo outfits lined up across the front of the stage. There hadn't been any visible security at the other rallies. The other difference he saw was a camera on a tripod. Someone was going to video the performance. Otherwise, it looked like the same set up.

He didn't run into trouble with people wanting his seats, but still he was happy to see Bill and the others. One of the guys was a no show, so he didn't need all the seats. It was not a big deal. There was even an empty seat in the front row. Dwight thought it was weird. *Maybe people all came with friends, so they needed more than one seat.* Finally, a guy who must have come by himself headed for the seat. When he tried to take the empty front-row seat, one of the security guys wouldn't let him.

About five minutes before the start time, a man and a woman came out from behind the stage. Dwight was shocked. The man was Clement Mincy, he'd swear to it. And the woman was Katerina. She was in a disguise, one including bright red hair, tattoos, and padding to make her look fatter. The disguise didn't fool Dwight. He'd taken a good look at her when she was walking back to the house after her swim. As the woman disappeared behind the stage, he kicked himself for not taking a picture now.

Dwight also saw the guy he'd seen in Cincinnati. He was standing beside the stage a few minutes before the show was scheduled to start. Dwight couldn't shake the idea he'd seen the guy somewhere before. Just like before, he thought the guy was focused on him, not just the crowd in general. Dwight didn't like the idea that he seemed to be the focus of this guy's attention.

The rally started just like the other ones. There was a boom and smoke poured across the stage. When the smoke cleared, the VM man stood on the stage. He gave the sign, and the cheering started. Dwight looked around and saw all the stands were full and quite a few people were standing. He didn't think the crowd was as big as the Cincinnati one, but it was close.

The masked man welcomed the crowd and then said he had a special guest. "Would you please come forward."

Clement Mincy got up from his seat in the front row and used a little ladder to climb up to the stage. Dwight wondered why he hadn't spotted the ladder before. When Mincy got to the guy in the mask, they shook hands, and the masked guy took a microphone out of his robe and gave it to Mincy.

"Please introduce yourself to the audience," the masked man said.

Mincy turned toward the audience and said, "My name is Clement Mincy."

Several people around Dwight gasped, and there was a general murmur in the crowd.

When the crowd settled, Mincy continued, "Most of you will probably recognize my name from the bogus newspaper story saying I am the VM masked man. As you can see, the story is false. I didn't know whether to be annoyed by the story or flattered."

Pointing to the masked man beside him, he went on. "I think this guy is incredible. He speaks the truth."

Applause interrupted Mincy, so he paused. "In any event, I am not behind the mask. I am here for all of you to see. I just wanted to set the record straight. I don't know why the newspaper reporter thought I was involved with the VM people, but it's not true. They were kind enough to give me this chance to explain things. Thank you for listening."

Mincy handed back the microphone, shook hands with the VM guy, and headed back to the ladder as the crowd broke out into cheers. Mincy stopped at the edge of the stage and waved at the crowd before climbing down the ladder and returning to his seat.

Illusion of Truth

Dwight thought, *Slick, just like the other stuff. The VM guy's voice sounded just like it had before, the deep baritone. Mincy's voice was very different. They must be using a recording somehow. You can't tell what's going on behind the mask.* He looked around and recognized he was probably one of the few people who still thought Clement Mincy was the VM masked man.

Cathy and Charlotte were having similar thoughts twenty-five rows behind Dwight. The appearance of Clement Mincy had come as a complete surprise to them. When he was walking back to his seat as the audience stood and cheered, the two women exchanged quizzical looks.

The remainder of the presentation was almost a carbon copy of the other VM rallies. The speaker soft pedaled the foreign wars bit, only wondering whether the soldiers who died in Iraq had died for the American people or for the big oil companies. The finale too was just like the other rallies, and the audience was, if anything, more enthusiastic. Many in the crowd yelled "keep the faith" before the man raised his hands. Dwight decided to film the finale. It was quite a show.

Daniel Vilsac had recognized Dwight as he was saving seats. He kicked himself. There was no way he could follow him this time. He was responsible for getting Clem out of the crowd. He was Clem's ride back. When the finale was over, Daniel rushed toward Clem. There was no way he could get close. People were coming up to Clem and shaking his hand. Daniel could tell Clem was enjoying the attention, so he backed off. He looked around to see if he could see the guy who'd been saving the seats. No such luck. He must have already left.

CHAPTER TWENTY

Back at the hotel, Dwight met Charlotte in the lobby. "Where's Cathy?"

"She's getting rid of her disguise. I don't know why she needs it."

Dwight looked around to see who he might know in the lobby. Fortunately, there was nobody. "She doesn't want her husband to know she has any interest in the VM thing. Also, it's eventually going to get out that Cathy and I are together. It's almost impossible to keep that kind of a secret in a small town. When that gets out, Cathy doesn't want to blow my cover as a VM enthusiast."

Just then, Cathy walked up. "What did you think?"

"Let's sit here," Charlotte suggested.

Dwight responded after they were seated, "It was convincing, at least to the people around me. They bought the presentation in every detail. I'm not sure how they did it. Even the voices were right. The VM guy sounded the same as the other rallies and the videos, and Clement Mincy sounded like someone else. You can't see lips moving behind the mask, so it could have all been recorded."

"The VM guy's gestures seemed like they fit the words," said Charlotte. "I guess they could have rehearsed enough to make that work. They're really good."

"I have something else." Dwight took out his phone. "I videoed the finale. I want to look at it again."

"Why?" Cathy asked.

"The final time the VM guy appears there are four of him, right? The way I count, with Mincy sitting in the front row, they're one man short. When I was in Michigan, I counted three people other than Mincy. I think Katerina had to step in to the fourth spot, and we might be able to tell if it's her."

They crowded their chairs together to look at the finale. When it got to the last part with four people, Dwight froze the video. "Look at the one on the right-hand end. He's not as tall, and his arms aren't as long. I don't have any video of the other finales, but I don't remember this kind of discrepancy the other times. They all looked the same. It's part of the illusion."

"We can check with the other times," Charlotte said. "Several people posted the other finales online. You might be on to something, Dwight."

"I agree, but I don't see how it's going to help us much," Cathy said. "At the moment, the VM guy is riding high, and none of his followers are going to believe he has anything to do with Clement Mincy. We're back where we started."

After a pause, Charlotte spoke up. "I agree. They shot a big hole in my story. I don't know what's going to happen when I get back to the newsroom. I can't back down. I know the story's true, and I'm not going to reveal my source. The whole thing is going to be a mess."

"You won't get fired, will you?" Dwight asked.

"I don't think that's likely."

"Look, if you need me to, I could reveal myself to your editor. I'd like to stay anonymous, but I could back you up."

"That's nice of you, Dwight, but I don't think it will come to that."

Waiting for her flight, Charlotte looked at the news feeds on her phone. A couple of right-wing ones ran short stories about the Toledo rally. They claimed Clement Mincy's appearance at the rally blew her story out of the water. Luckily for her, they didn't mention her name. Still, it was out there, and people would read it. She wasn't looking forward to the return to her office.

When Charlotte got home, she had several voice messages. She wasn't surprised, so she sat down to take her medicine. Two of them were from her boyfriend, and they made her smile. As she had feared, one of them was from her editor requesting a meeting as soon as possible. Three of them from VM supporters were obnoxious. She erased them before they were finished. The final message was from someone named Larry Green, who said he had information for her. He left a phone number.

Charlotte phoned Cathy, who told her she didn't know anyone named Larry Green, but she'd ask Dwight.

On her drive into the newspaper office, she received a call from Dwight. "I don't know anyone named Larry Green," he said. "Wait a minute, the girl I talked to in Michigan, the one who was killed before we could talk again, was Marcie Green. He might be related to her. I'd give him a call. You can hang up, if it isn't useful."

When she got to her office, Charlotte couldn't help but notice the looks the other reporters gave her. They all knew she was in trouble. No one greeted her. It was like she was poison. The normal buzz stopped as she made her way to her desk. She shared a room with the other seven reporters. She could tell they were trying to avoid eye contact, but they'd all paused what they were doing. Finally, everyone resumed their activities after she sat down.

Before she went to see her editor or take care of the other voicemails on her office phone, Charlotte called Larry Green's number. Several of the other reporters were now staring at her, but she ignored them. After they'd identified each other, Charlotte lowered her voice and said, "I don't have much time. Why did you want me to call?"

"My sister was killed recently, and I think Clement Mincy was responsible."

"Wow, you get to the point quickly, Mr. Green. That's a lot to absorb."

After Charlotte didn't continue, Larry filled the silence. "My sister Marcie used to date that no good Mincy, and after they broke up, she showed me a video, one where she played the mermaid. I didn't think much about it at the time. I was just glad she wasn't with Clem anymore. Someone showed me your story a couple of days ago, and I want to know what you know about Mincy. Marcie was killed in Michigan close to where your story said Mincy lived. I've been there and talked to the police, but they don't have much."

"I'm so sorry about your sister. You think Mincy is involved. Can you explain why?"

"I've been going over Marcy's stuff. It's a painful process. Anyway, I found her diary. I guess I shouldn't have read it. I mean, diaries are private, right? Anyway, I couldn't stop myself. The diary has quite a section on Clement Mincy and why Marcie broke up with him. It all fits with your newspaper story. Marcie was no liberal, but she couldn't go along with what Mincy was starting. Also, the last pages of the diary outline why Marcie was going to Michigan."

As she listened, Charlotte couldn't help smiling. *This is just what I need—independent confirmation of Mincy's involvement.* When he paused, she said, "Marcie's diary could be just what I need. Let me fill you in on the latest. The VM people had one of their rallies in Toledo, Ohio last night. Clement Mincy attended the rally and directly contradicted my story. I came to work today with the feeling I'd been completely destroyed. What you have could rescue me."

"You must have had other sources for your story. Are they consistent with what I found in Marcie's diary?"

"Yes, they are. In fact, my source met your sister in Michigan. What he learned from her confirmed what he already thought. I went out on a limb with my editor. I claimed I had two sources, but I didn't admit one of them had just been a murder victim. What you have solidifies my case."

"Where do we go from here?"

"Let me think about it. My editor wanted me in his office when I got to work. I bet he wonders what's holding me up. I feel a lot better about that meeting after talking to you. If I survive the meeting, I'll contact my other source. I'm quite sure he'll want to talk to you. Thanks so much for calling. One way or the other, I'll definitely be in touch, probably in a couple of hours."

Returning to her desk after her meeting, Charlotte didn't know quite what to think. The news about the diary saved her. Max, her editor, finally told her he'd stand by her, but he was firm. If she didn't uncover another way to corroborate her story, he'd take her off the assignment. He wasn't sure, but if she failed, his plan was to just drop the whole thing. He figured it would all blow over eventually.

At least I still have a job, she thought.

She wrote down Larry Green's number on a slip of paper, grabbed her purse, and walked out of the building. She wanted to have some private conversations, and she found the atmosphere in the newsroom stifling.

When she got to a park two blocks away from the paper's office, she called Dwight from her car and told him what she'd learned from Larry Green. Dwight was thrilled. "This is great. Now you have two sources. Isn't that important for a reporter?"

"Yes, but actually I don't have another source. Before it was you and Marcie. Now I have the same—you and Marcie. It's just that I have Marcie in writing now. Before what I had was your recollection of what Marcie said."

"Yeah, I see what you're saying. Still, if this guy Green will let us read Marcie's diary, we might have more stuff. If she wrote it out in her diary, she may have told some of her friends. The diary could be the break we need. He must be in Indianapolis."

"I guess so. We didn't talk long."

"I'd love to talk to him, but I just can't call him out of the blue."

"No problem. I told him I'd call him back. I can introduce you. Give me a few minutes. I'll message you with his number if it's okay for you to call him."

"Thanks so much, Charlotte. This could be just the break I need."

"You and me both."

Ten minutes later, Dwight was at his desk trying to figure out what to do next with Charles Dickens when he received the text with Larry Green's phone number.

Dwight's call was answered after the first ring. "Larry Green here."

"This is Dwight Kelton; Charlotte Mangum told you I'd be calling. I met your sister in Michigan. We both were spying on Clement Mincy. It was funny, actually. I was headed to get behind a bush I'd used the day before, but Marcie was already behind the same bush. Anyway, we talked."

Larry interrupted, "Yes, Charlotte told me your talk with Marcie was an important source for her story."

"She's right. After a brief talk, Marcie agreed to meet me and my partner at a restaurant in Grand Rapids, but she didn't show. The next morning, I saw a news story saying a car with a dead body in it had been found that morning. The story only showed the car, but it was Marcie's."

"A silver Audi TT is easy to recognize."

"I agree and seeing the Indiana plates clinched it."

Silence followed that remark. Dwight couldn't tell if Larry was upset. Finally, he said, "Charlotte told me you've found Marcie's diary.

Is there a chance I could look at it?"

"Before I give an answer, I guess I'd like to know more about you and why you are so interested."

Dwight described his background and how he got involved in trying to uncover who was behind the VM videos. Larry said he only knew about the mermaid video. Dwight advised him to look at a couple of them, so he had a feel for what was going on. Also, Larry told Dwight he still hadn't read all of the diary. After a long discussion, Dwight offered to meet Larry in Indianapolis the next day.

That evening, Dwight and Cathy rendezvoused at the back room in the Clayville store. Dwight had filled Cathy in about his trip to Indianapolis, and she'd told him she had something for him, but she wouldn't say what it was.

Dwight spoke after they'd shared a long kiss. "So, can you tell me this mysterious thing you've discovered?"

"It's not so much of a mystery. I just wanted to see your face when you saw what I've done. You know what you said about the VM guy at the end of the finale. I got copies of the other three finales on the internet, and I want you to look at them. Courtney arranged them in pairs. The Toledo one is always on top, and the other ones are on the bottom. I've looked at them, but I want to see what you think. Here, why don't you sit at the desk so you can see them?"

Cathy opened a laptop and moved behind Dwight so she could look over his shoulder. "Just click on the video, and it will go."

Dwight watched the video. "Can it run in slow motion?"

"Yes, I think so," Cathy said, leaning over him to hit the right keys. "There you go."

After he'd watched all three videos, both at regular speed and in slow motion, Dwight spoke up. "It's clear the right-hand person in Toledo is different. Whoever it is is shorter. I think they have lifts in their shoes, and the arms are shorter, too. They don't quite fill out the outfit the same."

"I think it's Katerina, like you said. I remember from the video you showed me, the one in the bikini. She's had breast augmentation surgery. It would be difficult to hide her big boobs, even in the warrior robes they wear."

"This is great, Cathy. I think you should forward it to Charlotte."

"Will do. When are you leaving for Indianapolis?"

Dwight turned away from the computer to face Cathy. "Early tomorrow morning. I've done the drive recently, and it's not bad. I'm leaving early enough so I can meet Larry at his office at one o'clock. He's a lawyer. If everything goes well, he'll let me copy the diary. I'm going to make two copies, one for us and one for Charlotte. Larry hasn't read the whole thing. At least he hadn't when I talked to him last. There could be some really useful information."

"I wish I could come with you, but I really can't take off on this short notice."

"That's okay. I think it will be a boring trip for the most part. I'm coming right back the next day."

Cathy wrapped her arms around Dwight. "Drive safely."

CHAPTER TWENTY-ONE

Dwight made it to Indianapolis in time for a quick lunch before his meeting with Larry Green. Green worked at a four-person law firm that had offices in downtown Indianapolis. When Dwight got to the office, Larry's secretary took Dwight to a conference room, telling him Mr. Green would be with him shortly.

Five minutes later, Larry Green rushed in. After they shook hands, he said, "I'm sorry to keep you waiting. I had a phone call I had to take."

As they sat down, Dwight thought he could see some of what he remembered of Marcie in Larry. They both wore thick glasses, and they had the same coloring. Larry was much taller, maybe six four, so the resemblance wasn't strong.

Larry started the discussion. "Let me be up front. I Googled you, Professor Kelton, and I was impressed. You're quite the author. I know you gave me a brief explanation of how you got involved in the VM business, but I don't quite understand. Also, I was surprised you could come to Indianapolis on such short notice."

Dwight explained that he'd quit his job at the university to help his mother, who was recovering from a stroke. He decided not to go into the full reason. He mentioned the Dickens book, which he said he could write at home as easily as if he'd stayed at the university.

Illusion of Truth

Actually, he explained, it was easier without a teaching schedule. Then he introduced Cathy, who had convinced him to get involved in her quest to expose the VM business.

"Okay, I understand. It didn't seem to fit with what I found out about you. That's all."

"No problem. I'd be curious if I were in your shoes."

Larry leaned back in his chair and tapped his pen on the papers a few times. "I looked at a couple of those VM videos like you suggested. They're quite well done. I guess I shouldn't be surprised. Clement has a theater background, and he also performed a magic show. That's where Marcie first got to know him. She worked as his assistant on the show. Anyway, it's clear he knows how to stage things. Also, he must have linked up with someone who knows how to produce high-quality videos."

"I agree, the videos are slick, but what did you think of the content?"

Larry shook his head. "It was crazy. Vikings, mermaids, and space aliens. I can't see how anyone finds it anything but wacky. People believe this stuff?"

"That's the horrible thing about it. People do, at least some people. I infiltrated a group where I live in Boynton, Ohio. It's not large, but our group has several true believers. Also, I've been to VM outdoor rallies. Like the videos, they are polished productions. The rallies draw enthusiastic audiences. VM has a large and growing following. We think it could grow into something very serious."

"It's just so strange. I can't see it."

"That was my first reaction, but the more I got involved, the more I saw its appeal. If you want to be depressed about our country, I recommend reading the VM message board. There are large numbers of people who aren't happy for lots of reasons. They believe the VM guy has identified the source of their dissatisfaction. He tells them they are being manipulated by the liberal elite. I always knew there were a small number of people who were completely alienated. You know, survivalists in the West. Now, I've come to understand a large group of people have similar thoughts, just not quite as extreme. The VM guy is trying to radicalize those people. If he's not stopped, he might just succeed."

Larry stood up and went over to a small refrigerator. He extracted two bottles of water. "Want one?"

"Sure."

He came back with the water and continued. "I haven't read all of Marcie's diary, but some of it echoes what you've just said. Let's cut to the chase. I'm willing to let you copy the diary. If I give it to you right now, you can take it to Staples or somewhere and make a copy."

"If it's okay, I'd like to make two copies, one for me and Cathy and another for Charlotte Mangum, the reporter from Knoxville who wrote the story about Clement being the VM guy. She needs the diary to convince her editor she's right."

"That's fine, but I would want to see anything she writes about Marcie before it gets printed."

"I think she can live with that."

"Good, let's go to my office."

After his meeting with Larry, he made two copies of the diary at an office supply store. Dwight then checked into the same hotel he and Cathy had used for their Indianapolis trip. He spent what was left of his afternoon reading the diary. Much of it wasn't useful, but some of it was. He made notes with references to pages much like he would have if he were doing literary research. The diary verified what he already knew and added considerable detail. Unfortunately, the diary included names of people who might be able to add important details, but Marcie only used first names. He was happy he'd agreed to meet Larry for dinner. It would give him a chance to see if Larry knew more about the people Marcie mentioned.

The most disturbing part of the diary was a description of a meeting Clement took Marcie to right before they broke up. Marcie, Clement, and Greg went to Atlanta, where the meeting took place. Marcie wasn't permitted to go to the actual sessions, but she accompanied Clem to the receptions and dinners. Marcie mentioned names of businessmen she met in Atlanta. The impression she left in her diary was that Clem and Greg were meeting with some kind of hush-hush group that shared their political views. She and Clement got into a big argument because he wouldn't tell her what it was about. That argument started their breakup.

Dwight found this part of the diary chilling. If the VM stuff was part of a larger conspiracy of some kind, it might be even more dangerous. He figured his first order of business when he got back to Boynton should be to see if he could find anything about the two names Marcie mentioned.

At seven, he met Larry at a steak house only a block from his hotel. They chatted amiably over drinks, and Dwight was delighted Larry could fill in some last names and descriptions for people mentioned in Marcie's diary. The most important full name Dwight learned about was Jocelyn Mason. Jocelyn was Marcie's roommate before she moved in with Clement. Marcie had moved back with her for a short spell after she broke up with Clement. The diary mentioned several long talks the two women had when Marcie was trying to get things back together after ditching Clement. Dwight could tell Jocelyn had met Katerina too.

Larry recognized a couple of other names but not many. Dwight was hoping he would know the names of some businessmen Marcie had mentioned from the meeting in Atlanta. Unfortunately, Larry didn't recognize any of the names.

When they'd finished with Dwight's questions, Larry wanted him to describe again how he'd met Marcie and what he thought happened to her in Michigan. Dwight repeated what he'd told him over the phone and described how he'd left a message for the police. "I'm sorry, that's all I know. She was killed several hours after I left her beside Mincy's house."

"I spoke with the Grand Rapids police. They told me they talked to Mincy, who admitted Marcie had come by the house that afternoon wanting him to pay her rent money. That was it. Mincy told them she left shortly after she came. He said he didn't have any idea about Marcie being killed. The girl who was with Mincy in the house, Katerina I suppose, backed up his story. So far, they don't have any suspects in the killing."

Daniel Vilsac was thrilled he was able to convince Helen Simons to go out with him again. Helen had been very angry with him when he'd disappeared on her to go to Michigan to keep watch on the house. He hadn't been able to explain where he was going, what he was doing, or when he'd be coming home. She'd blown him off the first two times he'd called but relented this time when he'd mentioned where he wanted to take her. They enjoyed the steak house and were having their first drink when Daniel saw the person who'd used his sports coat to reserve seats at the VM rally—the one who drove the car with the Ohio license plates. The guy sat down two tables away from them and was joined by a tall man who Daniel didn't recognize.

Daniel wondered what to do. He really should try to find out his identity, but he didn't want to abandon Helen. She was just starting to warm up to him. He'd explained his job to her in the past, but then he'd just been the head of security for the department stores. Now he was in the process of telling her he sometimes had special jobs for Greg Mincy, jobs he couldn't talk about.

"Okay, I can see that, but there are phones, you know. If you have to go on some secret mission again at least call me."

"I will," Daniel said. "It might happen again real soon."

"What do you mean?"

"See that guy over there, the shorter one?" he asked, gesturing in Dwight's direction.

Helen looked around and spotted Dwight. "Yes, what about him?"

"He's someone Gregory and I are very interested in. I've got to follow him."

Helen had a gleam in her eye. "Let me go with you."

"What? That's crazy."

Helen leaned over, reached under the table, and stroked Dan's knee. The touch, and the view of her cleavage the maneuver created, softened him up.

"Okay," Daniel said. "Here's what we'll do. When it looks like they're finishing up, we'll leave. You go to the lobby and pretend you're waiting for your date. When the guys come out, see if you can overhear what they say. They might say something about where they're going. Watch for my car after they get out the door and come out and hop in when you see me. I'll pull up right in front after they leave."

"Then we'll follow them."

"That's my plan. I don't know if it will work, but it's worth a try. Greg and I have been trying to find out who that guy is for quite a while. I know what his car's license plate number is, but it's a new one in Ohio, and they don't put them in their system for a while. I have a friend who's going to get me a name when they load the most recently purchased licenses."

"I don't suppose you can tell me what this is all about."

"No, sorry. I can't."

Helen and Daniel ordered dishes they knew wouldn't take long to prepare. Also, they told the waiter they were in a hurry, so they wanted the check a little early. Daniel had a good look at the two men, and he was convinced he and Helen would finish before they did, so he relaxed.

After he and Helen finished and paid the check, Daniel saw the dishes were being cleared from the other table. They might have dessert or coffee, but even if they didn't, they still had to deal with the check. He told Helen not to look hurried, but it was time to leave.

As they walked out, Helen said, "I'm a little nervous. All I have to do is try to see if they say anything about where they're going, right?"

"Yeah, try to act natural. Maybe you can look like you're annoyed your date hasn't brought the car around."

Five minutes after Helen got to the restaurant lobby and was pacing in front of the door, the two men came out. She overheard the one they were interested in talk about staying in the hotel just down the block. The two men shook hands, and the tall guy headed for the parking lot. The other guy started walking. Helen followed him out the door. Right after they got outside, Daniel drove up. Helen hustled over to the car and opened the passenger door. "He's walking to the hotel. See him down there?"

Daniel looked at where Helen was pointing. "Great work, Helen. Wonderful, I'm going to pause and then follow him. I want to be sure he goes into the hotel."

"I heard him say he's staying there. I bet he goes in."

Daniel was right beside him when Dwight went into the door of the hotel. "Great," Daniel said. "I know where he's staying. I should be able to follow him tomorrow morning. Let's head to your place."

Daniel left Helen's two hours later, very aware he was back in her good graces. Just to be sure of everything, he went back downtown. He parked near the Ohio guy's hotel and snuck into the underground parking. He wanted to be sure the guy had the same car. After a bit, he found it, the white Camry with the new Ohio plates. He'd be easy to follow in the morning.

CHAPTER TWENTY-TWO

*D*wight had a difficult time sleeping. Finally, he got up at four o'clock and decided to head home. He could get out of the city before it was busy and put in three hours of driving before stopping for breakfast. He'd had a good call with Cathy after dinner, and she'd suggested he leave early so they could meet for a late lunch. *If I leave this early, the lunch wouldn't even have to be late*, he thought.

Dwight wasn't aware he'd thwarted Daniel Vilsac's plans. At six-thirty, Daniel had positioned himself so he could follow any car leaving the underground parking. At nine-thirty, thoroughly frustrated, he'd finally gone into the garage and saw that the Camry wasn't there. *Wow, he left before six thirty.*

Dwight had two cups of coffee with breakfast and arrived in Boynton at eleven thirty, feeling fresh. He took the copies of Marcie's diary and met Cathy in the parking lot of the Clayville country club. They'd stopped going there a couple of months ago, thinking they were being too conspicuous, but still it seemed to Dwight that the hostess recognized them. She took them to a table close to where they'd eaten before.

After they ordered their drinks, he gave Cathy the package. "Here's the diary. I've read it once, so you can have a crack at it. I made two copies. I'm sending the other one to Charlotte. Is there somewhere in Boynton where I can send a Fed Ex package?"

"Sure. Use the Mailboxes Unlimited on Second Street. I use them sometimes when I have to send stuff in a hurry. You still think it's interesting, the diary, I mean?"

"Most of it's not relevant to what we're interested in, but some of it is. Reading Marcie's description of Clement Mincy is revealing. He comes across as fairly manipulative. They started going out when she was his assistant in the magic show. The most interesting part is about their breakup. She really unloads about him then."

"I think you told me she got suspicious after she saw the origins video."

They were interrupted by the waitress who brought their lunch orders. Dwight was hungry, so he took a few bites of his grilled cheese before he continued.

"Actually, the major dustup happened after the video. The big breakup started when he wouldn't tell her any details about a meeting in Atlanta. She went to Atlanta with Clement and his father, but girlfriends and wives were only allowed to go to the dinners and the receptions. Marcie couldn't get Clement to tell her what it was about. The diary mentions the names of a couple of businessmen she met there. I haven't had a chance to Google either of them yet. After I Fed Ex the diary to Charlotte, I'll see what I can find."

"Does she reveal other names? Girlfriends or anyone like that?"

"Yes, a few, but only with first names. Larry could only fill in one last name for me. She talks a lot about Jocelyn, whose last name is Mason. Jocelyn was Marcie's roommate before she and Mincy got together, and Marcie moved back in with her briefly after the breakup. I think we should talk to her. The only other one I could identify was Katerina, the other mermaid. We know she's still with Mincy."

"That gives us something to go on. I'll read the diary when I get a chance, and then maybe I can call Jocelyn. She'll probably know the other last names. Actually, Jocelyn might be a big help. Girlfriends sometimes share a great deal. Why don't you call Marcie's brother and ask him to give me an introduction to Jocelyn?"

"I can do that, and you might well learn something from her. What's got me bamboozled is we don't really have an end goal. I mean, we've learned a great deal about Clement Mincy, but I don't see what we're going to do with it."

"I guess you're right. I think we have to keep up our investigation. Something will come to us."

"I sure hope so." After they finished eating, they agreed to meet in the evening in the back room of the Clayville store.

Dwight stopped by the Mailboxes Unlimited, wrote a quick note, and sent the note and the diary to Charlotte in Knoxville. No one was at the house when he got home. It looked like his mother was out for a long lunch with some of her friends. He was tired. He'd rallied for Cathy, but his early morning was starting to show. He took off his clothes, put ninety minutes on the phone's timer, and crawled into bed. When the timer went off, he didn't feel rested, but he forced himself out of bed.

At his computer, he Googled James Bigelow, one of the businessmen Marcie mentioned in her diary. Dwight looked at his notes again and realized there was more than a quick mention. The guy Bigelow had maneuvered Marcie into a corner and propositioned her at one of the receptions in Atlanta. She tried to convince Clement to do something about it, but he refused. According to Clement, Bigelow was too important a guy to mess with. It was clear from her diary how much this response displeased her. Dwight figured it was one of the things that led to her breakup with Clement.

Googling James Bigelow generated a large number of hits. Dwight eliminated many of them because they were the wrong age, or prominent for some obvious reason. He was left with three who appeared to be successful businessmen. Dwight read all he could find about the three he'd picked out and finally selected James Bigelow of Atlanta. His choice was driven by an article this James Bigelow, who owned a large construction firm, had written for a local magazine. He was clearly very right wing. Dwight dug further and found that Bigelow had been a significant donor to many right-wing causes, particularly a militia group dominated by white supremacists. Dwight couldn't uncover any connections to right-wing politics for the other two James Bigelows.

The other name mentioned in Marcie's diary was William Whinston. Marcie didn't have an unpleasant encounter with Mr. Whinston, quite the opposite. Marcie was very impressed with him. She wrote that she'd never met anyone with as much natural charisma as Whinston. The entire gathering hung on his every word. She'd been incredibly impressed.

There were fewer William Whinstons than James Bigelows, so Dwight's task was easier. He found Whinston right away. He was from Charlotte, North Carolina. Posts described him as a spell-binding orator. He was a bank president of a regional bank with a large internet presence. He was in his fifties, younger than James Bigelow, who was sixty-two. Dwight watched a video of one of Whinston's speeches. The guy had a gift. He had the audience in the palm of his hand after the first five minutes. Dwight didn't think much of the content. It was not his brand of politics.

Dwight thought about what he'd found. The two people Marcie mentioned in her diary were clearly rich, right-wing businessmen. He wondered how many such people had been at the Atlanta meeting. Marcie didn't say anything about the size of the gathering.

As he ruminated, he recognized it made sense for Gregory Mincy to be at such a meeting. Like Bigelow and Whinston, he was a rich businessman. *Clement Mincy didn't fit. He was a struggling actor.* In his discussion with Greg Mincy, it was clear Clement wasn't going to inherit the business. Maybe Clement as the VM guy was somehow a spokesman for the group. From what he had just read about Bigelow and Whinston, they both would be very pleased with the thrust of the VM videos and rallies.

Dwight concluded it was quite possible he and Cathy were up against a much bigger conspiracy than they thought. It was clear the Mincys were right-wing extremists who were trying to gather a following, but Dwight had thought it was a small-time operation. Now, he wasn't so sure. The Atlanta meeting suggested it was a much bigger deal. He didn't like the smell of things.

Since progress on VM was stalled, Dwight decided to put it on the back burner by looking at his Dickens project again. He knew his subconscious would still be working away, but he was tired of directly thinking about VM.

Fifteen minutes after he'd made the switch, Cathy called. "Dwight, you said you could call Marcie's brother, so he could give Jocelyn a heads up about my call."

"Do you have time to call now?"

"Yes, I took the rest of the afternoon off at the store, and I've made a first pass through the diary. I'd like to see what Jocelyn can add."

"Great, I'll call Larry. He's a lawyer, so I might not be able to get to him easily, but I'll try. I looked up the two names Marcie mentioned from the Atlanta trip. I'll tell you what I learned tonight."

"Thanks. Goodbye."

Dwight was able to get through to Larry right away and arranged for him to call Jocelyn. Larry had Jocelyn's number, which Dwight realized he needed. After hanging up with Larry, he made a brief call to Cathy, giving her the number and telling her Larry was going to make the call.

Cathy received a call from Larry about fifteen minutes after she hung up with Dwight. Larry told her Jocelyn would be available in the evening. Cathy called Dwight and told him she might be late for their evening get together. They agreed she should call him after she'd completed her call with Jocelyn.

◇◇◇

At seven o'clock, Cathy sat down at her desk at home to call Jocelyn. Jocelyn answered her phone on the second ring. "Hello."

"Jocelyn, this is Cathy Wilson. Larry Green told you I'd be calling."

"Oh, yes. About Marcie."

"It's a little complicated, so let me give you an explanation. My boyfriend and I are trying to see what we can find out about Clement Mincy, Marcie's old boyfriend. Larry contacted us. He found Marcie's diary when he was cleaning up her place. You are mentioned frequently in it. Always in a good light, I should say. Anyway, you knew Clement, and I was wondering if you could tell me what you know about him."

"Do you think Clement had anything to do with Marcie's murder?"

"Maybe, but there's no way to know for sure. All we know is that Marcie had been spying on Clement's place in Michigan the same day she was killed."

"That sounds suspicious."

"It is, but beyond that, there isn't any evidence linking Clement to the murder. What we're interested in is what Clement was like. What can you tell us about him?"

"Sure, I can do that, but I should warn you, I was never a fan of Clem's. Marcie started working with him in his magic show the second year Marcie and I were roommates. I could tell right away Marcie was really into Clem. Frankly, I couldn't see the attraction. He was four or five years older than us, and not very good looking, if you ask me. The final straw for me was his politics. He's extremely right-wing and loud about it. If you ask him, he's always right. I don't think the politics bothered Marcie as much as it bothered me. After a while, the three of us didn't hang out much. It was just Clem and Marcie. Then the two of them got an apartment, and Marcie moved out."

"I understand she moved back with you when she broke up with Clem."

"Just for a month. It turns out Clem moved out of their apartment, but she was stuck with the lease, so she moved back to their old place. Also, I was starting to get close with my boyfriend, so my apartment was getting crowded."

"I'm interested in why Marcie broke up with Clem. Did she get tired of his politics?"

"I think that's most of it, but I think there was another woman involved too."

"Somebody named Katerina?"

"Yes, that's her. Anyway, Marcie showed me a video Clem did. It was wacky. He claimed to be a combination of a Viking and a mermaid. Did you ever hear of anything so looney?"

"I've seen the video. I think Marcie played the part of a mermaid in the video."

"That's right. That part of it was well done, but the rest of it, the space aliens and all the right-wing propaganda, was disturbing. Marcie told me she initially thought it was harmless, but eventually she changed her mind. It had something to do with a meeting she attended with Clem and his father."

"In Atlanta?"

"Yes, that's it. Anyway, after the Atlanta meeting, she got scared about what Clem was doing. She told me she hadn't known how serious he was about the politics. I thought she was a fool. Anyone could see how much his political beliefs mattered to him. I guess chemistry can overpower good sense. Anyway, she broke up with him when he told her he wasn't going to stop with the political stuff. At least that was

Marcie's story. She told me he took the breakup without much fuss. It hurt Marcie that he didn't seem to care. I think Katerina, she was the other mermaid, was moving in on Clem, so Marcie's breaking up with him wasn't a big deal for him."

"Did she reveal anything about the Atlanta meeting?"

"Not really. She just said there were a lot of rich guys there, and they were very pleased with what Clem had done in the video."

"Her diary mentioned two of the names of the businessmen at the meeting, Bigelow and Whinston. Do you remember any other names?"

"No, sorry."

"There's just one more thing. Marcie mentions a couple of other girlfriends in her diary. Do you know a Janet and a Barbara?"

"Janet Wilks and Barbara Conyers. I know both of them. Wait a minute, I can get their numbers for you."

After Cathy got the phone numbers, she thanked Jocelyn and said goodbye.

When Cathy greeted Dwight at the back door of the Clayville store, he noticed she had changed into the brief number she'd worn a couple of times before. They exchanged a passionate kiss. Then she shoved Dwight away when he tried for a second kiss.

"There'll be time for that later, Dwight. We each need to find out what the other person learned."

As they walked to the office, Dwight sat on the couch and volunteered. "I'll go first. I tracked down the two names we know from the Atlanta meeting. James Bigelow is an Atlanta native. As you remember, Marcie mentioned him because he made a pass at her. He runs a big construction company, and he's active in right-wing politics, particularly a militia group known to be full of white supremacists."

"Marcie made him sound like a dirty old man, if I remember correctly."

"That's him. The other guy, William Whinston, is a wealthy banker from Charlotte, North Carolina. One internet source called him a silver-tongued orator, and I'm inclined to believe it. I watched one of his speeches. While I didn't think much of the content, too right wing for me, I have to admit he has charisma. He had the audience in the palm of his hand. You could tell from her diary, Whinston charmed Marcie."

"Yeah, I remember."

"Thinking about the Atlanta meeting scares me. I thought the Mincys were running sort of a mom-and-pop operation in the Midwest. Clem was doing the VM stuff and Greg was financing it. Now I'm not so sure. We may have uncovered something much larger."

Cathy paused and took Dwight's hand. "I'd never thought of it quite like that, but what you're saying is consistent with what I learned from my call with Jocelyn. She told me Marcie broke up with Clement soon after the Atlanta meeting. The impression I got was that after the meeting, she took the whole VM business much more seriously, and in the end, she didn't like it."

"That seems a little strange. She should have known that Clement was a dedicated right winger."

"Jocelyn put that down to chemistry overwhelming good reason."

"I can see that maybe. He's not my type."

Cathy smiled and wiggled a little. "I think I know your type."

"I thought you said later."

"Yes, I did," Cathy said, scooting away from Dwight. "What I can't figure is what we do next. What good does it do us to know the VM stuff might be part of a larger conspiracy?"

"I've been trying to figure out an answer to just that question. So far, my only thought is that we need reinforcements. This whole thing might be bigger than the two of us can handle."

"I agree, we need help. I wish we knew enough to hand this off to the FBI or someone. Unfortunately, aside from maybe killing Marcie, which we can't prove, they haven't broken any laws. It's not illegal to have wacky extreme views."

"Yes, stupidity isn't against the law."

They laughed.

"I think we need to give Charlotte a chance to read the diary," Dwight said. "I sent it off to her right after lunch. She might have some ideas."

Cathy slid over next to Dwight. "Right now, I think you need comforting. I'm going to see if I can provide some."

CHAPTER TWENTY-THREE

Charlotte Mangum received the Fed Ex package at 2:45 in the afternoon the day after Dwight sent it. She had a string of meetings starting at 3:00, so she didn't have a chance to do more than verify the contents and read the first few pages. Dwight's note hadn't pointed her to any particular pages, so she figured she would have to at least skim the whole thing. As she gathered up her materials for the next meeting, she thought, *I'll have to tackle the diary after work.*

That evening, she read the diary. She was proficient at skimming through things of little interest and slowing down and taking notes when she got to the better parts. She dispensed with much of the first part of the diary very quickly this way. Marcie didn't meet Clement Mincy until the second year covered in the diary.

When she finished, she called Cathy Wilson's cell.

After the introductions, Charlotte asked, "What did you think of the diary?"

"Dwight and I both read it, and gosh, it's hard to summarize. I guess it's spooked both of us. We thought the VM thing was just the Mincys, you know, Clement the performer and Gregory the financier. What the diary says about the Atlanta meeting has us thinking it might be lots bigger. We're wondering what we've stumbled into."

"I understand. I was coming at it from a different angle." Charlotte twirled the pen in her hand, thinking about what Cathy had said. "The diary shows I was right—Clement Mincy is the VM guy. It's right there in black and white. I'm going to show it to my editor."

"Oh, yeah. I can see what you're saying. We've provided another source for you. I called Jocelyn, Marcie's roommate. She's seen the video, and she knows it was Clement behind the mask. I don't know if she'd want her name used, but I think you can count her as a source."

"I hadn't thought about the reaction you and Dwight had, but it makes sense. That Atlanta meeting was the thing that made Marcie see the VM stuff was dangerous."

"Yeah, that's what we figured. You sort of have to read between the lines to come to that conclusion, but I think we're right. When Marcie got a hint of the scope of what was going on, she wanted out."

Charlotte's mind raced with the implications of what Cathy was saying. "So, you think the VM thing might be the start of something big, something with nationwide backing?"

"That's what's got us scared. We don't think we can handle it on our own. Dwight looked up the two businessmen Marcie mentioned. They're both rich guys who lean very right wing. Whinston is quite well known around Charlotte, North Carolina, where he's from, and Bigelow is no slouch. He runs a big construction firm out of Atlanta. These guys are heavy hitters in right-wing circles. The Mincys are small time compared to them."

"I can see it. I guess my reaction was more self-centered. I was looking for verification for my story. In my defense, after the stunt the VM folks pulled in their last rally, my story has been battered around a great deal. My editor has been good. He says he believes me, but I don't know how sincere he is. The diary's going to help me with him. I really hadn't thought about the angle that's got you two worried."

"Dwight's idea is that we need reinforcements. We need to bring other people in. The VM nonsense should be stopped, but we're afraid we can't do it alone. As far as we can tell, they haven't broken any laws, so we can't go to the police. We're stymied."

She's right, Charlotte thought. *This could be huge.* After a long pause, Charlotte spoke up. "I might be able to help. One of my college friends is in the FBI. I think they have a task force focused on domestic terrorism. I remember several stories about them infiltrating groups and then swooping in with arrests just before the bad guys pull something off. My friend David might be able to put us in touch with the right people in the FBI. I don't know if the VM guy has caught their attention yet, but at least it's worth a try."

"That sounds wonderful, Charlotte. Dwight will be thrilled. He's been down since he read the diary and realized the magnitude of what we're involved in."

"Tell him I'll try to help. I think I can get you an interview at least. I'll let you know."

"Thanks, and I'm glad the diary will be useful with your editor."

"Me too. Goodbye."

Two days after the call between Cathy and Charlotte, Dwight's doorbell rang. It was odd. No one ever came to their house. His mother answered the door, and after a couple of minutes, called to him, "You've got a visitor, Dwight."

Dwight came downstairs from his office. A man in a suit stood next to his mother. He was about six foot tall, with red hair cut short, and looked very fit. Dwight walked up to him and said, "I'm Dwight Kelton. What can I do for you?"

The man took a side-long glance at Evangeline and said, "My name is Layton Billips. Is there somewhere we can talk privately?"

"Mr. Billips is with the FBI, Dwight," Evangeline said. "He showed me his badge. What have you gotten yourself into?"

Ignoring his mother, Dwight said, "Sure, why don't you come on up to my office?" Looking at his mother, he continued, "It will be private."

Layton shook Evangeline's hand. "Nice to meet you, Mrs. Kelton. And I should say, your son isn't in any trouble."

"That's a relief. With him, I never know what's going on."

When Dwight and the FBI agent got to the office, Dwight moved some books off the spare chair for the agent and swiveled his desk chair around so they were facing each other.

Layton started. "I'm with the Columbus office, and I work part time on the domestic terrorism task force. I understand you have some information about the VM group."

"Is the VM group one of the groups you've been looking at?"

"Actually, no. They just came to our attention recently. A group we monitor, the Midnight Patrol, a militia group out of Atlanta, appears to have started working with them. The Midnight Patrol guys provided security for a rally or something VM put on in Toledo recently. Why don't you just start at the start and tell me what's going on?"

Dwight began by showing Layton the first part of the origins video, ending after the mermaids. "There are a whole slew of other videos. I just showed you this one so you'd get a feel for them. The videos are their main recruiting device. As you can see, the guy is very good at play acting, and the videos are well done."

"Yes, the video looks very professional."

Next, Dwight introduced Cathy and told Layton about what he'd done. Layton mostly listened quietly. He interrupted when Dwight described Marcie's death. When Dwight couldn't give him any details, Layton had him continue. Similarly, he seemed to perk up when Dwight described the meeting in Atlanta, but he didn't ask any questions. When Dwight finished, he told Layton he could provide a copy of Marcie's diary.

Layton, who'd periodically taken down notes, sat back and responded,

"Mr. Kelton, what you've told me is fascinating, but unfortunately, I don't think you've uncovered anything illegal. You say these videos are rife with falsehoods, and I don't doubt you. But it's not against the law to lie. The same goes for the presentations at the rallies, and there is nothing wrong with forming clubs, even clubs that seem to be directed by a group that regularly deals in exaggerations and falsehoods. The only illegal activity you've talked about is the killing of this girl who used to go out with Clement Mincy, and you said yourself, you have no proof."

"I can't disagree, so this was just an FBI fishing expedition that came up empty?"

"I'm not sure I would characterize it that way. I'm here because it looks like VM is connected in some way with James Bigelow and the Midnight Patrol. They've been on our radar for quite some time. To the best of our knowledge, they are a fairly tight-knit group of very violent extremists. This activity, providing security for the VM rallies, is new for them. We didn't know much about VM, so you've been a big help. Also, we now know Bigelow attended a meeting in Atlanta with a bunch of other right-wing folks, and you've provided a couple of names we may not have known about."

Dwight got up from his chair and started to pace. He wondered what he'd gotten himself into.

"Where does this kind of information go from here?"

"It goes into a very secure database. While we do it, we don't want people to know the FBI spends much time spying on US citizens. We're on a knife's edge. If something bad happens and we didn't know about it, we're in trouble. On the other hand, if we're found snooping around some innocent group, we're in trouble for that. It's a tricky business."

Dwight sat back down. "I can see the difficulty."

"If the VM group and the Midnight Patrol are interconnected in some way, we'll want to know a lot more about them. If this security business is the only connection, I doubt we'd be interested. Let me cut to the chase. I'd like you to stay in the VM group here. See what you can find out about the direction the group is going. Is there talk about arming the group? Do they talk about linking up with other groups? Are the messages from the VM leadership suggesting violence against the government or anyone else?"

He paused, thinking over Layton's request. Finally, he decided he'd be okay with it. "If I maintain a low profile, I think I can do what you're asking. I don't think I'd be comfortable trying to climb up in the organization."

"That's fine. I can give you my contact information. I would only expect you to get in touch if something big is happening."

Dwight thought about getting up to end the meeting, but then he came up with a question, "If you don't mind, could you tell me why the Midnight Patrol bothers you so much?"

"Sure. Actually, it might be good to know, because from what we know, the VM connection to the Midnight guys might be how they get radicalized. The Midnight Patrol is a militia, basically a bunch of guys who like to play Army and strut around with their guns. They show up at rallies organized by liberal groups, particularly African American ones, and look menacing. They've been involved with several violent scuffles and have made some serious threats. Most of the guys are ex-military, and they actively try to align themselves with the military. Their propaganda says the enlisted men are being exploited by the officers. The brass doesn't like them at all."

"I can see how sowing dissent in the ranks would not be good for the military. And I can see how what they're saying fits in with themes VM pushes. It's all about experts and authority being untrustworthy. The VM guy preaches that the experts are all tools of the liberal elite who don't care about the welfare of ordinary people. Pushing the same idea in the military would not be helpful."

"Yes, I think what you've got ahold of is a talking point for a lot of these groups. When distrust of authority becomes anti-government, we get concerned. That's the tipping point. When that point is reached, it sets up the possibility of violence against the state. Mostly now it comes from the right, but in the past, it's come from the left. We need to see if VM joins up with other groups like the Midnight Patrol. They are very thoroughly anti-government, but it's not clear VM is there yet. It might be that this Atlanta meeting was the start of something. We have lots of sources, and I'm asking you to be one of them."

"Now that we've talked, I'd like to show you one more VM video. It's about guns and gun control. I found it very disturbing."

"Okay, but just one more."

After Layton had finished viewing The Solution, he said, "I can see why this bothers you, but it's like all the other stuff. People have freedom of speech, so they can say all sorts of weird stuff. A lot of what bothers you is implied, not said outright. I say it's all the more reason for you to keep track of these people, but there is nothing actionable for the FBI in what you just showed me."

CHAPTER TWENTY-FOUR

*D*aniel Vilsac finally received a call from his friend with access to the license plate information for Ohio. The plate Daniel was interested in was registered to a Dwight Kelton in Boynton, Ohio. After ending the call, Daniel fired up his computer to see what he could find out about Mr. Kelton. Dwight Kelton wasn't a common name, and Google only came up with a few possibilities. None of them lived in Ohio. After a few minutes, this made sense to Daniel. The plates were new. It had to mean Kelton had just moved into Ohio. *I'll have to go through all the Kelton entries to see if I can find pictures*, he thought. *Fortunately, I know what he looks like.*

Daniel found the Dwight Kelton he was looking for right away. He'd been a professor at a university in Pennsylvania, and he'd published several books. Daniel found a few pictures of him in commentaries about the books. Daniel wondered what he was doing in Ohio. From what he saw, he was sure the guy had tenure at his university. He was listed as a full professor.

Daniel called Greg Mincy at his office in Indianapolis. Greg told him he should get down to Boynton, Ohio, wherever the heck that was, and get the story on Mr. Kelton. There wasn't anything brewing at the store or with Clem that required Daniel's presence, so Greg told him to get right on it.

<><><>

That evening in the back room of the Clayville store, Cathy and Dwight discussed Dwight's meeting with the FBI agent in considerable detail. Cathy was disappointed. "I don't think your meeting with the FBI moved the ball at all. We're right back where we started. We're trying to stop the VM thing, and the FBI isn't going to be any help."

"Yeah, I could tell Layton thought the VM folks were small potatoes. They weren't a threat. My meeting with him reminded me a little of something I've experienced back at school. Every once in a while, one of the students I'd taught had a government job that required a security clearance. Someone would come around and ask us a bunch of questions. One of them was, 'Did the student ever advocate the violent overthrow of the government.' It seemed ridiculous to me. Layton was the same way. He was only interested in preventing violence."

"That's weird. What if your student was involved in a plot to violently overthrow the government? Who thinks he or she would talk it over with their English professor?"

Dwight scooted over and gave Cathy a quick kiss. "Precisely, honey. Layton was the same way. He wasn't interested in VM unless they'd made threats like that or were engaged in something illegal. I think he only wants me to report back about that kind of thing."

"It's frustrating. What VM is doing is more subtle. I'm shocked I'm using the word subtle in connection with VM, but I am. They're undermining people's trust in the government and in science. They're trying to tear apart common beliefs. The kind of beliefs that support trust, and trust is important for keeping our country together."

"Right. They don't have to advocate the violent overthrow of our government. They're digging away at the foundations so it will be easier for someone who does want to overthrow the government."

Cathy got off the couch and paced around. Finally, she said, "Ever since you called me and told me we'd run into a brick wall with the FBI, I've been thinking. Our ace in the hole on this whole deal is that we know Clement and Gregory Mincy are behind it. There's got to be some way to use that information to our advantage. We just need to figure out how to use it."

"You're right, but we tried, or at least Charlotte tried. Clement Mincy had a clever counter to her attempt to out him. You were there. You saw it. It worked with that audience, and it worked with his followers too. The message board is full of people who thought it was convincing."

"That's it, Dwight—the message board. We need to try to use it to undermine the Mincys. I've always thought your writing ability would be one of our assets. This is it."

"I don't see it. What are you talking about?"

Cathy smiled and sat back on the couch. "We need to mount an attack on the message board. We have information most of the VM people never saw. They don't read newspapers, so they didn't see the evidence that showed the lake used in the mermaid video was behind Mincy's house. And they don't know about Marcie's murder right after she was snooping around his house. We have to create posts that make the readers think Mincy is the VM guy despite the Toledo rally."

"We've got the evidence that suggests Katerina took Clement's place at the Toledo rally. I don't know how, but I bet we could put the video in a post."

"You're right, Dwight. Oh, I like this idea," Cathy said as she put her arms around Dwight.

"I like where you are headed with that hug, Cathy, but there's something else I've just thought of."

"Keep it short."

"I think we could use the fact that the guy is always behind a mask to cast doubt on the whole business. Why is he wearing a mask all the time? Why have none of his followers ever seen him? Why be so mysterious? I think it's a good line of attack."

"You're right," Cathy said as she started kissing him.

Dwight spent most of the next morning outlining a list of possible message board posts. He would have to do something to make his posts stand out, something that would grab the reader's attention. He needed a handle—a name people would recognize. He decided on THE SHADOW, all caps.

He started drafting his first entry. He decided it would be short. THE SHADOW would start by asking why the VM guy always wore a mask and why none of his followers had ever met him or seen him. He wanted to cast doubt. He didn't want to come out and be directly hostile. His plan was to develop credibility by asking questions before he presented any evidence he had about Clement Mincy.

After he sent a draft of his proposed first posting to Cathy for her review, he looked at the time on his computer and recognized he'd better get downstairs. He and his mother had a planned lunch together. He got down before Evangeline and was peering out the front window when he saw a car slow down as it passed the house. It was odd. The car almost came to a stop, so Dwight got a good look at the driver. It was the man he'd seen staring at him at the rallies. As he watched, the guy drove away. The car had Indiana license plates.

Dwight was instantly upset. *What is going on?* Before he could come to any conclusion, he heard his mother coming down the stairs. He turned to greet her.

"What's wrong, Dwight? You look like you've just seen a ghost."

Dwight didn't know what to say. He just blurted out, "Some guy, I don't know who, just drove by and seemed to be paying way too much attention to my car."

"Do you think he's going to try to steal it? I guess it's sort of exposed out there on the street. Maybe he's planning to come tonight. Don't car thieves work at night mostly?"

"I think you're right. It might be sensible to move my car. Where could I put it?"

Evangeline paused and sat down on the couch. "I was wondering what to do with my car. Actually, it's your father's car. He bought it right before he died. It's just been sitting in the garage. I don't think I'm going to be driving again. Maybe we could sell the old car, and you could use the garage."

"You still have the Caddy Dad bought?"

"Yes, I didn't see why I shouldn't keep it. It was a lot nicer than the Ford I was driving. The doctor says I shouldn't drive, and now that I've found out how easy things are without a car, I'm not sure I want a car, even if I'm cleared to drive."

Dwight gestured to his mother. "Come on, let's go to the garage to see if the Cadillac will start. We can talk about whether it's sensible to sell it at lunch."

They found the car was dusty, but otherwise in fine shape. It started on the third try, and sort of bounced out of the garage. "The tires get a little flat on one side when they've sat in the one place," Dwight said. "The ride will smooth out quickly."

"I forgot how nice a car this is," Evangeline replied. "How many miles does it have on it?"

Dwight peered into the dials on the dashboard. "Just over sixteen thousand. That's not many."

"Your father put most of those miles on. I hardly ever drove anywhere except to lunch or shopping. I'm not sure I ever had the car out of town since he died. I bet we could get a fair penny for a low-mileage car like this."

At lunch, Evangeline tried her hardest to get Dwight to reveal the name of the woman he was seeing. She knew there was someone. Still, Dwight maintained his privacy. Even though Cathy and Bill had officially separated, he didn't want to say anything yet. Evangeline would tell her friends, and then it would be all over town.

"Listen Mom, you're right. I am seeing someone, but she and I are not telling anyone."

"She's married, isn't she? Oh, Dwight, you know you shouldn't."

"You won't get another word out of me." Dwight hoped he hadn't given anything away. He'd tried to keep a straight face.

After Evangeline realized he wasn't going to say anything more, she concluded, "Just be careful, whatever you do. I'm afraid we all know your weakness. You lost your wife and your job over some young graduate student. Don't make the same mistake again."

Dwight felt like correcting her but decided changing the subject was the better approach. "Are you sure you want to sell your car?"

"So, you want to talk about something else, do you? Okay, I'll let you off the hook. Yes, I thought about it on the drive over. I don't need to keep paying for insurance. With the amount I pay for insurance and the amount I get for selling the car, I can afford lots of cabs and Ubers. There's no use for me to own a car."

"Does the Haggerty lot still exist?"

Evangeline looked at him quizzically. "I don't know what you're talking about."

"When I was growing up, a guy named Haggerty had a used car lot. It's where I bought my first car. It wasn't like many lots. Haggerty did it like a consignment shop. He sold the car for someone and then took ten percent. Craigslist could have put him out of business, but maybe not."

"I don't even understand what you're talking about. You'll have to check the yellow pages or look it up or something. Whatever, I'll leave the sale of the car in your hands."

On their way back from lunch, Dwight drove by where the Haggerty lot used to be, and it appeared to still be in business. Once they got home, he looked up the Kelley Blue Book value for the Cadillac. He was surprised it was so low. He thought his mom's car would be worth more. Then again, it had exceptionally low mileage and had always been garaged. It should be better than most of the ones the Kelley book had priced.

When he drove onto the lot, he was surprised to see who came out of the sales office to greet him. It was Stacy, Bill's girlfriend.

"Hi Dwight, what brings you here? Where'd you get this sweet ride?" she said when she reached him.

He hadn't noticed it before, but Stacy was one of those people who Dwight thought violated people's personal space. She came right up to him, way too close. She sort of grabbed his arm when she was talking. It was all he could do not to back away. "I want to sell this car. Does the lot still work the same way as it did when it was run by Mr. Haggerty?"

"Yep, he's my uncle, my mom's younger brother. He still owns the lot," she said as she moved away and started to inspect the car. "We don't buy used cars. We sell them for people. Our cut is fifteen percent of the price. If you go with us, we'll agree on a starting point, and a strategy for reducing the price if the car doesn't sell after a few weeks."

By the time she'd finished talking, she'd returned to where Dwight was standing, reached out her hand, put it on his arm, and smiled up at him. "Do you think we can do business?"

Dwight stepped away this time. "Yes. I think so. I guess I'd better take a look at the paperwork."

Stacy reached out, put her arm through his, and sort of pulled him toward the office. Dwight was not happy with all the touching, but then he thought it might be just the way she was. He'd only seen her with Bill, and she'd been plastered to his side all the time. Still, it wasn't right in this kind of a professional setting. *Surely, she isn't coming on to me*, he thought. *She knows I'm Bill's friend.*

In the small office, she had him go in and sit down before she brushed by him as she went over to a file cabinet on the far side of the small room. She then bent over at the waist, waving her behind at him. She took her time in this position, more time than Dwight thought was necessary. When she turned around with the papers she'd extracted from the file cabinet, she gave Dwight a big smile. She brushed against him again on her way to the desk, even though Dwight knew there was plenty of room for her to get by.

As she sat down, Dwight noticed that somehow the top button on her blouse had come unbuttoned. He didn't think it had come undone of its own accord. *Eyes up*, he told himself.

Throughout the proceedings, Stacy took every opportunity to bend over, exposing some cleavage. At one point, when Dwight wasn't sure of the meaning of one of the clauses, she came around from behind the desk and leaned over his shoulder to see what he was talking about. Again, she leaned in too close.

Finally, Dwight had had too much. He blurted, "Look, Stacy, I don't need whatever you are trying to do. Back away. This is a business transaction and nothing else."

She laughed and returned to the desk. "I guess I shouldn't let you steal two of Bill's girls."

Dwight was shocked. If Stacy knew, it's for sure Bill knew. "What's that supposed to mean?"

"It's nothing. Bill said Courtney's impressed with the way you are around your mother. Bill thinks she has a crush on you."

"She's young enough to be my daughter," Dwight said, incredibly relieved. "I've never heard of such silliness. Let's finish our business."

Dwight took an Uber home from the car lot and put his car in the garage. There was some paperwork he had to get to Stacy, but after that it was a done deal.

Daniel Vilsac was not having much luck in Boynton finding anyone who knew Dwight Kelton very well. From what he could find out, Kelton had moved in with his mother a few months ago. Mrs. Kelton had suffered a stroke, and her son had come to help her recover. This much he got from a talkative woman he'd sat beside at a deli counter in the middle of town. Before his lunch, he'd driven past Kelton's house, a big one in a nice neighborhood and verified the car was there.

From what he'd seen, there wasn't much going on in Boynton. He was getting bored. He'd poked around and talked to as many people as he could without arousing suspicion, and he'd only found out things he already knew. Kelton had been a professor at a university in Pennsylvania, and he hadn't been in town long. No one knew who his friends were. The only lead he got was one guy's comment that he'd seen Kelton a couple of times at the Red Dolphin, a bar on the outskirts of town.

Before he ate an early dinner in preparation for going to the bar, Daniel drove by the house again. The car wasn't parked in front like it had been before. He wasn't alarmed. The guy had to go out occasionally.

At the Red Dolphin, which Daniel found a little seedy, he didn't have any luck at first. The bartender had never heard of Dwight Kelton, and none of the other people at the bar had either. His story was that he was looking for Dwight because they'd been friends in college, but they'd lost track of each other.

Just when he thought he'd run out of luck, two men came in and sat down beside him at the bar. One of them, a big solidly built man about Kelton's age, said he knew Dwight. "Yeah, we went to high school together. He was a little pipsqueak then, maybe the shortest guy in our class. I used to push him around all the time, a real nerd."

Daniel was surprised by the description. The Kelton he was tracing wasn't short at all. "But he's not short now," Daniel said.

"No, you're right. When he showed up in town recently, he'd grown a lot. I think he's here because he lost his job at some university. He got caught shagging one of the coeds."

"What?"

"The school had a rule against sex between faculty and students, so Dwight got fired."

"That seems a little extreme."

"Tell me about it." He turned away from Daniel and started talking to his friend. Daniel overheard some of the conversation. The big guy, Tank, was talking about his chances of moving in on some woman who'd just separated from her husband. Tank wondered if it was a good idea because he was friends with the husband. The woman was really hot, so Tank decided he'd take his chances.

When the bar started thinning out, Daniel left. He hadn't learned much about Kelton. Only one guy in the bar knew him. The story about Kelton losing his job was interesting but not very revealing about why Kelton was showing so much interest in the Mincys. Daniel drove by Kelton's house again, but the car still wasn't out front. Daniel went down the street, did a U-turn, and parked across the street from Kelton's house. He wanted to see when Kelton got home. Four hours later, he gave up and drove to his motel. Kelton never came home.

After breakfast the next morning, Daniel drove by the house again and the car still wasn't there. He decided Kelton must have gone somewhere. He made the same maneuver he'd made the night before, but this time he parked a little farther from Kelton's house. He watched for three hours before something happened. A taxi pulled up and an older woman come out of the house. Then nothing. Finally, he decided Kelton might be out of town. There was no telling when he'd be back. Daniel scrawled a note, put it in an envelope, walked over to Kelton's house, taped the envelope to the front door, and walked back to his car. *It's time to blow this town.*

Dwight had seen the Indiana car drive by in the morning. He also seen it parked across the street all morning. He'd done checks every fifteen minutes, and he'd watched the man get out of the car with what looked like a piece of paper. As he stood looking out of the upstairs window, Dwight finally remembered where he'd first seen him. The outer office at Gregory Mincy's store. Dwight remembered this person paying a lot of attention to him as he walked out of Mincy's office.

What's he doing on my porch? Dwight couldn't figure what was going on. *Did he leave a note?* Thinking back, he remembered, as he was leaving Mincy's office, the secretary told this man to go right in, using his first name. There was something familiar about the exchange. Maybe he was a Mincy employee. Dwight decided to see what he could find on the internet.

Dwight found Daniel Vilsac immediately on the Mincy store website. The head of security for the Mincy stores, he appeared in a group picture of the administrative staff, in the back row. Dwight was sure he was the person in the car out front. It also made sense that he was at the VM rallies. What Dwight couldn't understand was why Vilsac was so interested in him. It could have been his meeting with Gregory. If Vilsac was in Boynton checking him out, he must have found out the story about his being a graduate student at Purdue was phony. Still, Dwight couldn't see how that was enough to send the head of security out to look for him.

Finally, Dwight's curiosity got the better of him, and after checking out every window and seeing nothing, he opened the front door and grabbed the envelope. Inside, he found a short, handwritten note. "Stop snooping around the Mincy's. We know where you live."

CHAPTER TWENTY-FIVE

*D*wight slipped out of the back door without turning on the light and walked down the alley at eight-fifteen. Cathy was in her car at the end of the alley where he'd ask her to meet him. "I feel a little silly sneaking around like this," he said when he slid into the front seat. "I think the Mincy security guy is gone, but I can't be sure."

"Since your car is in the garage, I bet he thinks you've taken off. You're probably okay. Still, better safe than sorry. I think your idea of using the back door and coming and going in the dark is good."

He turned his body to face her while she pulled out of the parking spot. "I sure hope so. What I can't figure out is how he found me. If I'm right, he was eyeing me at both of the VM rallies I've been to. It had to be based on my meeting with Gregory Mincy. Vilsac was there. I passed him in the outer office. Maybe he tried to verify my story about being a Purdue graduate student. He might have been able to find out I wasn't who I said I was. But how'd he discover my identity?"

Cathy glanced in the rearview mirror. "Didn't you say he really slowed down when he went by your house and car the first time you saw him here? Maybe he was checking out the license plate. You drove your car to both rallies. You'd have never known if he followed you after a rally. There's a mass of humanity heading for their cars. It would be easy to follow someone."

"Makes sense. I can't think of anything else. Actually, it doesn't matter how he found me. What's important is we've got to learn to live with it. I can't be front and center in anything we do. No, that's not right. It's Dwight Kelton who can't be front and center. There's no way anyone can connect Dwight Kelton to THE SHADOW."

"Absolutely." Cathy reached over and squeezed Dwight's thigh.

They drove in silence for the rest of the way to the Clayville store. When they got to the back room, they hugged and then sat down on the couch. Cathy spoke up. "You wouldn't believe who my first gentleman caller turned out to be."

"Huh?"

"People know about my separation from Bill, and I expected some guys to try to make a play for me. Who do you think was first?"

"Oh, I see. You are an incredibly attractive, recently unattached female, and the word is all over town. I never thought about it, but I guess lots of guys will show an interest. I have no idea who came first."

"Roscoe Anderson—you know, Tank. I couldn't believe it. He's been one of Bill's best friends since third grade or something. Frankly, I couldn't think of anyone I'd be less interested in. He gives me the creeps, always has."

Dwight draped his arm around Cathy and said, "I hope it wasn't difficult to brush him off. As gorgeous as you are, you must have quite a bit of experience getting rid of guys."

Cathy gave Dwight a squeeze and disengaged. "Thanks for calling me gorgeous. A girl likes to hear that once in a while. I've had some experience, but not as much as you'd think. Bill and I were a couple all through high school, and all the guys knew it. It was the same in college, and after that I was married. The ring didn't stop some bozos, but there weren't many. This afternoon I didn't have a ring to wave in Tank's face."

"And you couldn't tell him about me, either."

Cathy got up and wandered over to her desk and picked up a piece of paper.

"No, but I got rid of him anyway. I told him I wasn't ready to get back into dating."

"It worked, I hope."

"Yes, he was nice about it. Enough about my little encounter with Mr. Anderson." Then, waving the paper, she continued, "I haven't had a chance to tell you how much I liked the proposed first post from THE SHADOW. All caps. I like that, and the content was good. You can't start off with all guns blazing."

"Thanks, but we have a problem. We now know I'm on the Mincy's radar. We can't have the posts coming from my email. It's easy to find it on the university's website. I understand why the emails are all listed. They want people to be able to get in touch with the staff. In this case, it could be a disaster."

"You're right. I hadn't thought about that problem. Is there anything we can do about it? I guess I could post things."

Dwight got up and joined Cathy by her desk. "Thanks for offering, but I don't want to put you in jeopardy either. There has to be a way of posting to the message board anonymously. I think we should ask Courtney's friend. You know, the one who helped us find the lake."

"Yolanda?"

"That's her. She's a computer genius. I bet she knows how we can utilize an untraceable email. Now that we know the Mincy's head of security is suspicious, we have to be extra careful."

Cathy took Dwight in her arms. "You're really shook up about this, aren't you? Sure, I can ask Courtney to talk to her. I won't mention your name. I'll bet Yolanda can come up with something."

Dwight kissed Cathy. "Thanks, darling."

Five days later, Enrique knocked on Clement and Katerina's

bedroom door at seven thirty in the morning. "Is it okay if I come in? I have something to show you, Clem."

"Sure, come on in."

Enrique went in. Clem and Katerina were sitting up in bed. Katerina had the sheet pulled up to cover her top. Enrique could see the outline of her big breasts, but he quickly diverted his eyes to focus on Clem. "Boss, I thought you'd like to know. There was another post by that guy who calls himself the Shadow. I showed you the first one three or four days ago. The one that wondered why you're always behind a mask."

"Yeah, it was a little different from most of the posts, but it was no big deal. What's in this one?"

"Here, see for yourself." Enrique handed him the iPad.

Clement took the iPad and read, "You want to know what happened to the mermaids in the Origins video? I know what happened to one of them. She left the VM group and later was murdered in Michigan. THE SHADOW."

Clem passed the iPad to Katerina. Her sheet slipped a bit when she grabbed the iPad. Enrique noticed but had his eyes back under control when Clem turned to face him.

"Thanks, Enrique. Katerina and I will think about what we should do about this Shadow person. We'll see you at breakfast."

By the time the team assembled around the table, everyone was up to date about the Shadow post. Jake was the first to speak. "I think you should contact Vilsac. He's security. I know he's old and might not be very tech savvy. Still, I bet he could find someone who could trace the post. If we knew who'd sent it, we could decide what to do about it."

"I think Jake's right," Katerina added. "I certainly don't know how to figure out where a post is coming from. Do any of you know?"

Everyone shook their heads.

Clement concluded, "Okay. We're all agreed. I was going to be sure Daniel and my dad saw the post. I'll just add something to my email to Daniel. I guess I'll have to give him the information about how we set up the message board. You've got that, don't you Enrique?"

"No problem. I can put that together in ten minutes."

Daniel Vilsac saw Clement's email right before he headed out the door for a date with Helen Simons. Things were going swimmingly with Helen since he'd been able to be in Indianapolis on a regular basis. As he drove to pick up Helen, he wasn't bothered by the email. He knew just the person he'd put on the job. He pulled over a block from Helen's and called Oscar Lenten. Oscar was a computer geek who'd done some work for Daniel in the past. He was able to set up a meeting for nine the next morning. Daniel drove the rest of the way to Helen's with a smile on his face.

The next morning, Daniel showed up at Oscar's house. If Daniel knew anyone who fit a stereotype, it was Oscar. His living room was one great big computer center with a slightly unpleasant smell. There were two workstations, each equipped with a keyboard and three monitors, a couple of big computers, servers Daniel thought, two big printers, a huge screen on the wall, and on the floor, piles of computer printouts intermingled with pizza boxes and soft drink cans. Daniel picked his way through the mess so he could sit in front of one of the keyboards. Oscar had returned to the other one after letting Daniel in the door.

"I've been hired by a guy who runs a message board. Someone is posting stuff he doesn't like. We want to find out who's behind the posts. I don't have the faintest idea how to do what he wants, but I bet it would be easy for you. You know I'll pay top dollar for this help, and I know you'll never tell a soul about the work you're doing for me."

Oscar nodded and smiled. "It shouldn't be difficult. Forward me what you've got."

Daniel pulled out his phone and forwarded the email to Oscar.

A moment later a ding sounded, and Oscar scanned the email. "Do you want to wait? I ought to be able to track this down quick."

"Sure. Is it that easy?"

"Should be," Oscar said as he turned to his keyboard and started typing.

Daniel sat and watched Oscar's hands fly over the keyboard. Line of code started to scroll down Oscar's three screens. Oscar stopped the code and read a couple of lines and then typed something else, which started the code scrolling again. At this point, Daniel looked away. There was no way he could understand what was going on.

Twenty minutes later, Daniel got restless. "Why don't you call me when you have this figured out."

Oscar looked up. "Oh, you're still here. I forgot. Yeah, I'll get back to you. It's not as simple as I thought."

Daniel let himself out.

Two days later, Daniel received an email from Oscar telling him he'd failed. There was no way he could trace the posts. He was sorry, but whoever was doing the posting clearly didn't want anyone to know who they were.

After reading the email, Daniel called Oscar. "What do I owe you?"

"No charge. I found nothing, so I can't charge you. Whoever this is knows computers at least as good as I do. Good luck."

Daniel reported back to the Mincys. He couldn't find the Shadow. He knew they wouldn't be happy, but he was sure if Oscar couldn't trace the guy, no one could.

Clement and Katerina read Daniel's email together in the study, staring at Clement's screen. "Wow, Daniel's computer geek can't find this Shadow guy," Katerina said.

"I can read," Clement snapped, a little annoyed.

"Don't be so touchy. I know you can read. I don't think it's that big a deal. There are only a few people responding to the Shadow's posts, and half of them are very negative. You're not losing support because of this."

"I guess you're right. Whatever, I don't like having this guy out there and not knowing who he is. We've got the Peoria rally in less than a week. I don't need more screw ups. First, there was that stupid newspaper article and now this Shadow person. I don't like it."

The next day Enrique checked the message board in the early afternoon. After reading most of the posts, he found one from the Shadow. He went running to find Clement, who was sunning himself in a lounge chair in the back. "It's the Shadow again. There's another post."

"Let me see," Clement said, grabbing Enrique's iPad.

The post he read was about the finale of the rallies. It explained the finale was supposed to show the VM man in four places at once, but the Toledo finale showed it wasn't true. The right-hand guy was too short. The post ended with a link to a video. The video displayed the Cincinnati and Toledo finales stacked one on top of the other. Clement winced when he saw what the Shadow was talking about. Clearly using Katerina in Toledo hadn't worked.

Clement was furious. He jumped out of his chair and glared at Enrique. "This is a monster screw up! We have to find out who this Shadow is and shut him up."

Katerina came out of the house with two drinks in her hand, looking good in her bikini. Enrique couldn't help staring.

"Look at this," Clement said, handing the iPad to Katerina.

"Holy shit, I didn't think I was that much shorter than the rest of the guys."

"Well, you are. It's pretty obvious from this video. It looked okay from where I was sitting in Toledo, but maybe I wasn't focused on you. The Shadow has primed everyone to look at you, so it's obvious you're shorter, and you have shorter arms."

Clement wandered out into the yard, shaking his head. Enrique and Katerina shared a look. They didn't know what to do. Clement would eventually calm down, but it was going to be a rough afternoon. Three hours later, Clement wasn't in a better mood. He spent the afternoon looking at the message board. The Shadow's posting had generated a considerable response, and most all of it was bad as far as he could tell. It was clear that even several true believers were shaken. He wracked his brain and couldn't figure what to do. The finale had been a staple of his shows. He'd have to come up with something else. He just didn't know what.

Dwight had a difficult time doing anything other than checking the message board after he posted. It was clear that the Shadow had finally hit the bullseye. He emailed Cathy several times reporting on his success. She told him she was up for a celebration.

He finally went back to work on Dickens, whom he'd been neglecting recently. About an hour before he had to get ready for his evening out, he received a phone call from a number he didn't recognize.

The caller turned out to be Larry Green, Marcie's brother from Indianapolis. Dwight was shocked when, after the introductions, Larry asked, "Are you the Shadow?"

Dwight paused awkwardly. Recognizing his pause had been a dead giveaway, he finally spoke up. "Yes, as a matter a fact, I am. I think my last posting was effective. I'm not sure the others were."

"I agree, and it's given me an idea."

"What is it?"

Twenty minutes later, Dwight put down his phone. Larry had a wonderful idea. Now he had even more to celebrate with Cathy.

Dwight arrived in the parking lot at one of his and Cathy's favorite Italian restaurants in a nearby town and waited. The parking lot, not full, was bathed in the warm glow of the lighting that had been set up for safety. Cathy arrived ten minutes later. Leaning against his vehicle, he watched her pull in and get out of her car, looking fabulous in a low-cut blue dress. He rushed over to her, sweeping her into his arms.

"Wait a minute Hon, we have plenty of time," Cathy said with a smile.

Dwight put her down. "Okay, but I have more good news."

She took his hand and headed for the restaurant. "Tell me about it."

After they were seated, Dwight filled Cathy in on Larry's plan. Although nobody sat near them, he kept his voice low just in case the other diners overheard him. He didn't think anyone was paying attention, but it paid to be cautious. When he finished, Cathy smiled, thrilled. Right away, she said, "Can I be part of it? I'll use my disguise. Please, I want to go."

Dwight paused. "I can't go. You know I'm persona non grata with the Mincys. I bet Vilsac will be there. But I guess he doesn't know about you. Even if he does, that disguise works. I'm not sure I'd recognize you."

"Yes, and even if Bill's there, he won't recognize me either."

"Okay, I'll call Larry and tell him I've recruited someone else for his team. Then you can call him."

After dinner, Dwight and Cathy went to the backroom of the Clayville store and celebrated up a storm.

CHAPTER TWENTY-SIX

Cathy drove to Peoria for the VM rally. She felt odd leaving Dwight, but he was afraid to be in the same place as Daniel Vilsac. He was probably right to avoid Vilsac. Cathy met Larry and the others at the hotel they'd agreed on. Larry had recruited several of Marcie's friends. Cathy was happy to meet Jocelyn in person, and they hugged. There were seven of them in total.

Larry explained to Cathy what he had planned and gave her the equipment, a little microphone she could clip on her clothing and a small speaker to hide in a pocket. She went outside for a test. At first the speaker was too loud, but they were able to adjust the sound. They wanted it loud, but they didn't want it to sound like a loudspeaker.

Cathy knew Bill wasn't coming to this rally, but some of his group were. This meant she had to wear her disguise. She showed up in the lobby in her get-up and walked up to Jocelyn. "Ready to go?"

"What?" Jocelyn blurted. She looked closer. "Is that you, Cathy?"

"Yes. There may be some people from my hometown at the rally, and I don't want to be recognized."

"I don't think you've got a problem there."

They took two cars to the rally. They were among the first to get there, so they were able to grab chairs where they wanted. They had to spread out so that their little amplifiers wouldn't produce any feedback.

Cathy noticed Daniel Vilsac scanning the crowd as Dwight had predicted. The militia guys were there too. Everything looked much like it had at the other rallies. The start was also the same, the boom, the smoke, and then the VM masked man appeared. His talk was almost a carbon copy of the ones Cathy had witnessed before. *It looks like he's just going to ignore the Shadow*, she thought. *I guess I should have expected as much.*

When the VM leader had ended his talk at the other venues, he'd paused before cueing the "keep the faith" chant. His silence set up the spectacular finale with the chant, the booms, the smoke, and him popping up all over the stage. Cathy watched for Larry's hand to raise and then shouted along with the others, "Show your face!"

The same shout echoed from several places in the crowd, and then it grew into a chant. At first, the only participants were Larry's group, but then other people joined in. Soon it was a loud regular chant growing in volume. "Show your face. Show your face!"

Since he was behind a mask, there was no way to know his reaction, but it was clear the normal rhythm of the rally had been interrupted. Led by Larry and his friends, people started standing as they chanted. The VM guy seemed stunned, and he took a step back. Just then the smoke and the boom happened. When the smoke cleared, the audience saw the VM guy sprawled on the stage. *He took that step back, so he wasn't positioned correctly when his trapdoor opened,* Cathy thought.

Larry and the group kept up the chant, and the VM guy scrambled to his feet looking down to see where he should go. Then came the boom and the smoke, and another VM guy appeared off to one side. The second VM guy raised his arms a couple of times as if he was leading the chant. Then he stopped. The original guy just stood there with slumped shoulders. Cathy remembered; *the first guy shouldn't be there. Their timing is all off, and the second guy shouldn't be leading the chant. They've completely messed up.*

Nothing happened on stage. The two guys stood there, staring at each other. The chant Larry had started was the only thing going on. The VM guys didn't look like they knew what to do. Eventually, the second guy disappeared down his trap door, leaving the original guy standing there facing the chanting crowd. Finally, clearly frustrated, he yelled in a booming baritone, "Shut the fuck up." This riled the crowd more, and the chant grew louder. Finally, one of the trap doors opened, and the guy jumped down, disappearing from the stage.

The chant continued for a minute or two but then died down. People stood in silence, wondering what was going to happen next. When it was clear the show was over, they started walking to the exit.

Daniel Vilsac had monitored the crowd as it filed in. He didn't see the Kelton guy, but he did see someone he recognized, a tall man who'd been in the Indianapolis restaurant with Kelton. He didn't know who he was. He'd have to find out.

Daniel didn't have any real interest in watching Clem's rallies, but he had to. He did like the finale with all its razzle dazzle. When everything got interrupted by the sudden chant, Daniel stood up, trying to see who'd started it. He couldn't tell. It seemed to come from several places, but then it took over the entire crowd. He did notice the tall guy he was interested in was one of the first people to stand as the chant intensified, but that might not mean anything.

When Clem went down because he wasn't positioned correctly over the trapdoor, Daniel wondered about rushing on stage to help, but decided against it. It was up to Katerina to figure out what to do. She controlled things from backstage. After Clem lost it and yelled at the crowd, Daniel knew they had a monumental screwup on their hands. When nothing happened after Clem left the stage, Daniel decided he wasn't going to be any help backstage. He'd let them stew in their own juices. Instead, he followed the man he'd recognized. Daniel wasn't surprised when he got in a car with Indiana plates. He wrote the plate number in his notepad.

When he returned from his successful trip to the parking lot, he stopped in front of the stage and figured he'd better call Greg. He looked around. Almost everyone had cleared out. When he got Gregory on the line, he asked, "Have you heard anything from Clem about the Peoria rally?"

"No. It went well, I presume."

"On the contrary, it didn't go well at all. It was a total screwup."

"What happened?"

"You know how Clem pauses just before the finale? I think he's trying to build tension before he starts the chant. Well, at that point, a bunch of people in the audience started a chant. They kept repeating 'show your face.'"

"Show your face."

"Yes, that's it. Anyway, the rest of the crowd picked it up, and we had a shitshow on our hands. Katerina held off starting the finale, so all that was going on was the chant. The crowd was standing at this point, and Clem sort of took a step back. At that point, Katerina started things, but Clem had stepped partway off his trapdoor, so he fell down on stage instead of disappearing. He was lying there when the smoke cleared, and Jake was standing on the side. Everything but the chant stopped then. Clem lost it after a minute or two and yelled at the crowd, 'shut the fuck up.' Things finally stopped when, somehow, they got Jake and Clem off the stage. It was a total disaster."

"Oh God. I bet Clem is furious. He hates it when things don't work."

"I'm standing in front of the stage right now. I haven't tried to go into the set to talk to him. He's got a horrible temper, as you know. I'm going to let him calm down. I'd hate to be part of that crew right now."

"Do you think we should shut down the whole VM thing?"

"I don't know, Greg. The attendance was still strong tonight, but it was amazing how fast the crowd turned on Clem. I'll call again if I'm able to talk to him early enough."

As Daniel headed for the back of the stage, he saw Jake coming out of the door. *It's not right. They're not supposed to come out for another half hour.*

Jake approached him. "Good, Daniel, tell them I quit. Clem has gone berserk. I'm not putting up with the names he's calling me. They couldn't pay me enough to put up with what's going on in there. Clem is blaming everyone but himself. We all know you're supposed to stand right over your trapdoor. He's the one who screwed up."

"He didn't start the chant."

"No, but the chant started because he's afraid to let people know who he is. Something like this was bound to happen. It's his fault all the way, but he's in there ranting and raving at everybody. He almost hit Enrique. I don't know how he can stand the abuse. I certainly can't."

Daniel knew he couldn't stop Jake, so he didn't try. "At least take off the costume. A few people are still here."

Jake flung the robe he'd been wearing at Daniel. "Good riddance."

Daniel decided it was best not to knock on the backstage door, so he went to see who was still hanging around. Billy Rae Husted, the leader of the militia group, stood with his arms folded over his chest.

"Your guy screwed up big time. I think he's toast."

"I don't know. He might be able to recover. The audience seemed to be with him right until the end. I couldn't tell who started that chant. Could you?"

"No. The funny part is it started from several parts of the crowd at the same time. It's like it was rehearsed. Anyway, it just showed how thin your guy's support is. If the crowd could turn on him like that, his support couldn't have been that strong."

"You might be right. He's getting attacked on the internet too."

"Whatever. Contact us if there's going to be another rally. I'm not promising to come, though. That will be up to Mr. Bigelow. After this performance, I'm not sure."

"Will do."

Daniel stayed around as Billy Rae walked away. It was another hour and a half before Katerina came out. It was clear she'd been crying. Her makeup was a mess. She walked over to Daniel. "I think it's over, Daniel. He's said some things a person can't take back. Jake's already left, and I think the other two are only hanging around to help me."

"It can't be that bad."

"Oh, yes it is. Enrique and Wilhelm looked up to him, but the way he yelled at them destroyed any respect they may have had. He was a madman, still is. He even tore into me, but he backed off. He knows he needs me. I wouldn't go near him if I were you."

"It's probably good advice, but I'm supposed to be his ride home."

"Good luck with that," Katerina said, as she walked over to confer with the last fairgrounds people who were still hanging around.

While he waited for Clement to appear, Daniel paced back and forth in front of the stage. The fairground had turned off its lights. The only lights left were the ones connected to the stage and powered by the semi. Daniel wondered if Clement was going to want to stop or if he'd be stuck driving all the way back to the place by the lake. A half an hour after he started pacing, Clement came around the stage looking for him. "Let's go, Dan. I think those bozos can take it from here."

As Clement approached him in the dim light, Daniel looked at him. Clem looked haggard, and he walked with a slight limp. Maybe the fall had taken something out of him, or maybe it was the three hours of ranting at his crew. Whatever, his face had deep lines and his eyes were bloodshot. He appeared to be absolutely exhausted. Ten minutes after their drive started, Clement was sound asleep in the passenger seat.

CHAPTER TWENTY-SEVEN

When she arrived at the hotel, Cathy went to her room to take off her disguise. This made her at least one drink behind the others when she got to the hotel's bar. A celebration was clearly underway. Cathy was glad she'd texted Dwight on the ride back to the hotel. She wasn't sure she'd be able to compose a coherent text after trying to keep up with the young people.

The group had managed to commandeer a large round table in the half-empty bar. After things calmed down, Cathy asked Larry what he thought would happen next.

"I don't know; it's a good question. One thing I can tell you for sure. That was Clem Mincy behind the mask. I could tell it was his voice."

"You're right Larry," Jocelyn added. "The guy sounded just like Clem. I don't see how anyone who knows him would miss it."

"We've been sure of that for a long time," Cathy said. "The question now is, how will the Clement you know react to the humiliation we created tonight? Does he have a temper? Will he try to retaliate in some way?"

"Oh, he's got a temper for sure," Jocelyn replied. "Marcie told me she had to tiptoe around him when he got mad. I think it's part of the reason she left him. Well, that and the crazy stuff we heard tonight.

The more I think about it, the stranger tonight seems. The people sitting beside me were lapping up the junk Clem was pedaling. They jumped up and cheered a bunch of times. But when our chant started, they joined right in. Didn't they know we were trying to shame him?"

"The same thing happened where I was," one of the others said.

"There's two things going on here," Larry said. "First, I've heard about Mincy's temper. Like Jocelyn said, it was one of the things that drove Marcie away. So that's your answer, Cathy. He's got a big-time temper. I think he'll try to retaliate somehow. Now to the other thing you brought up, Jocelyn. I experienced the same thing where I was. His fans turned into his tormentors. I think it has to do with mass psychology. There were lots of us and we were spread out. And once we got going, people just went along. I don't believe there was much thinking involved."

"You're right, Larry," Cathy commented. "It's about being part of a crowd. Crowd psychology replaces clear-headed thinking sometimes. In a way, what we did was turn Mincy's trick on him. The finale of his other rallies all involved people chanting. I've been to a couple of them, and as much as I disagree with what Mincy stands for, it's difficult not to be swept up with the rest of the crowd."

One of the others sitting at the table, Roger, Cathy thought, joined in at this point. "If I were Mincy, I'd be mad at my crew. Granted, they didn't start our chant, but they messed up things by tripping him and putting that other guy on the stage. If he's got a big temper like you say, I bet he's all over them."

"Makes sense," Larry said. "Does anyone have an idea of who's on the crew?"

"There's a girl named Katerina," Cathy volunteered.

"Yeah," Jocelyn said. "I met her once and some other guy named Jack or Jake or something like that. I don't have a clear memory."

"That's probably Jake McDowd," said one of the girls, Sharon,

Cathy thought. "I know him a little, and he's a right winger like Mincy. I think they were in plays together back in Indianapolis. I haven't seen him around for the last few months. Not that I was looking."

"Sharon, don't I remember you were hot for some guy named Jake at one point?"

"That was before we talked politics at all. The more we talked, the more it became clear he wasn't my type. I'm just saying. I think he and Mincy were friends from the theater, and they're simpatico politically."

It was late when Cathy left the group. She wasn't up to one more round, as someone had suggested. Early the next morning, she decided to get up and start her long drive—half of Illinois, all of Indiana, and part of Ohio. It was dusk when she met Dwight behind the Clayville store.

"Welcome home, darling," Dwight said as he took Cathy in his arms. "I bet you're tired."

"Yes tired, but still triumphant. It was a real kick. Mincy made a complete fool of himself."

"The whole deal, which even some of his supporters called a fiasco, made a big splash on the message board. It even made some newspapers. One of the Chicago papers ran a picture of the guy on his knees getting up from his fall. THE SHADOW just added a short post. 'Ruined show makes us wonder if there's anything behind the mask. The Toledo show was probably a fake.' It didn't seem appropriate to rub it in too much."

"Take me to dinner, Dwight. We can talk there."

"Sure thing, I thought we'd go to Max's again. I called them after you messaged me the time you were getting in."

At the restaurant, Cathy told Dwight what she learned at the bar the previous evening. "I really learned two things. First, Clement Mincy is known to have a giant-sized temper. He's the kind of person who's going to seek revenge. Since we don't think he can figure out who we were, we felt safe. Somebody mentioned that he might take it out on his staff, whoever they are. They screwed up too."

"Shouldn't he be mad at himself? Telling the crowd to shut the fuck up wasn't a smooth move."

"You're right, but people didn't feel he was the kind of guy who would be self-critical."

"What else did you learn?"

"So, we know one name on Mincy's crew. The girl is Katerina, no last name, right?"

"Yeah."

"People thought one of the others might be a guy named Jake McDowd. They weren't sure, but they knew he was a friend of Clement's. They'd been in plays together, and McDowd's politics match Mincy's. Furthermore, Jake hasn't been seen for the last few months."

"Another guy from Indianapolis?"

"Right."

Katerina pulled the semi into its parking place late in the afternoon two days after the Peoria rally. Clem came out of the house to greet her, still looking angry. Katerina tried to give him a kiss hello, but he brushed her off. "What took you so long?"

"You know this rig is slow, and Enrique, Wilhelm, and I had some difficulties packing up. It usually takes four of us, but Jake took off, so we had to improvise."

"Things are awful. Enrique and Wilhelm got here in the middle of the morning. They cleaned out their stuff and left in an Uber. We lost Jake back in Peoria, so we got no crew. If that wasn't bad enough, we've been summoned to Indianapolis by my father. He wants to see both of us."

"Can we make it tomorrow? I've done all the driving I want to. I need to get to the house. I want to be in bed soon."

"Sure, I can put him off, but there are things we need to do. First, I need you to wipe out the message board. It's going crazy. Enrique told me to get lost when I asked him to do it before he left."

"I'm not sure I know how, but I can try."

Clement walked away from Katerina, but she followed him, putting her arms around him and pressing her breasts against his back. "Settle down, honey," she said, holding on tight.

After a minute or two in the hug, Clement turned around and kissed Katerina.

When they finished the kiss, Clement said, "I know it's not your fault. Everything has just gone to hell. There doesn't seem to be anything I can do. I'm incredibly frustrated. I've been pacing around for the last hour, waiting for you to get here."

"Let's go in the house. I need a beer. I'm parched."

After Clement and Katerina settled on the couch with a glass of beer each, Katerina asked, "Have you been reading the message board?"

"Yes, I couldn't help myself. Like I said, it's crazy."

"Crazy how?"

"People are calling me an idiot, a fake, and worse. Also, one guy named me. He said he recognized my voice. A whole bunch of people agreed with him. Then the Shadow guy said, I wouldn't take off my mask in Peoria because it would show the Toledo rally was a fake. The more time I spent on the damn message board, the madder I got. We've got to shut it down."

"I don't know. I think shutting it down is admitting defeat."

"You're right, but it's no use," Clement said glumly. "The whole thing isn't up to us. Dad and his friends control the money. They aren't about to invest any more in us. I'm sure our meeting with dad is about pulling the plug on us. They'll want our list of supporters, but VM is no more."

"Wow, are you sure? It was just one screwup."

Katerina got up, stretched, and yawned, looking at the hallway. She couldn't abandon Clem, but she was bone tired.

"I can't break down a brick wall, and my dad is a brick wall. You should have heard him. But I want revenge. Somebody engineered the Peoria stuff. That chant wasn't just one person. It started all over the place, like it was planned. Daniel has some ideas he's checking out. I want to get whoever it was."

"I hope he can find the person who's responsible, and I agree we deserve to get revenge."

"I knew you'd understand."

"We've got bigger problems you haven't thought about."

"How's that?"

"The crew all know about Marcie. That's our biggest liability. If one of them talks to the police, we're cooked. Right now, I understand why you're more interested in whoever started that chant, but for the long-term, avoiding a murder charge is more important. We can't have those guys out there. We need to make sure they don't talk."

"I don't know. I don't think they'll talk," Clement said.

"Are you convinced? You said some awful things to them in Peoria. Jake was really steamed. Think about it. You blew up at him. He was mad enough to storm out of the trailer with no ride home. He could very well want to get back at you."

"But he was leading the chant. The wrong chant. How could he do that to me?"

Katerina, who'd been standing, flopped down on the couch beside Clem.

"Maybe he couldn't hear when he was below the stage. At least that's what he claimed."

Clement's face turned red as he balled his fists at his side. "That was bullshit and you know it."

"Don't yell at me. I'm just saying Jake was awfully mad at you. You called him some awful names. And the others were the same. They only stuck around because I asked them to, begged them to. They both told me what they were going to do when they got here. They'd have taken off with the van if I hadn't told them we'd report the vehicle missing. You don't want to know what they were calling you."

"Holy shit. I guess you're right. It looks like we've got a lot of work to do."

Katerina wrapped her arm around Clement. "I'm just the girl to help you. I've been thinking about how to get rid of those guys. I've known them long enough to understand their weaknesses. Stick with me. We'll get the job done."

"I like the way you think."

CHAPTER TWENTY-EIGHT

Clement and Katerina's meeting with Clement's father, Gregory, was a disaster. He hadn't even asked them to sit. They were forced to stand in front of his big desk like two schoolchildren who'd been called into the principal's office. Gregory had heard from the other businessmen who had been helping to fund Clement. They were all pulling out. According to Gregory, they'd shouted at him and cursed him. One of them even said he thought the Viking and mermaid business was ludicrous from the start.

Clement spoke up. "But they were all on board after we left the Atlanta meeting. They had all seen the Origins video there. Nobody told us they thought it was ludicrous then."

"I know, boy, but when people turn against you, they get distorted memories. It was clear they only wanted one thing from us—the list of the people in your groups and the people who signed up after the rallies. They don't want to hear about you or the Vikings or the mermaids ever again."

"Do we have to give them the lists?" Katerina asked.

"You bet we do. These guys play hardball. If we give them a lick of trouble, I don't know what would happen, and I don't want to find out."

"Okay, I'll get you the list, and you can send it," Clement said.

"It might not be so easy, Clem," Katerina responded. "That's something Enrique kept track of. I don't know where he stored the lists. Just like a computer geek, his files have goofy names, and the important ones are password protected. We haven't had any luck finding anything."

"You'd better find this Enrique guy and get those names. I don't want any trouble from our former friends."

As Katerina and Clement walked out of Gregory's office, Katerina said, "Honey, let's go somewhere where we can have a private talk."

"There's a park a block away. We should be able to find an out of the way bench.

Clement was right, the park was deserted, so Katerina felt free to talk. "I've been thinking, and now I'm even more positive. We've got to clean up our leftovers."

"What do you mean?"

"All of our crew know too much. They know you and I drove off with Marcie, and they know she showed up dead the next day. We can't have people with that information running around loose."

"You think we should get rid of them."

Katerina smiled. "Precisely."

"We can't do in Enrique until we get the information on the computer files."

"I know, but Enrique will be the easiest to deal with. I know his weakness. The key to this kind of thing is knowing weaknesses."

"Okay, I'll play along. What's his weakness?"

"These," Katerina unbuttoned her top two buttons and wiggled her breasts. "You must have noticed how he stared at me all the time. He was always taking his break when I was in the lake. He'll be easy."

"What about Wilhelm?"

"It's the pride in his work. He's good, I'll admit, but he thinks he's great. I think it's a weakness I can work with."

"And Jake?"

"I've got nothing yet. I'm still thinking. He was your friend. You should think about how we can trap him. All these guys are really mad at us, so we have to think of a way to get them to talk to us."

"Yeah, and we have to find them."

"Let's get started on Enrique."

When he was settled behind the steering wheel of his car, Clement paused. Looking at Katerina, he asked, "Are you sure about this? Committing three more murders?"

"Don't wimp out on me, Clem. We got away with murdering Marcie so far. If we can finish off these three guys, we'll continue to get away with it. Look, they're really mad at you right now. I wouldn't put it past one of them to snitch on us."

"But aren't we putting ourselves in more jeopardy?"

"I don't think so. We just need to be careful. Everything about VM, all of our identities, were kept secret. That was one of the smartest things you did. You even had them wearing masks when we were setting up and tearing down. Marcie was the only one who knew who was on the crew, and she's gone."

"I guess you're right. I don't think anyone but my dad and maybe Daniel knew who was working with us."

"Right. If we're smart, we'll get away with it. Just to be sure, we should blow town after we take care of the guys."

"Good idea."

Dwight spent the two days after Cathy returned from Peoria polishing the Dickens manuscript. After sending it to his editor as an attachment to a long email, he felt a tremendous sense of satisfaction. He knew he was a couple of weeks late, but he also knew he'd be forgiven. Eventually, he would have to embark on another project, but for a week or two, he didn't want to think about it.

He'd taken short breaks from finishing up Dickens to check the VM message board. He was surprised it was still up. The initial furor over the fiasco in Peoria had died down. All that remained were some loyal followers with questions about why there had been no response from the VM people. They'd been completely silent. Dwight thought this was odd. They had egg on their face for sure, but they had found ways to wiggle out of a jam before. They'd made a great save from the article naming Clement Mincy. Dwight wondered what they were cooking up now.

A bit at loose ends, he wandered downstairs and followed the odor of perfume to the front room and found his mother all dressed up sitting on the chair by the door. As he entered the room, Dwight asked, "What's his name?"

"Oh," said Evangeline, a little startled.

"That's what you asked me. I've never seen you so dressed up and smelling so good when you had a lunch date with your lady friends. I'll repeat. What's his name?"

"I'm going to lunch with Andrew Nichols, if you must know. There, I've been more forthcoming than you have."

Dwight sat in a chair across from his mother. "Andrew Nichols, why do I know that name?"

"Andy was a friend of your father. He's the person at the bank who handled all the business loans. His wife died five years ago. All the girls, if I can still call them that, have been chasing after him ever since. I was astounded when he called and asked me to lunch."

"Very interesting. Since you've made such a great recovery from your stroke, I think you'd be a real catch."

Evangeline blushed. "Okay, boy, I've told you. It's your turn. What's her name?"

"I guess I can tell you, but you can't tell a soul. It has to be a deep secret," Dwight said, staring at his mother.

"I won't tell a soul."

"Good, I've been seeing Cathy Wilson, Courtney's mother."

"Oh, Dwight, she's married."

"I know, but that marriage has been over for a few years. Bill has a girlfriend he's living with, and divorce proceedings are underway. Before you ask, I was not the reason for the divorce."

"I understand why you want to keep your relationship secret. I'll be good. Does Courtney know?"

Dwight hadn't thought about Courtney. *Maybe she does know. Cathy said they shared a lot.* "I don't think so, but that brings up a question. What are we going to do when Courtney goes away to college? We'll need to find another cook."

"I don't know. Maybe I can cook again, and you could lend a hand. Right now, I've got to go. That's Andrew coming up the walk."

Dwight didn't know why he cared, but he inspected Andrew closely. He was tall, distinguished looking and had a full head of gray hair. He looked a little younger than Evangeline and seemed a bit nervous when he was introduced to Dwight.

Dwight watched the two of them head down the walk to Andrew's car, a big Cadillac. He didn't know what to feel about his mother having a gentleman friend. Finally, he decided it was none of his business. She deserved to be happy, so he resolved to butt out.

Still, he had an additional thing to talk about at dinner with Cathy. *She probably knows Andrew Nichols. Maybe she does business with him.*

Katerina and Clement had no difficulty tracking down Enrique. He had gone to his mother's house. They remembered how delighted he'd been to join their team and move out from under her wing. Despite that, they knew he didn't have another place to land. They parked across the street, and it didn't take them long to spot him.

Katerina chuckled as they drove away. "I'm sure it will be easy to get to Enrique. You'll have to stay in the background though. This will be my deal."

"Yeah, you said he stared at you all the time."

"It's no big deal. Lots of guys are attracted to my boobs. Enrique was just more obvious about it. The thing is, we, actually I, can take advantage of his weakness. I know just the outfit I can wear."

At seven that evening, Katerina drove to Enrique's mother's house. She wore a red skirt that was a little short, with high heels and a tight white blouse. She greeted the mother, who came to the door, and asked if she could speak to Enrique. The mother left her on the porch, but that didn't bother Katerina. While she waited for Enrique, she unbuttoned the top button on her blouse, exposing more cleavage. When Enrique came to the door, Katerina could tell her outfit was having the intended effect.

"Katerina, I didn't expect to see you here," Enrique said, stepping onto the porch.

"Enrique, it's good to see you," Katerina said, smiling and putting her hand on his arm. She tilted her head slightly. "Clement and I had a big argument, and I don't know what's going to happen. I need a friend right now."

"That guy's crazy. I'd stay away from him if I were you."

Katerina stepped closer to him with a troubled look on her face. "I just didn't know where to turn. It's so upsetting." She reached out to Enrique, hugging him. Somewhat surprised, he put his arms around her. She could tell pressing her breasts against him caught his attention.

"Is there somewhere we could go?" she asked.

Enrique extracted himself from the hug, but he was looking at her breasts as he did so. "Let me think," he said. "Have you had dinner?"

"No, I haven't. I went to a motel after Clem and I had our fight. I'd wash my hands of him if he didn't owe me so much money. Anyway, dinner would be nice."

"Let me tell my mom where I'm going. I'll be right back," Enrique said as he opened the door and disappeared into the house. Two minutes later, he came out.

"We can go in my car," Katerina said. "I bet you haven't had time to get any wheels."

"I was going to borrow my mom's car, but maybe it would be better if you drove. Let me take her keys back."

Enrique was back in a minute, and Katerina linked her arm into his as they walked down the driveway to where her car was parked. This arrangement allowed her left breast to brush into Enrique with every step. She could tell she had his full attention.

At the restaurant, a little local Mexican joint, Katerina guided Enrique to a table in the corner. They sat across from each other, and judging by the look on his face, Enrique liked the view.

After they ordered, they made small talk about the disaster in Peoria and the difficulties they'd had packing up without Jake's help. Their meals arrived quickly, stopping conversation. When they'd finished, Katerina moved the conversation to her supposed problem with Clement. "I don't know what I'm going to do about Clem. Even though his dad's rich, he never has much money. When this all got started, I loaned him five thousand dollars. Now that it looks like we've split up, I want to be repaid, but it doesn't look like he's going to be good for the money."

"Gosh, that's horrible. Five thousand is a lot. I don't suppose you have anything in writing."

"No, nothing. He was my boyfriend. As you know, I moved in with him right after Marcie left. We were solid then. I wish I had something he wanted."

"If I had a girl like you, I'd be straight with her all the time. The guy's crazy. I tell you."

Katerina smiled and pushed out her chest a little. Enrique noticed.

"My guess is the only way I can get my money back is in some kind of exchange. That's the way Clement works. Everything's a transaction."

"What kind of things could you trade with him?"

"I don't know. Everything is a mess back in Michigan. We have no crew, and I don't know how much damage has been done to the brand. Probably a lot. Peoria was a real mess. The message board is full of some bad shit, and since you left, we can't even answer back. Clement lost the password or whatever."

Enrique looked around the restaurant. There was a line to get in, so he said, "We'd better leave. These guys need our table."

They left, again arm in arm. When they got to her car, Katerina pulled Enrique to her and gave him a deep kiss. "Thanks for being so understanding. I knew you'd be the one to talk to."

Enrique was still reeling from the kiss. He stammered, "I wonder if I could help you."

Katerina pulled Enrique into a hug and whispered in his ear, "How?"

Enrique backed off. "Stop that for a minute. I can't think when you're holding me like that."

"What, you don't like it?" Katerina smiled.

"No, that's not it, and you know it. I just need a minute to think." After a pause, he continued, "Look, I have a whole bunch of passwords Clement might want. I'm the only one who can get into the message board and to the list of supporters. Stuff like that. I bet Clement needs the passwords. He doesn't know any of them."

"That's brilliant," Katerina almost shouted as she launched herself into Enrique. She hugged him and gave him a passionate kiss.

They broke apart when they heard someone heading toward their part of the parking lot. When they were in the car, Katerina reached over to Enrique, took his hand, and put it on her breast. "There you go. You've been wanting to do that all night."

"Oh my God, was it that obvious?" Enrique asked as he pawed her.

"Yes, but it's okay. They were ready for a good fondle."

When Katerina pulled up in front of Enrique's mother's house, she leaned over and gave Enrique a kiss. After she broke off the kiss, she said, "Look, don't do anything yet. I'm going to make Clem pay me before I give him anything. Give me your cell number. If Clem's willing to do business, I'll call you to get the passwords."

"Okay."

"Here, write your number on my palm," Katerina said as she got a pen out of her small purse and extended her arm.

Enrique wrote his number as requested. Then he said, "I'd love to invite you in, but it's my mom's house. I don't think it would work."

"That's all right. Just kiss me again. We can find a place later."

The kiss was long, and Enrique didn't want to stop, but eventually Katerina pushed him away.

Back in their motel room, Katerina told Clement about her night, leaving out the kisses and the fondling. "I've got him set up. He'll give me all the passwords if he thinks you'll pay me for them. All I have to do is tell him you've paid up. He'll give me what we want, thinking he's helping me finish the bargain. I say we should wait a couple of days. I'll tell him you weren't interested in the bargain initially."

"You're a miracle worker, babe."

"It wasn't too tough. I unbuttoned my top button, and Enrique was putty in my hands. I even made him think the exchange was his idea."

"Good. After you get the passwords from him, we'll have to figure out how to off him."

"Yeah, you know I'm up for that."

CHAPTER TWENTY-NINE

*D*wight drove Cathy to the restaurant by the river where they'd gone the night they'd first made love. After they'd driven out of Clayville, Dwight started the conversation. "Do you know Andrew Nichols? He's a banker or something."

"Yes, I do. Actually, he's the guy who suggested I take out the loans for my store in my own name. The divorce discussions have shown just what a good idea that was. Bill doesn't own any part of the stores. Andrew's a good guy, but I think he's retired now. Why do you ask?"

"It's the strangest thing. I think he wants to date my mother. They went out to lunch today."

"You should be pleased. Andrew is a straight shooter. It was tough for him when his wife died. If I'm not mistaken, it happened close to his retirement. It's hard losing your job and your wife close together. Too much change."

"I don't know if anything will come of it, but my mom was all dressed up and wearing more perfume than I remember. Nichols seemed nervous when he met me. It was like they were a couple of teenagers."

"I'll ask Courtney if she knows anything. Evangeline probably confides in her more than she does in you."

"Probably true. I certainly didn't get a post lunch report from my mom."

"Oh, by the way, congratulations on finishing the Dickens book. It must feel great to complete a big project like that."

"I like writing books. There's a beginning, a middle, and an end. I'm not at the end yet. I still have to respond to my editor's comments, but I'm close. It feels good."

They drove in silence for a few minutes before Cathy broke it. "So where are we on our VM project?"

"That's a good question. The chant in Peoria and their disastrous response to it certainly put a crimp in their operation. They had to think the reaction on the message board was awful. It's weird. They haven't responded in any way. It's possible they'll shut down. They've been exposed as frauds. You and Larry deserve a lot of credit."

"Even if they do shut down, I don't want credit."

"Well, you deserve lots of it. I'd have never gotten involved without you. I would have never met Marcie without you, and that led to Larry and his idea about the chant. It all starts with you."

"Dwight, my love, you'll make me blush," Cathy said as she reached over and stroked his thigh.

After a couple of minutes of silence, Dwight brought up another subject. "Suppose our efforts have been successful in eliminating the VM bunch. That's huge, because at least for a while they were a big deal. Unfortunately, if they leave, somebody is going to pick up where they left off. We may have killed the messenger, but we didn't kill the message. To me, one of the scary things about the whole bit is how easily they attracted followers. There are a lot of people out there susceptible to their type of thinking."

"You gave me one good explanation of their appeal, about the people left behind by the modern economy. I guess you're right, those people are still out there looking for some group to take up their grievances."

"Yes," Dwight continued. "There are still Southerners who want to keep fighting the civil war, people who think immigrants will take their jobs, people who think everything the government does is overreach, and people who don't trust experts. Lots of groups are looking for a champion. The VM guy was becoming the champion for lots of those people. Unfortunately, another champion will probably come along."

"It's a good thing the restaurant is just around the next bend. You're starting to depress me."

"Sorry honey, but I think we just won a small battle in a long war."

◇◆◇

Two days later, Katerina called Enrique, telling him Clement had finally caved. He'd paid her, and she wanted to follow through in a hurry. It wasn't a good idea for her to rile Clement up by being late. They agreed Enrique should write down a list of the passwords, and she would pick him up at five thirty. Enrique thought it was odd that she wanted him to meet her at the 7-11 two blocks from his house, but she explained they didn't want his mother to know what was going on. Enrique didn't understand, but he didn't argue.

Katerina greeted Enrique with a kiss when he climbed into her car. "Do you have the passwords in that envelope?" Katerina asked, taking the envelope from him.

"Yes, open it and see."

She opened the envelope and scanned the page. "This is perfect, Enrique. You've listed the passwords and the names of the files they work with. Clem will be pleased, and I can wash my hands of him."

"I thought it was what he'd want."

"You hit the nail on the head. Now let's head to my motel room to celebrate."

"I couldn't think of a better idea," Enrique said.

Katerina drove for about fifteen minutes and then pulled into the end unit of an old-fashioned, one-story motel. She used a key to open the door and motioned for Enrique to enter. When Enrique took his first step over the threshold, Clement, who'd been waiting inside, hit him over the head with a small baseball bat, and he crumpled to the floor. Katerina quickly closed the door and stepped over the body.

Clement lifted Enrique and Katerina slid a sheet of plastic under the upper half of the body. Then Katerina took the garrote out of her purse. It was the same one she'd used on Marcie, just a thin wire between two short dowel rods. She put the wire around Enrique's neck and pulled it tight. After a few minutes, it was clear Enrique was no longer breathing, so she released the pressure. There had been some bleeding, but the plastic sheet caught it all. Finally, Clement and Katerina emptied Enrique's pockets of all identification and rolled the dead body into a large carpet scrap they'd brought with them.

Katerina stepped back with a big smile on her face. "That was great. I get a big thrill out of this. It really turns me on."

"Let's get out of here," Clement said. "I'm not doing anything in a room with a dead body. We can't move him until it's totally dark." Clem stared at the body, his face drained of color.

"Fine. I'll put the do not disturb sign on the door, and we can find someplace else."

"Good, and then we should get that list to my dad. Oh my God. I sure hope we can work the passwords. It might have been a big mistake to get rid of him so quick."

Katerina smiled. "I wouldn't worry, babe. He wanted to please me big time. He wouldn't give us an inaccurate list."

"I suspect you're right. I guess tomorrow we can try to find Wilhelm."

"I don't think that will be hard. His father runs that cabinet making shop. I bet Wilhelm is back working for him."

Dwight went to the Red Dolphin on Thursday night to see if anyone would still come. He'd been to the meeting the previous week, and it had been interesting. Most of the group attended. None of them had been to the Peoria rally, so their only knowledge came from the internet. What they'd seen had made them very mad at the crowd. They wondered how the people in Peoria could turn on the VM guy so quickly. At the same time, they couldn't understand the response of the VM guy. He tripped and then shouted at the crowd. Everyone was disillusioned, to say the least. Dwight had found it easy to add to the gloomy mood. Very little had changed over the previous week, so he wondered how many people would show.

Bill and Stacy were the only ones at the bar when he arrived. They sat at a table in the corner. "Get yourself a beer," Bill said.

"Is anyone else coming?" Dwight asked as he returned with his beer and sat beside Bill.

"I don't know, but I doubt it. I think VM is finished. I don't know if you know this, but the message board is shut down. It was gone the day before yesterday. They never responded to any messages after Peoria."

"I'm not surprised. I stopped reading the message board on Monday. It had turned almost completely stagnant by then."

"Yeah."

Dwight took a swallow of his beer. "Do you think the VM guy is that Clement Mincy?" he asked. "That's what a lot of the posts said. After what we saw in Toledo, I find it hard to believe. The guy was there and so was the whole VM rally."

"I don't know what to believe," Bill said. "The whole thing has me really depressed. I mean, it had so much momentum, but then everything collapsed. How can one bad rally destroy the whole thing?"

Stacy shook her head. "The guy lost control when he fell. When he shouted at the crowd, I was shocked. For me, one of the things I liked was how he was always in control, both in the videos and on stage."

"You're right," Bill responded. "He lost it. Unfortunately for him there were lots of cameras shooting when his control disappeared."

"What's going to happen to all the groups like ours?" Dwight asked.

"Look around, dummy. What does it look like?"

"I guess I should rephrase my question. As our leader, you used to get emails from the VM guy. Has that stopped too?"

"Complete silence. Nothing. It's like they've completely gone away. I can't tell you how disappointed I am."

Silence descended. Finally, Dwight spoke up. "Stacy, has there been any action on my mother's car?"

"Lots of people have looked at it, but I haven't had any firm offers. We drop the price in a week, and I bet that will work."

"Do some people hold off, hoping you'll drop the price?"

"I expect so. We don't advertise when our price reductions will happen, but people know we eventually have to drop prices to move the cars. I still think you'll get top dollar for that car. It's a peach."

Dwight finished his beer and excused himself. What he learned confirmed his suspicions. VM was dead, at least for now.

CHAPTER THIRTY

Two days later at eleven thirty, Katerina sat at a café across the street from the cabinet shop owned by Wilhelm's father. Clement had been right. Wilhelm had gone back to work there. They'd seen him leave the store yesterday. She was going to try to make contact when he left for lunch.

Katerina thought Wilhelm was an odd duck. Unlike Enrique and to a lesser extent Jake, he didn't seem interested in her at all. One day she'd paraded around in her bikini in front of him, and he didn't react at all. *Maybe he's gay*, she thought.

Though she couldn't use the same approach she used with Enrique, she and Clement figured she'd be the best one to approach Wilhelm. They'd left on good terms in Peoria. She and Clement were counting on his pride in his work. She'd tell him he was so good that they still needed him.

At noon, Wilhelm left the shop and headed toward a sandwich place for lunch. He wasn't a big talker, but he had told everyone how much he missed the submarine sandwiches he was used to.

Wilhelm had to pass by where Katerina was sitting. When he got close, she stood up and hailed him. He'd been walking with his head down, so he stopped and looked around before he spotted her.

"Katerina, what are you doing here?" he said, walking over to her table.

"Looking for you," she responded. "Here, have a seat."

Wilhelm sat in the seat she was pointing to. "Look Katerina, I can't talk long. I only get forty-five minutes for lunch. My dad gets mad if I'm late. I'm on thin ice with him. He's still pissed at me for leaving with you guys."

"Okay. I'll keep it short. Clement would like to meet with you. He's incredibly mad at himself for blowing up at you guys, especially you, Wilhelm. You didn't do anything wrong. Your sets were perfect. You do incredible work. He figures the VM business might be finished, but he may want to revive his magic show. He wants to know if you'll work for him. It would be part time, so it wouldn't interrupt your job. He'll pay you double what he used to."

"Double?"

"Yes, double. If you're interested, he'd like to meet at the warehouse, the one where he stored his magic props. He's busy until seven tonight. Could you meet us there at seven thirty?"

"I don't know. I'm still bothered by some of the things he said."

"I don't blame you. He was out of control, but he's calmed down now. The big salary offer is his way of saying he's sorry. He knows he needs you. You're really good."

Wilhelm smiled and then paused thoughtfully. Finally, he spoke, "Sure, I guess I could give the guy a second chance. I can be there tonight. I remember where the warehouse is."

"Thanks so much, he'll be thrilled. You can take off for your lunch now. You should still have plenty of time."

Wilhelm checked his watch as he was getting up. "Yeah, I still got time. Nice to see you Katerina."

Katerina took out her cell phone and sent a message to Clement.

That night at seven forty, Katerina heard Wilhelm's car pull up to the warehouse. When she heard his car door open, she shoved open the door enough to lean out and motioned for Wilhelm to come inside. When Wilhelm squeezed through the small opening she'd made, Clement hit him over the head with his little baseball bat. This time his aim wasn't good, and Wilhelm only staggered.

"Hit him again!" Katerina screamed.

Wilhelm lunged at Clement, grabbed his left arm, and dug in his fingernails. Luckily for Clement, he was right-handed, so he was able to put all the force he had into another blow with the bat. Wilhelm crumpled to the ground, leaving a scratch on Clement's arm.

"Quick, give him another whack."

"Good idea."

The third blow cracked Wilhelm's skull, so Katerina had no difficulty draining the life out of him with her garrote.

"Wow, he was a tough little mother," Clement said, inspecting the scratch on his arm.

"He's a goner now. Let's roll him up in the carpet. Then we can go to dinner before we come back here to collect him when it's dark. Get his car keys so I can drive his car. I'll put on my gloves. Follow me. I know where to stash the car."

"Sounds like a plan."

"Two down and one to go," Katerina said as they rolled Wilhelm's dead body into the carpet.

"You get a charge out of this, don't you? I can tell you're still excited."

"Yeah, I guess I do. Do you think that means something is wrong with me?"

"Not from where I'm looking," Clement said, taking Katerina into his arms.

The next morning, Jake McDowd was jolted out of his morning grogginess by a story on the local news. The reporter's story was about a dead body found floating at the edge of a local creek. The person had been garotted. The TV showed an artist's rendition of a face, asking anyone who recognized the victim to call the crime line. The guy was grizzly looking, particularly his neck, but Jake felt certain it was Enrique. A chill went up his spine. He thought maybe he should call the police, but he didn't want to get involved. As he thought more, he decided he should contact Wilhelm. It was just possible Clement had killed Enrique. If he was right, Wilhelm might be in just as much trouble as he was.

Jake found the number for Wilhelm's dad's cabinet shop and called. The person who answered said Wilhelm hadn't showed up for work today, and no one knew where he was. Another chill went up Jake's spine. He had to find a place to hide. He'd temporarily moved in with Dave, one of his buddies from his days at the playhouse. Unfortunately for him, Clement knew Dave. It wasn't smart to stay here. He gathered up his stuff, wrote a quick note to Dave, and ran out to his car. At least he'd been smart enough to put his car in his folk's side yard when he went to Michigan.

Jake drove around aimlessly for a half an hour before he came up with a plan. He'd try Sharon Ridley. They'd dated a bit, but she'd broken it off. Still, they'd parted on good terms. Sharon lived in a house with a couple of roommates. The house was big, and Jake was fairly sure there were spare bedrooms. As far as he knew, Clement didn't know Sharon. It should be a good hiding place.

No one answered the door at Sharon's house, so Jake returned to his car and waited. As he sat there, he realized Clement would know his car. If he could get a room at Sharon's house, he'd have to park somewhere else. Maybe he'd trade cars or something. He got more and more worried as he sat there. He knew murder was not new to Clement and Katerina. He was pretty sure they'd done in Marcie Green.

After a couple of hours, during which he'd seen two other girls go into the house, he spotted Sharon walking up the street. Jake got out of his car and walked up to Sharon. She seemed startled to see him.

He didn't know what to say, since he was so nervous. Sharon started the discussion. "Jake, it's nice to see you. What brings you here?"

"I need a favor, Sharon, a big favor. I need a place to stay for a while, not long. Do you have a spare bedroom I could use?"

"I don't know. Honestly, I don't. I mean, there is a spare room, but I don't know if you could stay there. It would be up to the other girls. We have rules about guys staying over, but this is not that. Anyway, what's up? Why do you need a place all of the sudden?"

"It's complicated. I think some guy's got it in for me. I have to find a place to stay. One he doesn't know about."

"So, you want to use our house as a hideout? Is that it?"

"I guess you could put it that way. Sharon, I'm desperate. I wouldn't be any trouble. I'll pay rent. Whatever you say. You know me. I'll be clean and quiet. Your roommates won't even know I'm there."

"All we have is the attic room. There's no bathroom on that level. It's pretty basic."

"Sounds fine."

"Okay, I guess we should go see what my roommates have to say."

Jake gave in to every demand of Sharon's roommates. He would be home by ten every night, and he couldn't have any guests. He would only be able to use the stairs to the attic and the third-floor bathroom. He had no kitchen privileges, and he was on parole for a week. If he did anything objectionable during the week, he'd be kicked out.

After he moved his stuff into the room, he parked his car four blocks away and found a place to eat. After his dinner, he bought provisions for breakfast at a corner store. He didn't eat a large breakfast, so it wasn't difficult. It annoyed him that he couldn't use the kitchen, because he liked to make coffee in the mornings. Still, he was pleased. There was no way Clement could find him.

He called Dave, and just as Jake had feared, Clement had come by wondering if Dave knew where he was. Dave was glad he could honestly tell Clement he had no idea. Jake felt lucky he'd seen the picture of Enrique on TV. If he hadn't, he might have been there when Clement visited.

He got back to Sharon's house at nine thirty, well before the ten o'clock curfew the girls had set for him. About ten minutes after he got to his room, he was surprised by a knock on his door. It was Sharon.

"Do you have a minute or two, Jake?"

"Sure, what do you want to know? Come in and sit in the chair. I'll take the bed."

Sharon took the chair Jake had cleared for her. "Okay, I'll come right out with it. Are you mixed up with Clement Mincy?"

Jake was shocked, and he was sure Sharon could sense it. After a pause, he replied, "The answer is yes. Why do you ask?"

"I'll be straight with you, if I can count on you doing the same."

"Sure."

"I went to the VM rally in Peoria with a group of people. Were you there?"

"Yes."

"In that silly costume?"

"Yes."

"We were the ones who started the 'show your face' chant."

Jake looked surprised. "I was the second masked man. The one who raised my hands twice before I recognized what was going on. It was weird seeing Clem lying there on the stage beside me. He was supposed to be gone."

"What happened after everything stopped?"

"Clem went crazy. He has a volcanic temper, and he was spewing big time. I finally had enough of it, and I split. I just walked out of the trailer and left. I don't know what happened after that. I took a bus back here. I've been staying with a friend until I figured Clement was looking for me. He knows my friend too, so I relocated here. I'm not interested in Clem finding me just yet."

"Our group was organized by Larry Green, Marcie Green's brother. Did you know Marcie?"

"Yes, she was part of our group for a while. She and Clement were a couple, but then they split up, and she left."

"What happened to Marcie?"

Jake went silent and slid off the bed and went over to the window and stared out into the night.

"Come on. Larry thinks Clement killed her. Is he right?"

Jake turned around. "I don't know. Honestly, I don't."

"Tell me what you know."

"Okay, one day, Katerina, that was Clement's new girl. Anyway, Katerina saw Marcie spying on us. She ran after Marcie, and Marcie tried to get away in her car. She didn't succeed, because Clement got in his car and blocked her. When they caught her, they took Marcie into the house. I will admit I stood guard over her while Clem and Katerina decided what to do. I don't know what it was. All I know is that later that evening, Clem, Marcie, and Katerina left. They took Marcie's car and Clem's car. Much later, Clem and Katerina came back in Clem's car. That's all I know."

"You never heard Marcie's body was found?"

"Yeah, but I don't know any of the details."

"She'd been choked to death and stashed in her car. Whoever it was didn't manage to push her car all the way into a river. Given what you told me, the killers were most likely Clement and this girl Katerina."

"You don't know that. When did the killing happen?"

"It was the same day you guys caught her. We know that because she didn't make a dinner engagement she'd set up. And the body was found early the next morning."

"I guess I figured that was what happened. I was just fooling myself thinking Clem wasn't involved."

"So, tell me why, other than the fact he's a cold-blooded killer, you're so afraid of Clement."

"On TV this morning, they showed a picture of some guy whose dead body had been found. I looked at the guy, and I knew him. It was Enrique, one of the people who worked with us in Michigan. I think Clem killed him. And when I tried to find the other guy in the group, he hadn't shown up for work. Nobody knows where he is. It spooked me."

"Jake, you've got to go to the cops. For your own protection. And you have important information."

"I don't know, Sharon. I don't want to get mixed up with the cops. Nothing good is going to come of that. I didn't witness a crime."

"That's bullshit. You said you were guarding Marcie. That means she was being held against her will. That's a crime. And you damn well know that Clement killed her. On top of that, you know the identity of the body the police found. You have to go to the police."

"Will I need a lawyer?"

"I don't think so... but wait, maybe you should. Larry Green, Marcie's brother, is a lawyer. I think you should talk to him. I'm going downstairs and calling him. I'll be right back."

With that, Sharon hurried down the stairs. She came back five minutes later. "It's all set up. Larry will be here at eight tomorrow morning, and he will accompany you to police headquarters."

"Thanks, I guess."

CHAPTER THIRTY-ONE

The next morning, Larry Green met Jake McDowd in front of Sharon's house. Larry took Jake to a nearby coffee shop, and they discussed the role Jake played in the abduction and killing of Marcie. It was a difficult discussion for Jake, but Larry took it better than he'd expected. He just told Jake he would very likely have to repeat everything he said to the Grand Rapids police.

After discussing what Jake knew about Marcie's killing, they turned to Jake's current predicament. Jake told Larry about recognizing Enrique the previous morning, trying, without success, to find Wilhelm, and learning that Clement was looking for him. He admitted he didn't have any solid evidence, but what he did know scared him big time.

"I saw the picture of the body. You said his name was Enrique? Anyway, I was interested because it looked like he'd been choked by a thin wire. That's how Marcie was killed. Now you're giving me a connection."

"I didn't know how Marcie died. I just heard they found her body in her car."

"We've got to get the information you have to the police."

"Am I going to be in trouble?"

Larry told Jake he didn't think he was in any legal jeopardy. He had nothing to fear from the police. In addition, he would be a whole lot safer if Clement, and probably Katerina, were off the streets. In Larry's opinion, what he could report about Marcie's killing should be enough to have them picked up. Larry pleaded with Jake to go with him to police headquarters so he could tell them everything he knew.

Larry called ahead and made an appointment with a homicide detective, Ronald Hogan. Larry knew the detective because of an earlier case. He told Jake that Detective Hogan was a straight shooter who would be good to work with.

The detective turned out to be in his fifties, bald, and a little overweight. He had on a rumpled suit and sat in a room with four other detectives at their desks. Jake was a little startled. He didn't think he'd be telling his story in such a public setting.

Larry started the discussion. "Ron, this is Jake McDowd. I think he can be a big help with a recent killing and some other stuff too."

Hogan shook Jake's hand and pulled over a couple of chairs. "Have a seat."

Jake looked at Larry and asked, "Where should I start?"

"Start with the body. You can get to the Michigan stuff later."

"Okay, I saw the body on TV yesterday. The one who'd been found dead. I'm pretty sure I know who he is, or I guess was. He looked like a guy I used to work with, Enrique Hernandez. And I'm pretty sure I know who killed him."

"That's great. Why don't you tell me your whole story, and then I can connect you to the guy who has that case."

Jake looked at Larry again. "Should I start all the way back in Michigan? I think it makes more sense if I tell the whole thing."

"Sure."

Jake repeated the story he'd told Larry earlier, including Marcie's killing, the big blow-up after the Peoria rally, seeing Enrique's body, not being able to contact Wilhelm, and finding out Clement was looking for him. Detective Hogan took notes throughout Jake's story, but he didn't interrupt.

When Jake finished, the detective commented, "That's quite a story. We don't have jurisdiction on the Michigan murder, but I suspect what you've said is enough for us to pick up Mincy and the girl. We can hold them until Michigan decides what to do. You'll have to repeat that part of your story to a stenographer to get that process started."

"I can do that."

"Next, I think you'll have to do an identification on the body we've found. I'll get you together with the detective working that case. He'll be thrilled to have a name. It's really difficult to work a John Doe case. You don't have any real evidence on the case but providing a name along with the background will give him a leg up. I don't think he knows anything yet."

Larry said, "If Jake's suspicion is correct, another body's out there—Wilhelm Lawler. He was part of the crew who worked with Mincy, and Jake couldn't find him yesterday. He didn't show up for work."

"Right. I got Lawler here in my notes. If he shows up dead, Jake's story becomes critical. Any time there is a connection between two killings, it really helps. I'm not saying this guy Mincy, and what's her name, Katerina, aren't responsible for Hernandez's murder. What I'm saying is Jake doesn't have any hard evidence. He's right to be very suspicious, but that's all right now."

"I guess you're right," Larry admitted.

Detective Hogan made a phone call to another detective about a possible identification of the body. After a brief discussion, he turned to Larry and Jake. "Another officer, Stuart Lewis, will take you to the morgue. They have another person coming to identify him as well. If the both of you give the same identification, it'll be a lock. When you get back from the morgue, I'll have the stenographer set up."

Larry told Jake he'd have to leave at this point. He had an

appointment he couldn't reschedule.

"It's okay, Larry. Thanks for coming. I can handle things from here."

Jake waited patiently, looking at the other detectives. They all looked busy. Two of them were interviewing people, one was typing something, and the other one was on his phone. Five minutes later, Lewis turned up. He was a tall, African American about Jake's age.

After he introduced himself, Jake said, "Stuart Lewis. Your name sounds familiar. Did you play basketball?"

"Yes, for Franklin Central. Why do you ask?"

"I remember watching from the Decatur bench. You guys killed us."

"I think I had a good game against Decatur. But I don't remember many of the details. Basketball was so important in high school, but I've moved on. I know some folks haven't. All they want to talk about is their glory days in high school. It's crazy if you ask me. Come on, let's get you to the morgue."

It was a short drive to the morgue. Jake had an idea of what to expect from watching television. But it wasn't what he expected. They sat him in a room with a large screen television mounted to the wall. He was told that he would see the body on the screen rather than in person. Stuart talked into a phone that sat on the desk, letting them know Jake was ready. Although he was somewhat removed from seeing the body in person, it was still disturbing when the assistant pulled the sheet from the top of the body. Jake forced himself to look. While the body looked gross, particularly the neck, it was definitely Enrique.

Jake looked over at Stuart and said, "That's my friend Enrique Hernandez for sure."

"We're all set," Stuart said into the phone. The assistant pulled the sheet up, but Jake didn't watch. He'd seen all he wanted to see. As they walked out, they passed another detective and a short, middle-aged Hispanic woman. Jake recognized Enrique's mother. "Wait," he said, putting up his hand to stop Stuart. "That's Enrique's mother."

Jake and Stuart watched as the detective and the woman walked up to the room they'd just left. After a moment, Enrique's mother let out a huge scream and began sobbing. Jake took a few steps toward the room but stopped when Stuart put his hand on his shoulder. "Give her a few minutes," he said.

After Enrique's mother had composed herself, she had a short conversation with the detective and then they headed toward the door where Jake and Lewis were waiting. "Excuse me," Jake said. "I recognized you, Mrs. Hernandez. I'm Jake, I worked with Enrique. I'm so sorry."

Mrs. Hernandez looked up at Jake through her tears. "Do you know who killed my son?"

"I think so."

The detective with Mrs. Hernandez looked at Stuart. "Detective Lewis, you'd better take this guy back to headquarters. I'll be by later to talk to him."

After about forty-five minutes, the detective from the morgue came to where Jake was sitting. "Hello, I'm Dave Whitley. I've talked to Mrs. Hernandez. Follow me."

Detective Whitley led Jake to a small room and sat him down at a table. "You said you worked with Enrique Hernandez."

"Yeah, for almost a year."

"Mrs. Hernandez told me a girl, who she thought was a work friend of her son, came to see him right before he disappeared. Do you know who she was talking about?"

"That was probably Katerina."

"Katerina who."

"I don't know. I never heard a last name."

"Can you describe this girl?"

"Maybe five-six or so, dark hair, about shoulder length, big boobs, and quite a bit of eye makeup."

"Your description matches the girl Mrs. Hernandez told us about. Who is this Katerina?"

"It's like I told Detective Hogan. Enrique and I worked with Clement Mincy. I think he's the guy behind all this. Katerina is his girlfriend. They're a team, Katerina and Clement. She's a little slutty—fake boobs and tight clothes. All the guys were attracted to her, probably Enrique as much as any of us. If she came over to see him, I bet he'd have been happy to follow her."

"So, is it possible this girl took Enrique somewhere where he was killed?" the detective asked. "And Mincy was likely involved too?"

"Yes. I think it's thoroughly possible."

At five thirty, Katerina gave up her search for Jake McDowd. She hadn't been able to find him at any of the places Clem had suggested, and no one she spoke to had seen him. She thought maybe Jake had seen Enrique's picture on TV, and it had spooked him. He seemed to be hiding now. Maybe he wasn't in Indianapolis. It was time to link up with Clement and report her suspicions. He'd texted her that he was going to his father's house for dinner, and she was invited too.

When she approached the Mincy house, she was startled to see a police car in the driveway. Quickly, she backed up, so she didn't pass in front of the house. After she parked, she got out of her car and ran across the street to hide behind a car parked on the other side. She wasn't waiting long before she saw two policemen taking Clem out of the house in handcuffs. The policemen put Clem in the back seat of the patrol car and drove away. Katerina waked unsteadily back to her car and drove away.

What went wrong? she wondered. *We were always careful, and almost no one knows we're in town. How did the police find out about Clem?*

Katerina drove around, not knowing what to do. Finally, she realized she'd better get off the street. If the police had taken Clem, they might be looking for her. *Daniel, Daniel Vilsac, he'll know what to do.* Katerina pulled over and called Daniel on her cell. He didn't know anything about Clem's arrest, but he understood why she was spooked. He gave her his address and told her he'd meet her there.

Daniel directed Katerina to park in his garage, so her car couldn't be seen if the police came by. Instinctively, Katerina hugged Daniel when she got into his house through the door from the garage. Daniel seemed startled, and he backed away as soon as she let him go.

"I'm sorry," she said. "It's just I'm so scared. I guess I needed comfort."

"It's okay. I was just a little startled."

"Do you know what's going on?"

They stood in the kitchen, a few steps from the door to the garage. Daniel's kitchen was dark and outdated but clean, with a dish, coffee mug, and fork on a sideboard next to the sink. It didn't appear that Daniel cooked much. "I left a message with a friend on the police force. Gregory called me just after you did. I expect to hear from my police friend soon. What have you and Clem have been up to? Come into the living room and sit down. I think we need to have a serious talk."

When she was seated on the couch, Katerina decided she'd better come clean with Daniel. "Here's the deal. When everything went haywire in Peoria, the crew split. Jake left after the show, just walked out."

"I know," Daniel interrupted. "I saw him walking away. He told me Clement had gone ballistic. He said there was no way he was going to take the abuse Clem was spewing out."

"Yeah, Wilhelm and Enrique stayed around long enough to help me pack up, but they hit the road right after they picked up their stuff at the Michigan house. Clem and I were the only ones left. Gregory summoned us here and told us we were through. The money guys backed out. Clem was crushed, but there was no arguing with Gregory.

"Anyway, we were at loose ends, and I was worried. As long as we were all a team, everything was okay, but now that we'd split up, there could be trouble. All those guys knew we took care of Marcie back in Michigan, so we decided we had to get rid of them."

"All of three of them?"

Marcie angled herself so her boobs were slightly exposed. Her eyes were big when she answered him. "Yeah, but we were careful. Enrique was easy, but someone found his body faster than we'd expected. Wilhelm was even easier, and his body hasn't turned up yet. I went out looking for Jake today but didn't have any luck. I was headed to Gregory's for dinner when I saw the police taking Clem into custody."

"The people who found some reason to get Clem probably know about you too."

"Yeah, that's why I came here. I've got to hide, at least until we figure out what's going on. Please, can I stay here for a few days?"

Daniel gazed at Katerina. For a girl who always looked like she was in complete control of things, she looked scared. "Sure, I guess so. I've got a date tonight, and I was hoping to bring her back here. If I do, you'd better make yourself scarce. I've got a spare bedroom where you can hide."

Katerina exhaled. "No problem, you won't hear a peep out of me. But I wasn't planning on this, so I don't have any clothes or anything. I only took my purse when I left the motel this morning."

"You'd better give me the motel key, so I can fetch your stuff."

While Katerina searched around in her purse for the key, Daniel looked at his watch. "Look at the time, I've got to get ready for my date. Give me the key. I'll try to get your stuff on my way to pick up my date. Feel free to eat what you can find in the refrigerator but be sure to straighten up and be back in the spare room if you hear my car pull up. I'll show you the room."

CHAPTER THIRTY-TWO

The next morning, Dwight made it down for breakfast to find Courtney and his mother both sitting at the table. "What's the topic of conversation?" he asked.

Courtney got up to get his breakfast.

"I didn't mean to interrupt," Dwight said.

"It's not a problem, Professor. It was just girl talk," Courtney said from the kitchen.

She came out with a stack of pancakes for Dwight. "Sit down, Courtney. I'd like to hear what you two were talking about. Were you asking my mother about her date?"

"Aren't you the curious one," Evangeline muttered.

"Well, I am. I think it's great that you and Andrew went out for lunch. It was weird, the both of you were nervous. When he came to the door, I felt a little like a father looking over his daughter's date. The whole thing was unusual, but as I said, I think it's good for you. I hope you had a good time."

"I think Mr. Nichols is nice, and I'm glad he's asked you out for dinner," Courtney said.

"Dinner? I hadn't heard about any dinner."

Evangeline looked a little sheepish. "He called yesterday, and we're going out tonight. To answer your question, the lunch was just fine. Maybe better than fine. I agree with Courtney. Andrew is nice. We have a lot in common, and he's easy to talk to."

"That's wonderful, mother. I checked up on him, and he's got a sterling reputation."

Evangeline sat up straighter in her chair and glared at him. "You shouldn't have done that. I can take care of myself. I don't need you checking up on anything."

"You're saying back off. I get it. I'll be good."

Evangeline continued, "Now I want to get back to what I was about to ask Courtney before you came down. I'm curious about her mother. Cathy is a lovely woman. Now she's a lovely unattached woman. Surely every bachelor in town would be interested. Is she seeing anyone?"

Courtney's back was turned as she headed back to the kitchen, so Dwight glared at his mother, and she smirked at him.

"It's hard to tell," Courtney responded from the kitchen. "Now that she has two stores, she's busy. There have been quite a few late nights, but I don't know about any man."

"Lots of late nights. That's suspicious," Evangeline said.

Courtney returned with a new cup of coffee for Evangeline. "It's not a big change. Before, I thought she was out late because she was avoiding my father, but maybe the stores are more difficult to manage than I thought. Come to think of it, she has told me about a couple of local guys who've been sniffing around. From what little she's said, I think she's enjoyed turning them down. Maybe it's too early for her."

"Has the separation been hard for her?" Dwight asked.

"You know, it's odd, but she's been happier the last couple of months than I've seen her in years. I think separating from my father has been really good for her. It's too bad their marriage didn't last, but I could see it wasn't working for a long time."

Courtney cleared the dishes. When she returned to say goodbye,

Dwight asked, "What about you, Courtney? Do you have a boyfriend?"

"Nope," Courtney replied. "If there is one thing I've learned from watching my parents, it's that high school is way too early to pick a mate. I'm waiting until after college."

"But you've got to be one of the prettiest girls in the high school. I bet you've had lots of admirers."

"Thanks for saying that, Professor, and I guess it's true. But you've got to remember the roughest part of my parent's marriage happened just as I was starting high school. From my perspective, it was mostly my dad's fault. I think I took it out on some of the guys who asked for dates. I was really down on men. In retrospect, maybe that wasn't smart. Still, I think my plan of waiting until college, or maybe after, is a good plan."

"Yes dear," Evangeline said. "I think it's a great plan."

Courtney smiled at Evangeline. "I'm glad you approve. I've got to go now. See you this evening."

"Goodbye."

After Courtney left, Dwight said, "Cute, Mom. Asking about Cathy."

"Did I make you nervous, dear? I don't think you should be upset with me. It was just an innocent conversation. Actually, I think I did you a favor. Now you know that Courtney doesn't have a clue about you carrying on with her mother."

Dwight didn't respond because he didn't want to admit his mother was right. He just shook his head and went upstairs to his study.

He found an email from Charlotte Mangum. She'd attached a story she'd written for the Knoxville paper. It was a draft. She wasn't sure when the story would appear because she was waiting for more details.

Dwight didn't have any idea what details she could be talking about.

The story explained the apparent demise of the VM movement. Charlotte had found someone who used to be a follower. The guy said the VM websites had apparently been taken offline. Charlotte told an abbreviated version of the Peoria rally story. Dwight smiled when it was clear she took considerable glee in reporting the number of people who said it was obvious from his voice that the VM guy was Clement Mincy. The final paragraph of the story reported on the arrest of Clement Mincy. This was the source of the missing details. Charlotte didn't know much about the arrest.

Dwight was astounded. He dashed off a quick email to Charlotte, thanking her for the story and asking her to send him any details about Clement's arrest when she got them. Next, he went to the website of the *Indianapolis Star* to see if he could find anything. He came up empty. Then he looked back and realized Charlotte's email had been copied to Cathy, so he only sent her a short email. It just said "Wow."

Katerina stumbled groggily out of bed and found Daniel had left her suitcase in the corner of the room. She changed into a fresh outfit and walked into the kitchen, where Daniel sat at the small table.

"There's coffee," Daniel said in greeting.

With a cup of coffee in her hand, Katerina took a seat at the table. "Your date go well? I didn't hear you come in. I guess I was dog tired."

"I didn't bring her back here. We went to her house."

"So, the date went well."

"Super."

"Have you heard from your contact at the police department?"

"No, but that's not odd. Clement's arrest was late yesterday, so it might take my guy a while to find out what it's all about. I'm going in to the store in a few minutes. I'll ask Gregory what he knows first thing when I get there. If I were you, I'd stay here today. Your car is hidden, and you should be too."

"You think the police are looking for me?"

"I bet they are, or if they aren't now, they soon will be. Look, I've known Clement longer than you have. If he thinks it will help him, he'll rat you out in a second. I hate to say that, but it's true."

Katerina sat in silence for a while. Finally, she said, "I don't know, Dan. I'm not so sure Clem would do that."

"Okay, maybe he won't. Still, he might, so you'd better lay low for a while until I can find out what's going on. It's better safe than sorry."

"I get it, but it's going to be tough on me. I like action. I'm not good at being still."

"Just cool it until I find out more."

After Daniel left, Katerina explored his house. It was nice. There were three bedrooms: the guest room she was in, Daniel's bedroom, and a third one which had been converted into an office. She decided not to enter the office. Daniel might be one of those people who was finicky about people looking at his stuff. After investigating the house, she turned on the television. Daniel had cable and several premium channels. She found a movie to watch.

Katerina's phone rang just as her movie was reaching its climax. She paused the movie and answered her phone. "Hello."

"It's Dan. I finally got some details from my police friend. Gregory didn't know anything. I just finished telling him what I found out. Anyway, the police are holding Clem for two reasons. First, he's being held for the Grand Rapids, Michigan police. He is a suspect in the murder of Marcie Green. Green's brother is a lawyer, and apparently yesterday morning he brought Jake in, and Jake spilled the beans about how you and Clem took Marcie somewhere the day she was killed. Second, Jake identified Enrique as the body the police found. The police think Clement might be mixed up in that murder too."

"Why? Do they have evidence linking Clem to Enrique's murder?"

"Not really, but he used to work for Clem, and Marcie and Enrique were killed the same way, with a garrote. That's enough for them to hold him."

Katerina freaked out and didn't say anything for a while. Finally,

Daniel asked, "You still there?"

"Am I in any trouble?"

"For sure. I should have led with that. There's a warrant out for your arrest. They want you for the same two things they're holding Clement for. The Marcie Green murder and Enrique. Enrique's mother gave them a good description of you. The one thing going for you is that no one seems to know your last name, not even Clement."

"What am I going to do?"

"I don't know, but I wouldn't step out of my house at all today. I'll keep looking around. We can talk when I get back this evening. Maybe you can get out of town tonight."

After she got off the phone, Katerina wasn't interested in finishing the movie. There was no way she could sit still. She paced around Daniel's house, trying to think about where she'd go if she left this evening. As she walked around, she chuckled. *It was a good idea to only give people one name. I'm Katerina. Like Madonna or a Brazilian soccer player—no last name. They can't hassle my parents, not that I'm going to contact them anyway.*

The day dragged for Katerina, and she was almost frantic when she heard Daniel's door opening. She ran up to him. "What's happening? It's been hell being cooped up in here all day."

"Let me sit down and get a beer. I've got some things to tell you."

She almost ran to the refrigerator and opened a bottle of beer, so she was ready for Daniel when he returned from his room. He'd ditched his jacket and taken off his tie.

Daniel sat and took a slug of the beer. "You're in big trouble babe. They've got a really good picture of you."

"Where'd they get it? I don't like to have my picture taken ever. I guess I was in that mermaid video, but I don't think my face showed."

"I don't know where they got the picture, but my contact said Jake McGowan told them it was you."

"Holy shit. I guess I'm in big trouble."

"I'm afraid you're right."

"What should I do? Should I try to run? I'm not sure I'd know where to go. I still can't figure where they got a picture of me."

"You can't just take off tonight. I bet they know what kind of car you're driving, and they know what you look like. If you're going to run, you need some prep. You've got to change your looks and what your car looks like."

Katerina sat back in her chair and exhaled a long breath. "You've got a better handle on this than I do. How do I make those changes?"

"I'll go out later and get some stuff you can use to change your hair color. We might need to cut your hair too."

"What about my car?" Katerina interrupted.

"That will take a little longer. I'll get some paint, and we can do a quick paint job. It will take a day for it to dry, but that's okay. I won't be able to get a new set of plates for you until tomorrow at the earliest."

"New Indiana plates?"

"No. I know a guy who can get me just about any state. I have an appointment with him tomorrow. He has the plates and can print up the required registration documents. What name do you want to use?"

"Kate. That way I can use some jewelry I have. It has Ks on it."

"Last name?"

"Morrow, like Edward R. Morrow."

"That works. What state?

"Surprise me."

CHAPTER THIRTY-THREE

That same evening, Dwight and Cathy met at the Clayville store and headed off for an early dinner. "You wouldn't believe what my mother did this morning," Dwight said when Cathy got in his car.

"I guess I wouldn't."

"She asked Courtney if she thought you were seeing anyone."

"But you told me she knows about us."

"Yes, but she was putting me on the spot. Very effectively, I might add. Anyway, Courtney didn't think you were involved with anyone, but she did say you had been happier the last few months."

"She's right, and you're the reason," Cathy replied, reaching over and patting Dwight on the leg. "But I thought you were going to lead off telling me about the call you got from Larry Green."

"My email said most of it. Larry wanted me to send the video I had of Clement's girlfriend; you know Katerina. I took a video of her coming out of the water after her swim. Anyway, I was able to email it to him, and he gave it to the Indianapolis police. They're holding Clement Mincy, but they haven't found Katerina yet. They can make stills from my video. I don't know how good they'll be. She wasn't close to the camera, but the focus was good."

"I remember the video. I bet they'll help. So, it looks like the VM business is wrapped up. They've disbanded, and Clement Mincy is in jail. Charlotte wrote a good story. I bet she feels vindicated by what's happened. I feel great about the small part I played in their downfall."

"You should. Everyone who chanted at the Peoria rally should feel the same. We'd made some chinks in their armor before that, but it was the killer stroke. They fell apart. According to what Larry told me, all their staff left after the Peoria rally. Mincy has a big temper, and he blamed them for the mess. One of them, Jake somebody, turned state's evidence, and Mincy and the girl are in big trouble."

At dinner they talked about their future. They decided there was no reason to keep their relationship secret any longer, but they'd pretend they had just started going out. There was no reason for Bill to think Dwight had been doing anything behind his back. They had fun planning their first date in Boynton.

Katerina slept in after she and Daniel had worked late the previous evening. She had no idea painting a car was so much work. Daniel made her help him masking the car, so the paint wouldn't get on the windows or any of the chrome. Next, they hand sanded the car. When she'd complained, Daniel told her the new paint would stick better. When they finished, the paint job looked a little shaky up close, but they'd made a tan car dark green. Katerina was sure it would make it easier for her to get out of town.

Her task this morning was to cut, bleach, and dye her hair. She'd put in rinses before. She hadn't wanted to look the same at the different rally locations. Giving herself a haircut was harder than she thought, but when she finished, she thought it looked decent. It certainly changed her look. Bleaching her hair was smelly and messy, but it wasn't too hard. When she was finished, she liked the strawberry blonde look. She'd need to change her make up, but she didn't have the right stuff now. She'd have to stop in a drug store when she got out of town.

With her hair done, she went back into the garage and went over the car with a flashlight. There were a couple of places she touched up with the spray can Daniel had left. Katerina didn't think it was something that needed doing, but she knew Daniel would ask her if she'd checked the paint job.

Daniel surprised her by appearing at three thirty. He carried a bag with him. "Here, I've got some stuff for you," he said.

Katerina took the bag from Daniel and looked inside. She took out a set of Virginia license plates, a stack of papers, and a package. The papers were for the car, title, and registration. After she looked at the papers, she said, "So I'm Kate Morrow from Lynchburg, Virginia. I've never been to Virginia. How am I going to play it?"

"Get on the internet tonight and study up on Lynchburg. Actually, you probably won't ever have a conversation with anyone about it. The Virginia plates were what my friend had handy, so we went with it and used the name you gave me."

"What's in the package?"

"Open it."

Katerina opened the package and found a dress. She held it up in front of her and frowned. "This is nothing I'd ever wear. It's black, and it looks like it would be too loose."

"That's why I got it. The whole point is to get something that's not your style. It will be loose, not tight like the things you usually wear. The cops are looking for a girl with long dark hair and big boobs. There's nothing we can do about the boobs, but this dress won't draw attention to them like your normal outfits do. By the way, you did a good job on your hair."

"Thanks. I guess I'll go try the dress on."

"You do that, and I'll change the license plates."

When Daniel got back, he said, "I smelled fresh paint."

"I went over the whole car with a flashlight, like you said. Only a couple of places looked like they needed a little more paint."

"The dress fit?"

"There's not much fit to this kind of thing. I think it makes me look ten years older. Is it okay if I don't like it?"

"You don't have to like it but wear it at least until you get out of town. I don't think it's smart for you to look like the hot number we all know you are. There's one more thing we need. I need to take a picture of you. A head shot, so my guy can make a fake driver's license. I couldn't do the picture until you had your hair fixed."

She posed for the picture, which Daniel took with a little camera. He reviewed the picture and said, "This looks good enough. The next thing I need is a copy of your signature. Kate Morrow, isn't that it?"

Katerina made a few practices at the signature and then put one on the paper Daniel had provided her.

"I'll be back in half an hour," Daniel said. "We should have the driver's license by the middle of the day tomorrow."

Katerina paced the apartment in her dowdy black dress, counting the minutes until Daniel returned. She knew he was being incredibly helpful, but still she was annoyed with him for taking so long.

He arrived after about an hour.

After she greeted him, Katerina asked, "You learn anything more about how Clement's doing?"

"Get me a beer, and I'll fill you in."

They went into the kitchen and sat at the table. Katerina got two beers and they clinked bottles. "I visited him this morning. He wasn't happy, to say the least. The people from Michigan are questioning him tomorrow, and he's upset. Also, I had a tough time getting him to focus on what will help him. He kept wanting me to tell you to go after Jake, but that won't do any good. The police already have Jake's statement."

"I guess you're right."

"Oh, he learned where the picture of you came from."

"Where? I've been wondering about that."

"This guy in Ohio, Dwight Kelton. He was spying on us in Michigan. It was the same time Marcie Green was there. He took pictures of you getting out of the water after your swim. Actually, it was a video, but the cops got a still out of it."

"Who's he? I've never heard of him."

"I don't know for sure, but we think he's behind a lot of the trouble Clement had. Like I said, he was spying on you guys the same day Marcie was there. I think they may have met. He was the one who got the police in Michigan to come talk to you. And he shows up later."

"What do you mean?" She stood up and went over to the mirror. She couldn't get over how different she looked.

"He went to two of the rallies, but I don't think he was a supporter. I'm pretty sure he was connected to the woman in Knoxville who wrote the news story, and I think he had something to do with the chant in Peoria. Also, I saw him having dinner with Larry Green, Marcie's brother, and I think he talked to Gregory using a concocted story. He lives in a hick town in Ohio. I went there once but couldn't locate him."

She returned to join Daniel. "You think he was stalking us?"

"Investigating might be a better word."

Katerina looked pensive and took a long drink of her beer. "I've been doing a lot of thinking about what to do, and you've been incredibly helpful. Still, I've got one problem. I'm almost broke."

"I wondered. I know Greg kept Clem on a short string money-wise. I'll go to him tomorrow morning and make a plea for you. I think Clem will be in better shape if you completely disappear. Greg might be able to give you a stake."

"You think so? I've never been sure Gregory liked me."

"I don't know, but I'll give it a try. Greg should understand the bind you're in. You'd better hope he helps. After him, I'm out of options."

CHAPTER THIRTY-FOUR

Cathy lay in Dwight's arms on the couch at the back of the Clayville store. Looking at his neat stack of clothes on the chair, he recognized they were past the stage of tearing off each other's clothes. It was strange, since they were discussing how to manage their first date.

"I think Friday night will work. Call me tomorrow and ask me out."

"You'll say yes."

"We'll see," Cathy laughed. "Yeah, I think so. Anyway, it's time. Courtney goes off to college in a couple of weeks. All the fall sports teams get to school two weeks before the rest of the students. She's excited. I think we should have had at least a couple of dates before she leaves. I don't want her hearing things at college that will surprise her. I'm sure she'll be in touch with her friends back here. This is a small town, and our dates will be all over town."

"Our divorces are all but final. I wonder what Bill will think."

"I don't know. Maybe he'll try to warn you away. At times, he's still really mad at me, but it's boiled to the surface less often since he's moved away."

"We'll tell everyone we're taking it slow, right?"

"Yes. We're not serious, just getting to know each other. The dating can be intermittent for a while, then we can get serious."

Cathy slid off Dwight, got up, and started to get dressed. Dwight followed suit. "I was thinking we would be able to meet between dates," Dwight said with a smile.

"We're on the same page, my dear. Speaking of dates, what do you hear from your mother?"

"It's interesting—she was quite talkative the morning after her first dinner with Andrew Nichols. She knew I was curious. I think she and Andrew are both in the same place. They miss their spouses, and they're at a loss to know what to do about dating. She said it was sweet when she recognized how nervous he was. When I asked her if she wasn't a little nervous too, she said she guessed she was, but she thought she hid it better."

"Are they going out again?"

"Andrew called the next day and arranged for another dinner date. I think they'll be going out the same night we are."

"Wow, that proves Andrew's nice. I understand the worst part of dating is waiting for a call after a date. The woman just has to wait. I don't know from experience. Since Bill and I hooked up so early, I never had to go through it. The waiting, that is."

"You didn't have that problem with me either."

"I guess you're right, but it wasn't just about dating with us. I wanted to recruit you to look into the VM stuff. It turned into dating pretty fast, but at least I had more than one motive for being so aggressive."

"You got no complaints from me."

When Dwight got home at ten thirty, he recognized he'd forgotten his cell phone in his hurry to make it to Clayville for his meeting with Cathy. When he found it sitting on his desk, there was a message from Larry Green asking him to call, no matter how late it was.

"Larry, this is Dwight Kelton returning your call."

"Oh good, Dwight. Things here are moving fast. Clement Mincy has started to talk. He's saying he isn't the killer everyone is worried about. His girlfriend Katerina is the one who did the killing. She's the one with the garrote. He admits he was with her when Marcie and the others were killed, but he didn't do it. It was Katerina."

"I was going to say, that's great news, Larry, but I'm not sure that's right. I mean, it's good news that Mincy broke down and admitted he was involved in Marcie's killing. On the other hand, the killer is still on the loose. Not such good news."

Dwight walked out of his office and into his bedroom.

"It turns out this Katerina is a bit of a mystery woman. It's Katerina, no last name. Mincy swears he doesn't know what it is. Also, he doesn't know where she's from. The way he tells it, this hot chick comes up after his magic show and comes on to him. He was going out with my sister at the time, but that doesn't deter him. He hooks up with her and invites her to come be part of the VM crew in Michigan."

"She was in the first VM video. She and Marcie played the mermaids."

"Right. Marcie broke up with him right after that, and Katerina took her place. Mincy's story is consistent with the account given by Jake McDowd. He was part of the VM crew, and he's cooperating."

Dwight went over to his chest and extracted his pajamas.

"So, when they catch this girl, they'll have the case wrapped up. It sounds like good progress."

"I think you're right. The reason I'm calling is that we may need you to come to Indianapolis to testify about where you got the video of Katerina. It's just a detail, but the police might need it."

"Just let me know when. I can be there whenever you need me."

"Thanks for returning my call."

"No problem. I'm sorry it was so late. Goodbye."

Back in Indianapolis, Katerina was having a hard time waiting for Daniel to return. As far as she knew, the only holdup was the fake driver's license. She didn't know how hard it would be to make, but Daniel had a picture of her and a copy of her signature as Kate Morrow. She'd already packed all her stuff and pored over a bunch of maps she'd found. She wanted to confer with Daniel about where she should head. If he didn't have any suggestions, she wasn't sure where she would go.

Daniel finally showed up in the middle of the afternoon. He handed her an envelope with the new driver's license. Katerina inspected it. It looked authentic. It was even scratched up a little. She went to her purse and inserted the driver's license in her wallet.

"You don't have any other ID with your real name, do you?"

"No, I took it all out. I'm Kate Morrow now."

"Okay, Kate. I've got something else for you. Take a look in this," Daniel said, handing her another envelope.

"Wow, how much is it?"

"There's five hundred in bills and look more closely. There's a Visa card. It's already got five thousand loaded on it. That's all I could get out of Gregory. He says he never wants to see you again, and I assured him he wouldn't."

"It's more than I expected. Now, I want to talk to you about where you think I should go. I'm ready to leave, but I'll wait till after dark."

"Actually, Greg had a suggestion about where you should go."

"Why does Greg care where I go?"

Katerina nervously took the driver's license out of her wallet and inspected it closely. "The license is good, don't worry. Anyway, Greg is convinced the guy in Ohio is responsible for all the troubles VM ran into. He wants you to off him." Katerina started to talk, but Daniel held up his hands, stopping her. "If you can get rid of this guy, Gregory will load twenty-five thousand more on that Visa card. Think about it. With what you've already got, twenty-five thousand more will go a long way. You'll have enough to set yourself up real nice."

Katerina walked around the living room, thinking about what she'd just been offered. "I've never done anything like this by myself. Clem was always there to help me. I'm not sure I could do it alone."

Daniel shrugged. "I don't see the problem. You get this guy in a place where you hit him over the head before you use your garrote. He's not big, and if you're smart about it, he's not going to see you coming."

"I don't know."

"Go to the hick town in Ohio—Boynton—and follow him for a few days. I'm sure you'll be able to find some time when he's alone. Night would be better, but you could probably find him during the day too. Look, I have a file on him I can give to you. I've got his car license, his home address, and the layout of the town. Think about it, twenty-five thousand. You really can't get far with the 5,500 you've got."

Katerina knew Daniel was right. She needed a bigger stake. She tried to bargain. "Do you think twenty-five's all Gregory would give? Call him and tell him I'll do it for fifty thousand."

"He's not going to like it."

"Call him."

"I'll do it, but I'm handing the phone to you. You can do the bargaining." Fifteen tense minutes later, they split the difference between forty thousand and thirty-five thousand, settling on thirty-seven thousand five hundred. Daniel, who'd listened intently, was amazed at Katerina's ability to stand toe to toe with Gregory.

When she hung up, he congratulated her on the result.

"The way I see it, I'm taking all the risk. He's got no exposure, so I ought to get paid more. I might have settled for a lower amount, but he caved pretty fast."

"Let's figure out the best way for you to get out of Indianapolis headed toward Ohio."

CHAPTER THIRTY-FIVE

Cathy worked in the Boynton store the morning before her first "official" date with Dwight. One of her clerks, Clair, could tell she was distracted for some reason, and after getting the customer she was working with situated in the dressing room, she finally got up the nerve to speak to Cathy. "What is it boss? You don't seem to have your focus today. Something going on?"

"Oh Clair, I'm just bursting to tell someone. For the first time since my separation, I'm going on a dinner date."

"That's wonderful. Who's the lucky guy? I've seen quite a few guys coming around trying to interest you, but you've been pretty brusque with them. Who finally pierced your defenses?"

"It's Dwight Kelton, if you must know. He came back to live with his mother a few months ago. We went to high school together. We're going to Johnny's for dinner. I don't expect anything to come of it."

In the dressing room, Katerina almost jumped out of her skin when she overheard the conversation. She'd just gotten to Boynton that morning, and she hadn't been able to spot Kelton yet. Now she knew where he was going to be tonight. It was too good to be true. She kept quiet as she tried on the clothes, black, tight-fitting things, which should be good for snooping around at night.

Back in the main store, Clair asked, "Johnny's, isn't that close to your house?"

"Yes, it's about five blocks. We're going to walk. Okay, Clair, that's it. Don't go spreading it around. I know this little town will be all abuzz soon enough. There's no reason to accelerate the process."

"You can count on me to keep a secret."

Back in the dressing room, Katerina smiled. *They're walking. It will be easy to attack Kelton after he drops her off. Unless he drives to her house, but that doesn't seem likely. It would be silly to drive to the girl's house and then walk to some restaurant. They must live close.*

Katerina picked up the pieces she wanted and walked out of the fitting room. Clair came up to her and asked, "Find something?"

"Yes, I'll take these two. I left the other ones in the fitting room. Is that okay?"

"That's fine."

As Katerina followed the clerk to the cash register, she looked around and spotted the other person in the store. She was a good-looking blonde. Katerina couldn't tell her age with any precision. She looked young, maybe in her late thirties, but very well preserved. The woman glanced up and smiled at her. Katerina looked away. Then she remembered the clerk calling the other woman boss, so there was nothing wrong with the smile. *She's probably glad I'm buying something.*

Cathy thought the girl with the short blonde hair looked familiar, but she couldn't place her. She had been surprised when it appeared the girl was staring at her. *It's probably nothing.*

When Katerina left the store, Clair came up to Cathy and said, "Did you see the size of her chest? It must be hard to find clothes that fit. If a blouse fits over her top, it's going to look sloppy around the waist. I guess that's why we sold her an outfit that's mostly Lycra."

"I didn't recognize her. Has she been in the store before?"

"No, I don't remember her. She paid with a card. I can find out who she is." Clair walked back to the desk. "Nope, it was a pre-paid card. I don't have a name for you."

Cathy couldn't help feeling the girl looked familiar for some reason, but she didn't remember where she'd seen her. Clair was right—she had big fake boobs, but that wasn't all that unusual, even in Boynton.

Katerina walked to her car, excited about what she'd learned. She'd be able to take care of Mr. Kelton tonight and blow this hick town. She still hadn't quite figured out where she was headed, but she knew it wasn't a small town like this. If nothing else, it was easier to hide in a big city, and she knew she needed to hide. Daniel had made that clear.

That evening, Dwight spent more time that usual getting ready. It was funny, but something was different. He and Cathy had been together quite a bit, but this was a public date. They were sure to run into people they knew. When he went downstairs, his mother was all dressed up, waiting for her date. They complimented each other on the way they looked.

Across the street, Katerina watched Kelton leave. She was hiding behind a parked car. He turned to his right and walked down the street. Katerina waited for him to get half a block away before she started to follow. After two blocks, he crossed the street and went up to the corner house. Five minutes later, Kelton and the dress-store lady came out of the house and walked down the street away from where Katerina stood behind a tree.

Katerina knew where they were headed from the scouting she'd done that afternoon, so she didn't need to follow them. She had the information she needed. She decided to go back over the route between the two houses and figure out where she could stage her attack. It didn't take her long to find a tree that would work. It was a big oak just about halfway between the two houses.

Dwight and Kathy couldn't help noticing that several people stared at them when they came into the restaurant. It was all they could do not to laugh. They tried to act like a couple on a first date. There was no hand holding or anything like that. They kept their voices low and talked about what they'd been doing since high school. It was play acting, and they were enjoying themselves.

After they'd been at the restaurant for about an hour, Cathy saw a reflection in the mirror across from them. Someone was checking out the restaurant from outside. She recognized the girl from the store this morning. She wore the black outfit she'd bought then, and she had a black scarf over her hair. Suddenly it struck Cathy—the girl looked like Katerina, Clement Mincy's girlfriend. *What could she be doing here? Then again, the blonde hair wasn't right. Maybe I'm imagining things.* She glanced back in the mirror, and the girl was gone.

Katerina didn't know why she went to check out the restaurant. She knew Kelton and the woman were there. Maybe she was just using up nervous energy. Anyway, she'd seen them briefly before she got control of herself and walked away. Having Clement there the other times made it easier. She went over her plan once more in her mind as she walked back to her tree. She couldn't see a flaw. It was a dark night, and this sleepy little town was as quiet as could be.

Cathy tried to push her suspicions out of her head. *I'm being silly*, she thought. *Still, if it is Katerina, she's probably up to no good.* After some thought, she knew what she needed to do. After she and Dwight had ordered dessert, she excused herself and went to the lady's room. Inside the stall, she quickly called Courtney.

"How's your date going, Mom?"

"Fine, just fine. Listen, I have a favor to ask. I know it's crazy, but could you follow Dwight when he leaves our house? I want to be sure he gets home safely."

After a pause, Courtney spoke up. "What?"

"I know I'm being paranoid, but I think someone might be out to get him."

"Oh, you mean Dad?"

"No, not him, someone else. It's probably nothing, but could you just do it?"

"Sure, it's only two blocks. He'll never know I was watching him."

"Wonderful. Thanks."

Cathy returned to the table relieved. Their apple pie appeared right after her return, and they continued their first date playacting.

Twenty minutes later, they were walking back to Cathy's house.

"Here comes the difficult part of the first date, the drop off," Dwight said. "Should I try to kiss her? Will she invite me in? Should I tell her I'll call?"

"Well, you're not going to be invited in, but I think you deserve a kiss. It's been a lovely first date."

Courtney was looking out the back door when her mother and Professor Kelton walked past. When they'd gone by, she let herself out the door quietly. Since she was being a bodyguard, she decided to take her hockey stick. She thought the whole thing was silly, but her mother sounded serious. She headed across the street and hid behind a tree in the neighbor's side yard. She smiled when she caught the end of a kiss on her front porch. Professor Kelton looked happy as he walked across the street and headed toward his house. Courtney let him get three quarters of a block ahead before she started following.

When Dwight passed the tree Katerina was hiding behind, she sprang out and wacked him on the head as hard as she could with a short pipe. He crumpled to the ground. She dropped the pipe into her purse and took out the garrote. Before she could apply the garrote, she had to rearrange the body. It was a little difficult moving the limp body to expose the guy's neck, but Katerina managed. She reached for the garrote, which she'd placed it on the ground.

Courtney had seen someone jump out behind the Professor and clobber him with something. She started running toward the action, staying on the grass so her footsteps wouldn't make much noise. She saw the woman—it was a woman—propping up the Professor's head and reaching for something. Courtney didn't have time to think, she swung her hockey stick at the woman's head and made contact. She'd been running so fast that she couldn't help but crash into both the woman and Professor Kelton. She rolled over and sprang to her feet. Neither of the other two appeared to be conscious. Courtney realized that the woman was bleeding profusely from the wound inflicted by her hockey stick.

Breathing hard, Courtney tried to figure out what to do. She heard a police siren and saw her mother running up the street. Good, her mother could sort all this out. Cathy arrived just when the police car pulled up and went to check on Dwight, feeling for a pulse. "Oh, Mom, the woman down there hit Professor Kelton over the head. I don't know what she was going to do to him, but I clobbered her with my hockey stick before she could do anything more."

Cathy got up and put her arms around Courtney. "You did great. Dwight's got a strong pulse. When I saw you start to run, I called 911 and headed your way. I think an ambulance is coming too."

The policeman, a portly, round-faced man in his late fifties, approached them and asked what was going on. Cathy answered, "That woman attacked my friend. He's the one on the ground over there."

"How'd she get all bloodied up?"

"I hit her with my hockey stick," Courtney answered.

They heard a groan from Dwight, and Cathy rushed over to him and put her hands on his back. "Don't try to move, darling. I think you may have a concussion. Just lie still. Help is on the way."

Right on cue, they heard the siren from the ambulance.

The policeman checked for a pulse. "She's got a strong pulse, but it looks like she's lost a lot of blood. Do either of you know who she is?"

Cathy turned from where she was kneeling beside Dwight. "I think her name is Katerina something, she's wanted in Indiana—for murder. At least that's who I think she is. She attacked Dwight here. And if it hadn't been for my daughter and her hockey stick, I don't know what she would have done."

The ambulance pulled up and medics ran up to the two bodies. "Hi Evan," one of them said to the policeman. "What have we got here?"

"The best I can make out is that the woman with the bloody head attacked the man down there, and this young lady came to protect the guy. She slugged the woman with her hockey stick. I've called for backup, and you'd better call another ambulance. Both people need to get to the hospital."

Katerina rolled over at this point and tried to get up.

"Watch her, officer," Cathy yelled.

"Stay down, ma'am. You're in no shape to try to get up."

Katerina was panicked. Blood was running into her eyes, she had a splitting headache, and she didn't quite know where she was. All she knew was that she had to get away. She lay still, trying to get her bearings. As her head cleared a little, she heard a siren, so either the police or an ambulance was coming. Finally, her head cleared enough to see. A medic headed toward her. She got up as fast as she could, pushed the medic down, and started running down the sidewalk.

"What the heck," the policeman said, and he chased after her.

A moment later, Courtney ran past the policeman and caught up with Katerina, who wasn't running very steadily. This time Courtney tripped the fleeing woman with her hockey stick, causing her to crash to the sidewalk.

"Thanks," said the policeman. "I'm not up to chasing people anymore." He took out his handcuffs, grabbed Katerina's hands, pulled them behind her, and slapped on the cuffs. Katerina glared at Courtney after the policeman got her to her feet.

Another police car arrived, and two new policemen joined the group.

Cathy and Courtney described what had happened. Meanwhile, the medics had strapped Dwight onto a gurney and were wheeling him toward the ambulance.

Cathy broke away from Courtney and the policemen and rushed to be at Dwight's side as he entered the ambulance. "I'll come to the hospital as soon as I can, darling."

When Cathy returned to Courtney and the police, Courtney raised her eyebrows and asked, "Darling?"

"I'll explain later."

Just as the first ambulance pulled away, another one showed up. The medics loaded Katerina onto a gurney and attached one of the handcuffs to the side of the bed. One of the policemen got into the back with the medics, and the ambulance headed to the hospital.

To get a better view of the scene, the police got a bright light out of the trunk of one of the police cars. They found the short pipe in Katerina's purse and put it in an evidence bag. A little while later, they came across the garrote.

"Oh, God," Cathy blurted. "She was going to use that on Dwight."

CHAPTER THIRTY-SIX

Two days later, Dwight grumbled as the nurse forced him to sit in a wheelchair for the trip out to the hospital's front door, where Cathy's car was waiting. *Why,* he wondered, *do they force you to use a wheelchair when you are perfectly able to walk? The doctors told me to be careful, but this is ridiculous.*

"How are you feeling, darling?" Cathy asked after he was in the passenger's seat.

"A little rocky. I still have a lump on my head and a bit of a headache. I've found it's better if I keep my head still. I just have to watch what I do for a while, but otherwise I feel fine."

"You up for a lunch at Haden's before I take you home?"

"Sounds great. I've had enough hospital food."

Cathy parked her car behind her store, and they walked slowly down the street to Haden's Deli. Dwight was surprised when Cathy steered him toward a table in the back where someone else was sitting. When they arrived at the table, Dwight recognized Charlotte Mangum, the reporter from Knoxville.

"Charlotte, it's good to see you," Dwight said.

"Great to see you too." They exchanged a brief hug. "You look pretty good for someone who's just been released from the hospital."

"I'm on the mend, but I'm not up to any sudden movements."

After they were seated, Charlotte continued, "As I told Cathy, I'm not staying long. I made a side trip here on my way to Indianapolis. My editor agreed I deserved to try to follow up since I was the one who wrote the first VM story."

"What's happening?" Dwight asked. "I've been out of the loop lying in the hospital."

"It's fascinating. I haven't been able to do as many interviews as I would like, but here's what I know. Clement Mincy is being held in Indianapolis for the murders of Marcie Green, Enrique Hernandez, and maybe some guy they just found, Wilhelm something. Clement claims he didn't commit the murders. Your friend Katerina did."

"That makes some sense," Cathy said. "The police here found a garrote where Katerina attacked Dwight. My daughter got there just in time to stop her from using it on Dwight."

A waitress interrupted them at this point. Dwight and Cathy knew what they wanted and Charlotte made up her mind in a hurry. After the waitress left, the conversation continued.

"My understanding is that Katerina is livid at Clement for throwing her under the bus, so she's telling the police here he was involved in all the other murders. Her story is that he clobbered the people over the head before she used the garrote. She even says one of them was dead before she did anything."

"Doesn't she have a lawyer telling her to shut up?" Dwight asked. "I thought any competent lawyer wouldn't want his client confessing like that."

"She only has a public defender," Cathy said.

"Yeah, I talked to the guy, Edgar Nice, earlier today," Charlotte said. "He says she's totally uncontrollable. She's so mad at Clement she's not listening to any of his lawyerly advice. It's the perfect set up for the police. Both of them want to turn state's evidence, so they're incriminating each other."

"How does all this affect the legacy of VM?" Dwight asked. "Cathy and I got involved because we wanted to take VM down. Have either Clement or Katerina admitted they were behind the VM videos and shows? Is there some way all this mess can be linked to VM?"

Their sandwiches came, and they paused their conversation to eat. After she finished, Charlotte continued. "I think I can make the connection between the two murder suspects and VM. There's a guy, Jake McDowd, who worked with Clement and Katerina on the VM project. Larry Green, you know Larry, called me, and told me McDowd was willing to talk. He was a full part of the VM group. Apparently, he was the one who played Clement's role in Toledo. You know, when Clement appeared in person claiming he wasn't the VM masked man. Anyway, this guy knows everything, and he's willing to spill his guts."

"Will he know who financed the VM project?" Cathy asked. "There had to be quite a bit of money behind the whole thing. Maybe it was all the father's money, but I wonder."

"You hit on one of the crucial questions. If I can find out all of VM's sponsors, it would blow the whole thing wide open. It will be easy to discredit the VM guy. We'll have compelling evidence. He is a two-bit actor well on his way to being a convicted murderer. That much will be easy. Finding who funded his activities is going to be harder. Maybe this guy Jake will know."

"I think Larry can help you there," Cathy said. "He knows some of Marcie's friends, and I think she talked to some of them about other people who might have been financial supporters."

"I'm going to talk to Jake and whoever else Larry thinks will be useful. If I can get people to cooperate, it's going to be a big story. It has all the components to be huge: murders, a big-busted bimbo, a website full of conspiracy theories, lying, cheating, and weird politics. It's hard for a story to offer more to a reporter. As far as I know, I'm the only reporter with an inside to Jake. I couldn't be more thrilled."

"You deserve it Charlotte," Dwight said. "You took a lot of heat when Mincy's performance in Toledo appeared to blow your first story out of the water. It must have been tough to live through."

"You're right, I wouldn't want to live through that again."

"We'd better leave soon," Cathy said. "I don't want Dwight to get tired. He's still recovering. But before that I want to ask a favor. Could you send us your story before you're done? Dwight and I might be able to add some stuff."

"Sure, as long as it's okay for me to use your names. I thought there was a problem with that."

"That's all behind us now. Our relationship is out in the open. I've heard my ex-husband isn't too happy about it, but I don't care."

Cathy took Dwight home after lunch, and Charlotte headed to Indianapolis. Evangeline made a big fuss over Dwight when he got home. She didn't seem happy to see Cathy, but she suppressed any comments.

"Hospitals aren't safe places," Evangeline said. "He needs his rest."

"I agree completely," Cathy responded. "You can check your email later. I'm sure whatever is there can wait. Put on your pajamas and get to bed. I'll see you later."

Dwight obeyed. He didn't see any percentage in fighting the two women. As he was lying there, a depression fell over him. *It's odd. I should be elated. We vanquished VM. Clement Mincy and Katerina are in jail, and they won't be out for a long time, if ever. Charlotte is getting a great story. If this guy Jake really was an insider, she'll blow VM to bits. Then why can't I shake this feeling?*

Dwight fell asleep, not satisfied but unable to put his finger on why he felt depressed. The headache didn't help, but it was more than that.

That evening, Evangeline and Courtney brought up Dwight's dinner on a tray to his bedroom. He was still in his pajamas, but he was in his office checking his email.

"Get back in bed," his mother commanded.

When Dwight complied, Evangeline pulled over a spare pillow, put it on Dwight's lap, took the tray from Courtney, and set it on the pillow. "Here, this should be much better than the hospital food."

Dwight looked at Courtney, who hovered in the doorway. "I haven't had a chance to thank you. The way I heard it, you saved my life. Thank you."

Courtney blushed. "You should thank my mom. She's the one who had me follow you that evening. She thought something was wrong."

"Let's hear it for women's intuition," Evangeline said, smiling.

"I guess that's right," Dwight admitted. "Anyway, thanks, and I guess I should apologize for keeping my relationship with your mother secret. It's not nice to keep secrets, but we had our reasons."

"Mom's had a chance to explain all that, Professor. It's fine. I'm just happy for her. She and my dad haven't been getting along for years."

After a pause, Dwight asked, "You're headed to college soon. When do you leave?"

"One week from today. I'm excited. The hockey team and some other teams get to school before the rest of the students. I think we'll have intense practices for a couple of weeks. I'm kinda nervous about that. Some of the girls on the team are really good. I hope I can compete."

"I'm sure you'll do fine," Evangeline said.

"Thanks, you're sweet. I'm rooming with one of the other first year players. I don't know her, but we've emailed, so we're not complete strangers. Still, that's got me a little nervous too."

"We'd better let him eat in peace," Evangeline said, motioning for Courtney to leave.

CHAPTER THIRTY-SEVEN

A week later, Dwight could tell Cathy was disappointed. Bill had won the coin flip and was taking Courtney to college. Luckily, just before Dwight headed over to her house to keep her company, he'd received an email with a draft from Charlotte. He gave Cathy a quick call, alerting her to the email and telling her he'd be right over.

Dwight was pleased they'd have the email to talk about. There were drafts of two articles. He started reading the first article on his phone while he walked to Cathy's. Apparently, Jake McDowd had been the mother lode. He knew the workings of Clement Mincy's entire operation.

Cathy yelled for him to come in. She was at the dining room table, staring at her laptop.

"I haven't read the whole thing yet," Dwight said.

"Neither have I. Come sit beside me and finish the first story."

The first story outlined the way a VM rally worked. It was all very closely choreographed, particularly the finale. Jake described how he and Enrique and Wilhelm were dressed in outfits like Clement's and they stood on spring-loaded risers, making it seem as if they appeared on the stage out of nowhere. Charlotte described how it looked from the audience perspective with the booms, the smoke, and the VM people appearing all over the stage. After the discussion of the mechanics of the rallies, Charlotte described it all fell apart in Peoria, and Enrique and Wilhelm were allegedly killed by Clement and Katerina. She had considerable detail from interviewing the police. She didn't include any details of Katerina's attack on Dwight.

Dwight looked up from his phone and could tell Cathy was still reading. A few minutes later, she shifted her eyes to Dwight.

"There's a bunch of great details," she said. "This guy Jake added a lot we didn't know."

"And it looks like both Katerina and Clement are talking to the police. They're blaming each other."

"Let's read the other story. I guess it's a follow up."

The second story was more about what VM stood for and how the whole operation was funded. Charlotte reviewed some of the VM videos. Most interestingly, Clement had talked to Jake in some detail about the funding and his basis for the claims he made during the videos. Frist, Charlotte had descriptions of the main funders: Gregory Mincy, James Bigelow, and William Whinston.

Dwight interrupted their reading. "I bet there will be articles coming out soon describing how Greg Mincy and the other two are denying the whole thing."

"Yeah, you're probably right. Those guys will deny everything. The sad thing is that it will probably work. They'll have some unpleasant times, but they didn't do anything illegal, so it will all blow over."

"I'm really interested in this next part."

"Me too."

Apparently, Jake and Clement worked together on the videos, both the production and the content. According to Jake, Clement did the first drafts of the scripts, and Jake did some polishing. Charlotte had asked him about some of the wild claims in the videos. Jake told her all of them: the notion that water supplies were poisoned, medical implants having transmitters in them, the idea that the Civil War didn't have anything to do with slavery, and the claims about Vikings and the mermaids, were all Clement's inventions. He just made them up. Jake claimed Clement even told him he knew they weren't true, but that didn't matter. Clement included them for the effect they had. He wasn't interested in the truth.

The article ended with Jake's chilling description of a conversation he'd had with Clement about his hopes for VM. As Dwight and Cathy had feared, Clement's final objective was a revolution. After he'd built up a large enough following among the general populace, Clement planned to move his rallies to locations close to military bases. The article ended with Charlotte detailing one final chilling fact: Clement had had grand plans to enlist many members of the army in his plot.

"What do you think?" Dwight asked.

"The articles are wonderful. The whole VM thing is exposed for the fraud it was, and Clement and Katerina are going to be in jail for a long time. It's great." Cathy got up, plopped herself in Dwight's lap, and gave him a big kiss.

"You're right," Dwight said after the kiss.

"What is it honey? You don't seem as pleased as I am."

"Yeah, while I was spending time in bed trying to keep my head still, I've been thinking about all this. We've certainly been able to extinguish VM. They're done, but I don't know. It's like we're playing Whac-a-mole. VM reared its ugly head, and we whacked it, but another group will appear soon spewing similar nonsense. We've won the battle, but I don't think we've won the war."

"Dwight, it's not like you to be such a pessimist."

Cathy got off Dwight's lap and sat on a chair across from him. She didn't understand the serious look on his face. "What's got you down?"

"We've talked about this before. The appeal of VM is based on some people's dissatisfaction with what's happening in mainstream America.

Some of the people will fall for radical ideas. As long as there is the illusion of truth, those people will fall for lots of crazy ideas. There are lots of susceptible people out there, and someone will come along and try to exploit their vulnerability."

"Isn't it important that Charlotte got Jake to say Clement just made up a bunch of the stuff? Most of the things he said were lies. VM has been exposed."

"I wish it were that easy. A bunch of right-wing websites will try their hardest to discredit Jake. They'll say he's lying, trying to ingratiate himself with the police. They will have to distance themselves from Clement, who's admitted to being an accessory to murder, but they will try to hold on to as much of the VM message as they can."

"So, you don't think we accomplished much?"

"That's not it exactly. It's just we attacked a symptom, not the disease. There are people out there who don't trust the mainstream media, or experts, or the government. Some of them are going to fall for the next charlatan who comes along. As I said before, it's Whac-a-mole. We took care of one, but there will be others."

"I suppose you're right, but we can't solve all the country's problems. Still, I say we celebrate. We sure as heck whacked that one mole."

ABOUT THE AUTHOR

Robert Archibald was born in New Jersey and grew up in Oklahoma and Arizona. After receiving a BA from the University of Arizona, he was drafted and served in Viet Nam. He then earned an M.S. and Ph.D in economics from Purdue University. Bob had a 41-year career at the College of William & Mary. While he had several stints as an administrator, department chair, director of the public policy program, and interim dean of the faculty, Bob was always proud to be promoted back to the faculty.
He lives with his wife of 50 years, Nancy, in Williamsburg, Virginia.

CPSIA information can be obtained
at www.ICGtesting.com
Printed in the USA
BVHW080909251122
652759BV00019B/956